Implementing an Inpatient Smoking Cessation Program

Implementing an Inpatient Smoking Cessation Program

Patricia M. Smith
Northern Ontario School of Medicine

C. Barr Taylor
Stanford University School of Medicine

2006
LAWRENCE ERLBAUM ASSOCIATES, PUBLISHERS
Mahwah, New Jersey   London

Camera ready copy for this book was provided by the authors.

Counselor acted by Erin O'Grady, BS
Patient acted by John Forsayeth, PhD

Lawrence Erlbaum Associates, Inc., Publishers
10 Industrial Avenue
Mahwah, New Jersey 07430
www.erlbaum.com

Cover design by Tomai Maridou

Library of Congress Cataloging-in-Publication Data

CIP information for this volume may be obtained by contacting the Library of
Congress

ISBN 0-8058-5490-8 (cloth : alk. paper)

Books published by Lawrence Erlbaum Associates are printed on acid-free
paper, and their bindings are chosen for strength and durability.

Printed in the United States of America
10 9 8 7 6 5 4 3 2 1

Contents

Foreword

The hospital has increasingly been recognized as an important gateway for smoking cessation interventions that meet and surpass the quality measures provided by national policy-making organizations. These organizations, including the Joint Commission on Accreditation of Healthcare Organizations (JCAHO), National Committee for Quality Assurance (NCQA), and Centers for Medicare and Medicaid (CMS) have developed performance measures that track the advice, counseling, and pharmacotherapy provided to smokers within hospital settings. This book is the most comprehensive guide yet published to help administrators and program staff implement smoking cessation interventions at the bedside.

Written by two colleagues who have more than three decades of experience in hospital-based smoking interventions, the book offers a systems approach for managing hospitalized smokers. It is based upon the efficacy of numerous randomized controlled trials and dissemination studies undertaken in the United States and Canada during the past twenty years. The authors' hands-on experience and the close relationships they have developed with hospital staffs have enabled them to produce a definitive guide. The authors offer numerous approaches to resolving problems of implementation and define the resources needed to implement appropriate interventions. They make strong recommendations for achieving appropriate patient outcomes.

The past few decades have seen significant progress in smoking cessation, yet much work still needs to be done. The ability to identify patients at the time of hospitalization offers a key opportunity to initiate smoking cessation interventions at a time when patients are focused on their health, want to quit, and can be attended by numerous health care professionals experienced in providing appropriate services. This book provides the roadmap for ensuring that ALL hospitalized smokers receive adequate counseling and follow-up. It is an essential resource for those committed to conquering the single most preventable cause of death and disability in the United States, Canada, and worldwide.

December 2005

Nancy Houston Miller, RN, BSN
Associate Director
Stanford Cardiac Rehabilitation Center
Palo Alto, California

Preface

In the early 1990s, inpatient smoking cessation programs were called "an idea whose time has come". It is even truer today. Inpatient smoking cessation programs have become quality assurance indicators for hospitals and healthcare plans, are recommended by clinical practice guidelines, and program costs are covered by many private insurance companies and absorbed into hospital operating budgets.

Since the mid 1980s, we have, in collaboration with a number of other researchers, clinicians, hospitals, patients, and funding agencies, developed and tested a systems-based inpatient smoking cessation program in a series of studies in the United States and Canada. The smoking cessation program, called Staying Free, is a theory-based intensive intervention designed to be delivered by a tobacco cessation counselor at the bedside during hospitalization and followed up post-discharge by telephone. Although the development of Staying Free precedes the U.S. Department of Health and Human Services Treating Tobacco Use and Dependence clinical practice guideline, it has from its inception, covered all the recommendations now in the guideline for hospital-based programs.

Staying Free has worked consistently well across diverse populations, hospitals, healthcare systems, and even countries, and has evidenced among the highest confirmed one-year cessation rates reported in the scientific literature—48%-70% among post-myocardial patients, and 27-49% among general patients. The program is relatively inexpensive to deliver, appears to be acceptable to the majority of smokers who are hospitalized, and can be extended to hospital employees and their families, work-sites, and communities on a cost-recovery basis. We believe that the success of the program hinges on the synergistic effect of a centralized systems-based case-managed approach, an effective theory-based intervention, and the unique situation created by hospitalization—removal from cues to smoke, surrounded by non-smoking cues, the saliency of disease, and undergoing the worst withdrawal during the first 2-3 days of hospitalization.

Why We Wrote This Book

With the advent of increased tobacco policies and healthcare guidelines supporting hospital-based tobacco cessation initiatives, there is a growing need for a "how-to" implementation book. Although government and scientific publications provide an evaluation of the evidence for tobacco treatment and systems-based programs, none of them identify all the collective and sequential steps required to implement a sustainable program. This book is also in response to the many requests from researchers and clinicians who want to know how to proceed with the implementation of an inpatient smoking cessation program.

By sharing our experience, our hope is to increase the number of inpatient smoking cessation programs that are implemented, shorten the learning curve for others, and help create realistic expectations for providers, patients, and hospital management teams. Although the program featured in the book is smoking cessation, the process is applicable to the implementation of most, if not all, behavioral interventions in acute care or long-term care settings.

Perspectives of the Book

The focus of the book is on the implementation process and start-up phase of a program, and what could be called the "business of doing business" aspects of implementation. It is written more for the program administrator than the delivery provider, although they could be the same person. The approach taken is based on a program that will have a dedicated position for a tobacco cessation counselor. The book is not a "how to" for counseling patients, although there is a chapter on what should or can go into a tobacco cessation intervention.

Staying Free, the inpatient smoking cessation program on which our experiences are based, is not unlike other theory-based interventions. Our intent is not to suggest Staying Free as the only option for an inpatient smoking cessation program, but to provide a heuristic model for translating tobacco cessation guidelines and quality assurance indicators into practice based on our experiences with Staying Free.

Goals of the Book

The goals of this book are to provide a documented step-by-step reference guide on how to design an inpatient smoking cessation program, implement it, evaluate it, modify/evolve it, and maintain it over time with continuous quality improvement. The book identifies all the pieces, links them together, and integrates them into a logical and sequential series of steps. It incorporates the lessons and systems learned from over 20 years of research and development, thereby offering to drastically reduce the readers' learning curve and save vast amounts of time, money, effort, and frustration involved in the implementation of behavioral interventions. The book is written in a style that researchers and clinicians, even those outside the area of smoking cessation, can understand and use. Our extensive underlying research over the years provides rich examples throughout the book, and the providers who have been responsible for running the research provide insightful interviews that help bring to life the steps, barriers, and rewards involved in implementing an inpatient smoking cessation program.

Audience

The book is intended for disciplines involved in the field of healthcare, public health, community and health psychology, behavioral medicine, medicine, nursing, health promotion, respiratory therapy, disease prevention, risk factor modification and management, and rehabilitation. Within those disciplines, it is intended for a wide audience of healthcare and behavioral medicine professionals including administrators, researchers, health educators, students, public health officials, physicians, nurses, respiratory therapists, psychologists, and others interested in, or in need of, implementing an inpatient smoking cessation program. It might also serve as a valuable text or reference for courses in healthcare, public health, and community and health psychology.

Organization of the Book

The book is organized to provide the steps involved in conceptualizing, developing, implementing, evaluating, and maintaining an inpatient smoking cessation program. Each chapter works somewhat like a lab assignment, providing practical advice, and where appropriate, step-by-step procedures and case studies and examples, and requiring individual input, which if followed, will result in a series of linked pieces. Collectively, the linked pieces can be formatted into a program proposal for funding or approval, as well as serve as the blueprint for a tailor-made systems-based program. The linked pieces also provide the detailed work plan for implementation, evaluation, and maintenance. The book can be used as an ongoing resource to develop and/or fine-tune various aspects of a program.

Implementing an Inpatient Smoking Cessation Program includes:
- An overview of the clinical practice guidelines that support a hospital-based approach to cessation and how to tailor them to meet the needs of individual hospitals.
- Advantages of an inpatient program and the evidence and cost-effectiveness to support its use.
- Strategies for obtaining the necessary institutional buy-in for the program.
- Checklists for the implementation work to be done.
- Checklists for the program administrator.
- Tips on how to find a program champion, develop an advisory committee, and capitalize on community resources.
- The steps involved for a successful launch and sustainability of the program.
- Step-by-step instruction for delivering the program, including training the staff, setting up the infrastructure to support program delivery, and daily operations from the first 48 hours through the first year and beyond.

- Insight into where bottlenecks might occur, and how to plan for, avoid, and/or overcome them.

This book is written and organized from the perspective that readers will be asking the question "Where do I begin?", and looking for the starting points and steps for developing and implementing an inpatient smoking cessation program. The book is divided into three parts. Part I, Foundation, is designed to clarify the important supporting information and structures that need to be in place prior to developing and implementing an inpatient smoking cessation program. It provides an overview of the evidence and clinical guidelines supporting tobacco cessation and inpatient programs, the resources to consider, the administrative role involved, how to define the parameters of the program, and how to finance it. Part II, Program Development, provides information on the work involved in defining what the program will look like, who will provide the program and how to train them, how to evaluate the program, and how to promote it. Part III, Ramp Up and Delivery, provides information on working with hospital policies and procedures, and developing protocols and systems that will facilitate implementation, delivery, and maintenance. It also provides an overview of the rollout of the program, from the first 48 hours and beyond.

Acknowledgments

We begin by thanking our families for all they have done to make our work possible: Verna, Michael, Dale, Donna, Suesan, and Megan.

We owe deep gratitude to all the researchers, cessation counselors, research assistants, and technical staff who have worked with us on our various projects over the years and without whose work this book would not have been possible. Their collective depth of knowledge and experience far exceeds the expertise that we can claim between ourselves. We especially want to thank our long-time research colleagues at Stanford: Nancy Houston Miller, Bob DeBusk, Lynda Fisher, Emily Wien Fagans, Beth Sherman, Darby Cunning, Erica Froelicher, Rebecca Cameron, Kelly Reilly, and Helena Kraemer, and our research colleagues at Waterloo: Linda Corso, Roy Cameron, Steve Brown, Doris Winfield, Janice Farhood, Jill Bailey, Kathryn Campbell, and Jennifer Frood. We want to thank Joan Schoonover and Christine Vo, not only for their continued inspiring work in helping people quit smoking, but for providing data and examples for this book. We also want to thank Kim Sakis for providing examples for this book, Dale Smith for his help with the references, and Scott Sellick for help with the indexes.

We want to thank the following people who played a central role in establishing the *Staying Free* program in their healthcare settings in the U.S and allowing us to study and report on their efforts: Alfonzo Banuelos, Helen Chaknova, Frances

Conley, Ellen Feeney, Peggy Fleming-Crane, Maureen Forrester, Erin O'Grady, George Greenwald, James Guetzkow, Robert Hall, Maria Hamm, Nancy Janssen, Jeanne Kennedy, Caryn Kunkle, Ware Kuschner, Dennis Low, Sue Murphy, Jim Neil, John Phan, Stephen Pope, Nancy Sciutto, Javaid I. Sheikh, David Sobel, Lorriane Sundquist, Christine Vo, Clifford Wang, John Wehner, Michael Wood, and Judy Yanda. And in Canada: Michel Bedard, Carol Douloff, Nancy Martin, and William Wong.

The work, which has led to this book, would not have been possible without generous support from the National Heart, Lung, and Blood Institute (NHLBI), the State of California Tobacco-Related Disease Research Program, the Robert Wood Johnson Foundation, the American Heart Association, Andy and Eva Grove, and the National Cancer Institute of Canada with funds from the Canadian Cancer Society.

We thank the people at Lawrence Erlbaum Associates, Inc., who worked with us on this book—Debra Riegert, Kerry Breen, Nadine Simms, and all those behind the scenes for their help, support, conscientiousness, and good-natured patience. We also thank Belinda Borrelli, PhD, Brown Medical School, and Dana Busch, PhD, University of Pittsburgh Cancer Institute for their feedback in the development stage of the book.

Most importantly, we want to thank the many people who have volunteered to be part of our studies, often with the expectation of little personal benefit but with the wish to help others.

We hope that you find this book helpful. We would appreciate hearing from readers about their experiences developing and implementing an inpatient smoking cessation program.

Tables and Figures

Part I Foundation

1

Evidence Base for Tobacco Cessation and Inpatient Tobacco Cessation Programs

Tobacco use is a major health and healthcare issue. It is the leading cause of preventable mortality and morbidity in the United States (U.S.), Canada, the majority of other high-come nations, and increasingly, in low- and middle-income nations (U.S. Department of Health and Human Services [USDHHS], 2004). It is also responsible for staggering healthcare costs (USDHHS, 2004).

The focus of the most recent Surgeon General's report concludes that future reductions in tobacco-related morbidity, mortality, and healthcare costs will require a continuing and sustained effort (USDHHS, 2004). Because tobacco is the root or contributing cause of a large proportion of hospitalizations (USDHHS, 2004), we suggest, backed by the support of clinical practice guidelines (e.g., Fiore et al., 2000) and empirical evidence of the efficacy and cost-effectiveness of inpatient tobacco cessation programs (e.g., France et al., 2001), that hospital-based programs can play an important role in that effort, especially given the unusually high receptivity and long-term cessation success among patients who receive a tobacco cessation program during hospitalization, and the immediate benefits of quitting during hospitalization.

In this chapter we provide a broad overview of the evidence for the human and healthcare costs of tobacco and the potential cost savings with cessation, both from a general perspective as well as specifically for hospitalized patients. We conclude the chapter with empirical support for the high reach and efficacy for inpatient tobacco cessation programs in hospitals. Taken together with information in Chapter 2 on guidelines, quality assurance, and insurance coverage, the evidence base can help to build the business case for implementing programs in hospitals.

This chapter is not exhaustive of the empirical evidence available, but rather it provides a broad overview using review articles, where possible, to capture the state of knowledge. If more detailed information is required to help build the business case for implementing an inpatient tobacco cessation program in a particular hospital, it is advisable to begin with the information in the Surgeon General's report (USDHHS, 2004) and then supplement where necessary with individual articles from the literature. The key evidence in the report, representing over 1,600 scientific articles, is available to the public through the office on Smoking and Health at the Centers for Disease Control (CDC) in a searchable database (CDC, 2004; USDHHS, 2004).

HUMAN COSTS

The first Surgeon General's report in 1964 documented the causal relationship between smoking and chronic bronchitis and cancers of the lung and larynx (U.S. Department of Health, Education, and Welfare, 1964). Since 1964, there have been 27 Surgeon General reports that address tobacco (USDHHS, n.d.). Over the years, the documented negative health consequences of tobacco use supported by scientific evidence have continued to grow to such an extent that the most recent Surgeon General's report concludes that smoking harms nearly every organ of the body and causes generally poorer health (USDHHS, 2004).

Tobacco-Related Mortality

The tobacco-related mortality statistics are grim. Tobacco is responsible for one out of every five deaths in Canada[1] and the U.S., resulting in an estimated 45,000 and 440,000 deaths/year, respectively (Makomaski Illing & Kaiserman, 1999; USDHHS, 2004). The loss of life attributable to smoking in the U.S., is 13.2 years for men and 14.5 years for women (CDC, 2002).

Tobacco-Related Morbidity

The most recent Surgeon General's report (USDHHS, 2004) shows a *causal* relationship between smoking and myriad adverse health effects, ranging from a variety of cancers, cardiovascular diseases, respiratory diseases, and reproductive effects, to diverse other diseases/conditions such as eye-cataracts, hip fractures, and periodontis (Table 1). The report also suggests a strong relationship between smoking and various adverse health effects, such as a variety of cancers (colorectal, prostate, liver, brain, and breast), pregnancy outcomes (ectopic pregnancy, spontaneous abortion, and oral clefts), low bone density in older men, root-surface caries in teeth, erectile dysfunction, neovascular and atrophic age-related macular degeneration, onset or progression of retinopathy among diabetics, and ophthalmopathy associated with Graves' disease. Among children and adolescents who smoke, there is a suggestive relationship for a poorer prognosis with asthma.

Tobacco-Related Morbidity and Mortality Among Hospital Patients

The tobacco-related health effects in Table 1 have obvious significance for hospitalization and healthcare costs. But there are also tobacco-related risks that are specific to hospital patients. For example, surgical patients have an increased risk of a variety of intra-operative and postoperative complications and

---

[1] The population of Canada is approximately 1/10 that of the U.S.—many Canadian morbidity, mortality, and health cost statistics are approximately 1/10 that of the U.S.

infections (Egan & Wong, 1992; Thalgott et al., 1991). They also have an increased risk for in-hospital mortality, post-surgical admissions to the intensive care unit, lower respiratory tract infections, and failure rate for some surgeries (An et al., 1995; Brown et al., 1986; Delgado-Rodriguez et al., 2003; Egan & Wong, 1992).

Table 1. Causal Effects of Smoking On Disease

Disease	Causal Effects the Smoking
Cancer	bladder, renal cell, renal pelvis, cervical, endometrial in postmenopausal women, esophageal, kidney, laryngeal, leukemia, lung, oral, pharynx, pancreatic, stomach
Cardiovascular	abdominal aortic aneurysm, atherosclerosis, stroke, coronary heart disease
Respiratory	COPD, pneumonia, premature onset of and an accelerated age-related decline in lung function, poor asthma control, and all major respiratory symptoms among adults, including coughing, phlegm, wheezing, and dyspnea
Reproductive effects	sudden infant death syndrome (both for maternal smoking during and after pregnancy), reduced fertility in women, fetal growth restriction and low birth weight, premature rupture of the membranes, placenta previa, placental abruption, pre-term delivery and shortened gestation, and reduction of lung function in infants due to smoking during pregnancy
Other effects	eye-cataracts, adverse surgical outcomes related to wound healing and respiratory complications, hip fractures, low bone density in postmenopausal women, peptic ulcer in persons who are Helicobacter pylori positive, periodontitis, and diminished health status that might manifest as increased use of medical care services and increased absenteeism from work
Effects among children and adolescents who smoke	impaired lung growth during childhood and adolescence, early onset of lung function decline during late adolescence and early adulthood, respiratory symptoms (coughing, phlegm, wheezing, dyspnea), and asthma-related symptoms

Tobacco Cessation and Decreased Human Costs

All cause mortality decreases with tobacco cessation (USDHHS, 2004). At 35 years of age, the estimated life extension with cessation is approximately 8 years for men and women (Taylor et al., 2002). The incidence of tobacco-related morbidities also decreases with tobacco cessation, most notably heart disease, chronic lung disease, and various cancers (USDHHS, 2004). A rapid reduction in the risk of acute myocardial infarction (MI) is evidenced among asymptomatic persons as is reduced risk of re-infarction among post-MI patients (Samet, 1992; Sparrow et al., 1978). Among the smoking-induced abnormalities resulting in coronary heart disease—atherosclerosis, promotion of thrombosis, increased risk of coronary artery spasm, production of arrhythmias, and reduced oxygen delivery, all but atherosclerosis are believed to reverse within a short period of time following smoking cessation (Samet, 1992).

Tobacco Cessation and Decreased Human Costs Among Hospital Patients

Tobacco cessation during hospitalization results in immediate benefits such as significantly fewer intra-operative and postoperative complications (Egan & Wong, 1992; Moller et al., 2002; Sorensen et al., 2002) and decreased recovery time (Simon et al., 1997). Longer-term health benefits of cessation include decreased redo surgery and post-surgery death following coronary artery by-pass graft (Cavender et al., 1992; Voors et al., 1996), decreased re-stenosis after percutaneous translumian coronary angioplasty (Galen et al., 1988), and decreased acute MI, reinfarction, cardiac mortality, and all cause mortality (e.g., Critchley & Capewell, 2003; Hermanson et al., 1988; van Domburg et al., 2000). Improved prognosis and survival among some specific patient groups, such as those with head and neck cancer (Browman et al., 1993), are also evidenced. When adults who have children quit smoking, pediatric morbidity and hospitalizations decrease (DiFranza & Lew, 1996; Leung et al., 2003; Lightwood et al., 1999).

HEALTHCARE COSTS

The direct and indirect costs of tobacco-related illness are estimated to be $16 billion/year in Canada and $157 billion/year in the U.S. (Stephens et al., 2000; USDHHS, 2004). People who smoke are more likely to be hospitalized than those who do not, and will incur higher medical expenditures over their lifetimes than never-smokers (Hodgson, 1992).

The major tobacco-related illnesses account for a relatively high percentage of all hospital days. One study estimated that more than 3 million hospital days (approximately 7% of all hospital days) in Canada resulted from tobacco-related causes (Single, et al., 1998).[2] Another study showed that if smoking was completely eliminated among all American men aged 45 to 64, hospitalizations

---

[2] The study was based on 1992 data and is now out of date. In 2003, Health Canada funded CCSA to carry out a two year updated cost study. Results were not available at the time of this writing. See Canadian Centre on Substance Abuse, http://www.ccsa.ca/NR/rdonlyres/73A85C26-466C-4A7A-86E8F9D701284F99/0/ccsanewrel20040510e.pdf.

would decrease by as much as 12.5%, amounting to about $5.4 billion in healthcare savings (Miller et al., 1998).

Exposure to second-hand smoke also increases healthcare costs for children. Passive smoking is estimated to result in an excess of 160,000 pediatric hospitalizations each year in the U.S. for respiratory syncytial virus bronchiolitis, tympanostomies for treatment of middle ear infection (otitis media with effusion), asthma, and burns resulting from cigarette-related fires (Aligne & Stoddard, 1997). Annual smoking-attributable neonatal expenditures are between $366 million and $4.6 billion U.S., and loss of life costs are estimated at $8.2 billion U.S. (Aligne & Stoddard, 1997; Annual smoking attributable mortality, 2002).

Decreased Healthcare Costs with Quitting

Estimates suggest that a 1% absolute reduction in smoking prevalence in the U.S. would result in immediate first year savings of $44 million in healthcare costs ($\pm$ $26 million) due to decreased hospitalizations for acute MI and stroke alone (Lightwood & Glantz, 1997). Over a seven-year period, the estimates rise to $3.2 billion in savings for MI and stroke ($\pm$ 0.59 billion). The impact of cessation accrues rapidly for MI and stroke so these estimates are likely higher in the short-term than they would be for other diseases like cancer and emphysema.

Similar estimates have been made in Canada and England (Group d'analyse Economique, 2002; Naidoo et al., 2000). Canadian estimates suggest that an absolute 1% decrease in smoking prevalence plus a decrease of one cigarette per day for daily smokers who do not quit would translate, conservatively, into a savings estimate of $40 to $80 million for heart disease and lung cancer alone. Across all diseases, the Canadian estimate is $65 million in direct healthcare cost savings for each percentage point decline in the prevalence of smoking (Group d'analyse Economique, 2002).

In addition to estimated decreased hospitalizations for MI, stroke, and cancer, healthcare savings can be seen immediately with cessation during hospitalization due to shorter hospital stays, decreased recovery time, and decreased intra-operative and postoperative complications (Egan & Wong, 1992; Moller et al., 2002; Simon et al., 1997; Sorensen et al., 2002). Over time, cessation also results in decreased utilization—decreased number of hospitalizations and decreased number of hospital days (Wagner et al., 1995; DiFranza & Lew, 1996; Leung et al., 2003; Lightwood et al., 1999). In contrast, patients who do not quit tobacco at the time of their hospitalization show a steady increase in healthcare utilization over a five-year period of time—7%-

15% increase in outpatient visits, 30%-45% increase in hospital admissions, and 75%-100% increase in hospital days/year (Wagner et al., 1995).

There are also potential savings for children's healthcare costs when parents quit smoking (or at least stop exposing their children to second hand smoke). An annual drop of 1% in the adult smoking prevalence in the U.S. is estimated to prevent 1,300 low birth weight live births and save an estimated $21 million in direct medical costs per year. Over seven years, the savings would amount to an estimated $572 million (Lightwood et al., 1999).

Despite the compelling healthcare cost argument for cessation, the aggregate cost savings from cessation will depend on how many tobacco users quit, at what ages, and in what state of health (Hodgson, 1992). However, as Barendregt and his colleagues (1997) so aptly note, the argument as to whether or not tobacco users impose a net financial burden on the healthcare system should be approached with caution. Public health policy is concerned with health not just cost. Since tobacco use is a major risk to health, the objective of a health policy or recommendations to reduce tobacco use should be to decrease the risk to health.

COST-EFFECTIVENESS OF TOBACCO CESSATION

As a society, we value extended years of life and healthier years, so the choice for evaluating medical interventions is to compare the cost-effectiveness or the cost per year life saved (YLS) (or quality adjusted year of life saved [QAYLS]) among interventions rather than simply estimate the absolute cost savings to the system. Cost-effectiveness analyses allow decisions to be made to implement interventions that yield the highest return in health for the budget (Murray et al., 1994). Interventions costing $20,000/YLS are considered cost-effective (Goldman et al., 1996).

Interventions that foster tobacco cessation are among the most cost-effective applications of healthcare resources (Goldman et al., 1996; Tsevat, 1992), and are estimated to save more in lifetime medical expenditures than they cost (Cromwell et al., 1997). Unlike interventions which entail lifetime treatment, such as medications for hyperlipidemia and hypertension, tobacco cessation is often lifelong after a relatively brief period of treatment (Goldman et al., 1996). Estimates of the cost-effectiveness of smoking cessation with the general population have shown a broad range, from $1,000/YLS for smokers receiving advice to quit smoking during routine physician visits (Cummings et al., 1989) to $13,000/YLS when nicotine replacement therapy is added to physician advice during routine doctor's visits (Oster et al., 1986).

The cost and cost-effectiveness of implementing the original Agency for Healthcare Research and Quality (1996) *Smoking Cessation Clinical Practice Guideline* recommendations into physicians' offices and hospitals have been estimated (Cromwell et al., 1997). Analyses suggest that it would cost an estimated $6.3 billion in the first year for implementation if treatments were provided to 75% of American smokers 18 years and older who were willing to a make a quit attempt. This would result in a gain of 1.7 million new quitters at an average cost of $3,779 per quit, $2,587/YLS, and $1,915/QAYLS. The analyses showed that the more intensive the intervention, the more net benefit (i.e., the lower the cost/QALYS)—intensive counseling supplemented with transdermal nicotine generated the largest estimated number of quitters and cost the least per QALYS ($1,108).

Staying Free, our inpatient tobacco cessation program, has been estimated to cost $220/year life saved (YLS) for post-MI patients (Krumholz et al., 1993). The assumptions of the cost-effectiveness analyses were based on a 26% difference in biochemically-confirmed one-year cessation rates between the intervention and usual care groups (71% vs. 45%, respectively), and program costs of $100 per patient enrolled in the intervention (assuming no costs for usual care). Although a 26% difference between treatment groups is rare, sensitivity analyses showed that if the cost remained at $100 per patient, the program would remain cost-effective even if the difference in one-year cessation between groups fell to as low as 0.3% (i.e., 3 quitters for every 1,000 patients enrolled). Sensitivity analyses also showed that if a 26% difference between groups could be maintained, the cost of the program could increase to as high as $8,840 per patient, and still remain cost-effective.

The cost-effectiveness of Staying Free for post-MI patients not only compares favorably to interventions currently considered highly cost-effective (i.e., less than $20,000/YLS), but is also reported in a review to be one of the most cost-effective interventions for heart disease risk management (Goldman et al., 1996). For example, the review estimated hyperlipidemic medication to cost between $4,700 and $2 million/YLS (in 1993 dollars), and hypertensive medication to cost between $16,900 and $111,600/YLS. Balloon angioplasty ranged between $8,700 and $109,000/adjusted YLS, and coronary artery by-pass surgery cost between $18,200 and $1.1 million/adjusted YLS.

Return on Investment

In addition to favorable cost-effectiveness analyses of tobacco cessation programs, economic analyses also suggest the potential for substantial economic return on investment (ROI) of program costs. One study showed that for as little as $328 per recipient, a healthcare plan could save upwards of $6,000 per patient per year that would otherwise be spent treating preventable disease (Curry et al.,

1998). The study further showed a positive correlation between the level of benefit provided and the results achieved. There is now a new website calculator to estimate the ROI of tobacco cessation programs (Fellows et al., 2004). It was developed by America's Health Insurance Plans (AHIP) and the Center for Health Research, Kaiser Permanente Northwest (CHR), and can be accessed free of charge (http://www.businesscaseroi.org).

USING HOSPITALS FOR TOBACCO CESSATION

As suggested in the introduction to this chapter, hospital-based programs can play an important role in the effort to reduce tobacco-related morbidity, mortality, and healthcare costs. Inpatient tobacco cessation programs have shown both high efficacy and high reach, and therefore provide high population impact. The common measure for population impact of a program is a function of the percentage of people who access the program (reach) and how well the program works to help people quit smoking (efficacy).

Using hospitals as a delivery channel for tobacco cessation is consistent with ecological models for health behavior change (Green et al., 1996; Stokols, 1996) and the "*planning cube*" that is central to the National Institutes of Health blueprint for tobacco control planning in public health (USDHHS, 1991). Ecological approaches are based on the assumption that health behavior change programs established in key community channels, such as hospitals, have the potential to facilitate initial and sustained change in large numbers of individuals.

Efficacy of Inpatient Tobacco Cessation Programs

Results from two recent meta-analyses show that intensive inpatient tobacco cessation programs evidence among the highest one-year cessation rates in the published literature, ranging from 14% to 70%, depending upon the patient population, with post-MI patients evidencing the highest abstinence (France et al., 2001; Rigotti et al., 2003). Even patients receiving minimal intervention during hospitalization (often called "usual care") tend to have relatively high long-term abstinence rates—8% to 54%, depending on the patient population (France et al., 2001). These rates compare favorably to the estimated 3% of the general population of tobacco-users who quit on their own (Cohen et al., 1989), the 10% who quit with physician advice (Fiore et al., 2000), and the 11%-20% who quit using various other techniques (Fiore et al., 2000). The increases in quit rates over usual care attributed to intensive interventions have ranged from –1% to 10% (median 4%) among general hospital patients and from 7% to 36% among cardiac patients (median 15%; France et al., 2001).

The main conclusion from the inpatient tobacco cessation intervention meta-analyses was that high intensity interventions initiated in-hospital and followed up with post-discharge contact are more effective in promoting long-terms abstinence than brief intensity interventions with no post-discharge follow-up (France et al., 2001; Rigotti et al., 2003). The optimal "dose" of intervention is not entirely clear, but the data suggest that some follow-up post-discharge is indicated, particularly over the first month during which time the risk of relapse is greatest. The Rigotti et al., (2003) meta-analysis concluded that at least one month of follow-up contact was necessary, whereas the France et al., (2001) meta-analysis concluded that 3 to 5 months of post-discharge counseling was necessary[3]. The latter also concluded that the more successful programs had a dedicated tobacco cessation counselor. Both meta-analyses showed that programs that have tested either a brief in-hospital intervention and/or offered little post-discharge follow-up have not significantly increased one-year cessation over usual care.

Reach of Inpatient Tobacco Cessation Programs

Since smokers are more likely than non-smokers to be hospitalized (Haapanen-Niemi et al., 1999), offering a tobacco cessation program during hospitalization has the potential to reach large numbers of smokers. The dissemination study of Staying Free enrolled 52% of inpatients identified as smokers (Smith et al., 2002). One of the relative advantages of the program that results in such high reach is that the program is brought to the patient at the bedside—the patient does not have to seek out treatment. Typically, less than 2% of the patients who enroll in our inpatient tobacco cessation programs report that they would seek out a program to help them quit. A recent population study using a modified telephone-only version of Staying Free was able to recruit only 0.6% of estimated smokers in the general population across 10 communities (Smith et al., 2004). Based on these low enrollment numbers for population-based programs, the acceptance rates we have evidenced for the inpatient tobacco cessation program suggests that tobacco cessation programs offered as part of inpatient services have the potential to reach high numbers of smokers, many of whom would not otherwise seek treatment.

---

[3] The two meta-analyses share most, but not all, of the same studies. Also, France et al., (2001) provide more detail than Rigotti et al. (2003)—they include the actual cessation rates found in the studies, differentiate among the various patient populations, and differentiate between self-report and confirmed cessation rates by period of follow-up (i.e., 6 and 12 months).

2

Clinical Guidelines, Quality Assurance, and Insurance Coverage

Hospitals direct a large portion of their effort and resources to the treatment of tobacco-related illnesses. Until the 1990s, however, little had been done in hospitals to actively and systematically address the root cause of the problem—tobacco use. In the 1990s, that began to change with the introduction of clinical practice guidelines, insurance programs to cover tobacco cessation programs, and tobacco cessation counseling included as quality assurance indicators in hospitals. The surge of interest, guidelines, quality indicators, and insurance coverage for tobacco cessation programs in primary healthcare were and are a result of the well-documented heavy cost tobacco extols on human life, the mounting healthcare costs to treat tobacco-related illnesses (USDHHS, 2004), and the strong evidence base for the efficacy and cost-effectiveness of tobacco cessation programs (Fiore et al., 2000).

This chapter provides an overview of clinical practice guidelines, insurance coverage, and quality assurance indicators for hospital-based tobacco cessation programs. The information provided here is meant as an introduction to the various topics to help those not familiar with the issues to get acquainted; a more in-depth review is beyond the scope of this book. The information in this chapter can provide a starting point for individual hospitals to build the business case for implementing an inpatient tobacco cessation program.

CLINICAL GUIDELINES

The tobacco-related health and healthcare costs, and the efficacy and cost-effectiveness of tobacco cessation programs, have resulted in the development of a series of clinical practice guidelines for treating tobacco. The most well known, and arguably the most extensive, guideline was initially sponsored in 1996 by the Agency for Healthcare Policy and Research (now the Agency for Healthcare Research and Quality [AHRQ], 1996), *Smoking Cessation Clinical Practice Guideline No. 18*. This guideline was updated in 2000 by the U.S. Department of Health and Human Services (USDHHS) as *Treating Tobacco Use and Dependence Clinical Practice Guideline* (Fiore et al., 2000).

It is important to note that a number of professional associations, such as, but not limited to, the American Psychiatric Association (1996), the American

Medical Association (1994), the American, British, and Canadian Thoracic Societies (O'Donnell et al., 2003; British Thoracic Society, 1998; Celli et al., 1995), and the Health Education Authority (West, et al., 2000), have established their own clinical practice guidelines for tobacco use and treatment. Most guidelines are consistent with, and in some cases identical to, the USDHHS guideline. For example, the Canadian Thoracic Society guideline specifies:

> "....*Even brief counseling lasting less than 3 min should be offered to every smoker, with the understanding that more intensive therapy (individual and group counseling, nicotine replacement and the antidepressant bupropion), which results in the highest quitting rates, should be used whenever possible*" (Celli et al., 1995, p. 3).

TREATING TOBACCO USE AND DEPENDENCE CLINICAL PRACTICE GUIDELINE

The 2000 Treating Tobacco Use and Dependence guideline, although published by the USDHHS, was sponsored by a consortium of seven federal government and nonprofit organizations (Fiore et al., 2000). The organizations include the AHRQ, Centers for Disease Control and Prevention (CDC), National Cancer Institute, National Heart, Lung, and Blood Institute, National Institute on Drug Abuse, Robert Wood Johnson Foundation, and the University of Wisconsin Medical School's Center for Tobacco Research and Intervention.

The USDHHS guideline is the result of a systematic review and analysis (primarily meta-analysis) of the scientific literature of tobacco use, dependence, and cessation between 1975 and 1999 (Fiore et al., 2000). The first guideline by the AHRQ in 1996 covered articles published between 1975 and 1994. The updated 2000 Treating Tobacco guideline added articles published between 1995 and 1999. The guideline originated with a screening of 6,000 published articles on tobacco treatment and dependence that were then winnowed down to a smaller number of articles on which the data analyses and panel opinions for the guideline were based. The guideline was written by a panel of private-sector experts, consortium representatives, and staff, and then peer-reviewed by 70 external reviewers.

Guideline Recommendations for Patient Intervention

On the basis of evidence, the USDHHS guideline recommends that all clinicians intervene with all patients who use tobacco on every encounter using the "5 As" (Fiore et al., 2000). All patients should be *asked* whether they use tobacco, and if they do, they should be *advised* to quit and *assessed* for their interest in quitting. Clinicians should *assist* patients willing to try to quit tobacco by providing treatments identified in the guideline as effective, and follow-up sessions should be *arranged*. Patients who are unwilling to try to quit should be assisted by clinicians providing a brief motivational intervention based on the "5 Rs":

1. *relevance* of quitting to the patient
2. personalized and general *risks* of continuing to smoke
3. *rewards* of quitting
4. *roadblocks* or barriers to quitting
5. *repetition* of the motivational interview every time an unmotivated patient has an encounter with a clinician

According to the guideline, the minimum tobacco service offered should be brief counseling because even brief counseling has been found to be effective. However, there is a strong dose-response relationship between the intensity of interventions and cessation rates such that more intense interventions, especially more minutes of face-to-face contact, should be offered when available. The guideline also recommends first and second line pharmacotherapy to be used with all patients attempting to quit smoking.

Guideline Recommendations for System Changes

The USDHHS guideline states that it is essential for clinicians and healthcare delivery systems, including administrators, insurers, and purchasers, to institutionalize the consistent identification, documentation, and treatment of every tobacco user seen in a health setting (Fiore et al., 2000). There are six specific systems-based strategies recommended in the guideline. Each carries with it specific recommended actions. The six strategies are:

1. Every clinic should implement a tobacco-user identification system.
2. All healthcare systems should provide education, resources, and feedback to promote provider interventions.
3. Clinical sites should dedicate staff to provide tobacco dependence treatment and assess the delivery of this treatment in staff performance evaluations.
4. Hospitals should promote policies that support and provide tobacco dependence services.
5. Insurers and managed care organizations (MCOs) should include tobacco dependence treatments (both counseling and pharmacotherapy) as paid or covered services for all subscribers or members of health insurance packages.

6. Insurers and MCOs should reimburse clinicians and specialists for delivery of effective tobacco dependence treatments and include these interventions among the defined duties of clinicians.

Both the original AHRQ guideline and the updated USDHHS guideline identified hospitals as important delivery channels for smoking cessation programs. The specific recommendation for hospitals is:

"*Smoking cessation treatments have been shown to be effective for hospitalized smokers. Therefore, hospitalized patients should be provided smoking cessation treatments shown to be effective in this guideline.*" (Fiore et al., 2000, p. 98).

INSURANCE COVERAGE

Studies have demonstrated the benefit of providing insurance coverage for tobacco cessation counseling and medications, although coverage varies substantially across insurance plans and often remains limited (Curry et al., 1998; McPhillips-Tangum et al., 2004; Rigotti et al., 2002). The good news is that increasingly more insurance plans and hospitals are beginning to include coverage/reimbursement for tobacco cessation services and pharmacotherapy (e.g., McPhillips-Tangum, 2004). Being aware of the types of initiatives that are developing can provide potential resources for exploring ways to pay for tobacco cessation programs. Case examples of insurance coverage and strategies for working with healthcare plans in the U.S. to design a tobacco benefit are available from the Addressing Tobacco in Health Care (ATHC)[4] National Technical Assistance office (http://www.aahp.org/atmc/ntaosum.htm).

In general, tobacco cessation coverage will often include both counseling and pharmacotherapy. Counseling can include participation in either an individual and group program, and is often limited to one program per calendar year. Clinicians can also bill for tobacco dependence counseling. The USDHHS guideline provides examples of diagnostic (ICD-9-CM) and billing codes for the documentation of tobacco cessation treatment for reimbursement purposes (Fiore et al., 2000). Diagnostic codes can include, for example, tobacco use disorder (305.1) and history of tobacco use (V15.82). Billing codes for counseling will vary across plans and payors, and can include (Fiore et al., 2000):

---

[4] ATHC was established to advance integration of tobacco cessation/prevention programs into routine healthcare (Rosenthal, 2000; http://www.athc.wisc.edu).

1. preventive medicine treatments—as part of the initial or period comprehensive preventive medicine examination
   a. new patients (99383-99387)
   b. established patients (99393-99397)
2. preventive medicine treatments as specific counseling and/or risk factor reduction intervention
   a. individual (99401-99404)
   b. group counseling (99411-99412)
3. psychiatric therapeutic procedures, office or other outpatient facility (90804-90809)
4. psychiatric therapeutic procedures, inpatient hospital, partial hospital, or residential care facility (90816-90822)
5. psychiatric therapeutic procedures, other psychotherapy (90853)
6. dental code (01320)

Coverage for pharmacotherapy can include both prescription agents and over-the-counter nicotine replacement therapy (NRT), although not all health plans cover the latter. Regular prescription co-payments often apply to pharmacotherapy, with coverage limited to one course of medication (e.g., 3-month supply) per calendar year, although the benefit may be repeated in subsequent years. Pharmacotherapy coverage in some plans requires evidence of concurrent behavioral counseling for tobacco cessation.

U.S. Centers for Medicare and Medicaid (CMS)

Until recently, CMS coverage for tobacco cessation services in the U.S. was regional, not national. CMS has now added national coverage for smoking and tobacco cessation counseling for Medicare beneficiaries who have an illness caused or complicated by tobacco use, including heart disease, cerebral-vascular disease, lung disease, weak bones, blood clots, and cataracts—the diseases that account for the bulk of Medicare spending (USDHHS, 2005a). The benefit also applies to beneficiaries who take any of the many medications whose effectiveness is complicated by tobacco use—including insulin and medicines for high blood pressure, blood clots, and depression. As this initiative was put forward, there was an extra push to extend coverage to hospitals (e.g., Rigotti, 2005).

In order to be eligible for CMS coverage of tobacco services, patients must be competent and alert at the time that services are provided. Intermediate and intensive tobacco cessation counseling services will be covered for both outpatient and hospitalized beneficiaries who are smokers, as long as those services are furnished by qualified physicians and other Medicare-recognized practitioners. Minimal counseling is covered at each evaluation and management visit. Beyond that, Medicare will cover two cessation attempts per year. Each attempt may include a maximum of four intermediate or intensive sessions (the practitioner and patient have flexibility to choose), with the total annual benefit covering up to eight sessions in a 12-month period. An overview of what is covered is provided in Table 2.

Medicare's upcoming prescription drug benefit will cover tobacco cessation treatments that are prescribed by a physician (USDHHS, 2005a). Self-administrable pharmacotherapy for the purpose of tobacco cessation is not currently a covered benefit. Under the Medicare Modernization Act (MMA) of 2003 Part D, however, drugs are defined to include certain tobacco cessation agents beginning in January of 2006.

Table 2. Overview of CMC Coverage of Tobacco Services (USDHHS, 2005a)

Services Covered

Section 1861(s)(1)	Physicians' services.
Section 1861(s)(2)(A)	Service furnished as an incident to a physician's.

Professional Service

Section 1861 (s)(2)(B)	Outpatient hospital services.
Section 1861 (s)(2)(E)	Rural health clinic services and federally qualified.

Health Center Services

Section 1861(s)(2)(K)	Services that would be physicians' services if furnished by a physician and that are performed by a physician assistant (subsection (i)), nurse practitioner or clinical nurse specialist (subsection (ii)).
Section 1861 (s)(2)(M)	Qualified psychologist services.
Section 1861 (s)(2)(N)	Clinical social worker services.

Insurance Coverage in Canada

In Canada, tobacco cessation counseling and pharmacotherapy are often covered through employee benefits (extended health insurance), so employees should talk to employers and employers should talk to the insurance companies about coverage. The ROI calculator introduced in Chapter 1 might be a helpful tool to make the case (http://www.businesscaseroi.org). Coverage often has an annual cap for counseling (up to $500). Since inpatient tobacco cessation counseling services are still not offered in most Canadian hospitals, coverage for counseling would most likely involve outpatient services, such as group or individual counseling with a therapist. However, physicians, in all but two Canadian provinces (British Columbia and Alberta), can bill for tobacco counseling services through the provincial health insurance plans (Sullivan & Kothari, 1997), so counseling during hospitalization could potentially be covered. Coverage items vary by province (Table 3).

Table 3. Overview of Provincial Insurance Coverage of Tobacco Services (Sullivan & Kothari, 1997)

Province	Billing Options
Manitoba	medically necessary initial visit
Nova Scotia	lifestyle counseling
Northwest Territories, Yukon, Saskatchewan	general counseling
New Brunswick	office visit
Ontario	minor office visit nicotine dependence, regular office visit nicotine dependence, counseling nicotine dependence, psychotherapy nicotine dependence
Prince Edward Island	health promotion counseling

In extended health benefit plans, prescription pharmacotherapy is often covered separately from counseling under prescription medications, and usually includes some level of prescription co-payment or dispensing fee. Coverage of over-the-counter NRT remains a challenge but is covered by some plans, such as Non-Insured Health Benefits for First Nations and Inuit (for an alphabetical listing of NRT medications covered see: http://www.hc-sc.gc.ca/fnih-spni/pubs/drug-med/2005-10_drugmed_list/intro2_e.html#listings).

QUALITY ASSURANCE

In the U.S., the institutionalization of the consistent identification, documentation, and treatment of tobacco users is being "fast-tracked" into existence due to hospital quality assurance indicators, at least for some patient populations. Beginning in 2001, the Joint Commission on Accreditation of Healthcare Organizations (JCAHO)[5] and CMS (2003) worked together to create a common set of measure specifications for quality assurance indicators (JCAHO, n.d.[b]). Part of the quality assurance measures were the identification,

---

[5] JCAHO is an American standards-setting and accrediting body in healthcare. Accreditation is a distinction given to an organization when its performance meets or exceeds the JCAHO's standards and quality expectations. JCAHO makes comparison information publicly available (JCAHO, n.d.[a]).

documentation, and treatment of tobacco use for patients diagnosed with acute myocardial infarction, heart failure, and community-acquired pneumonia.

The JCAHO measures are documented in the Specifications Manual for National Hospital Quality Measures (JCAHO, 2005). Ultimately, the data collected with these measures will be used to improve the healthcare delivery process and permit comparison of local hospitals with others on state and national levels, allowing private and public purchasers, oversight and accrediting entities, and payers and providers of hospital care to make informed healthcare choices based on the quality of services provided by hospitals.

The JCAHO rationale for providing smoking cessation advice and/or counseling during hospital stay as a quality assurance indicator is based on the evidence included in the AHRQ (1996) and USDHHS (2000) guidelines. The rationale specifically highlights the efficacy of smoking cessation treatments, the cost-effectiveness of smoking cessation treatments relative to other commonly used disease prevention interventions and medical treatments, hospitalization being an ideal opportunity for a patient to stop smoking, the findings that smoking cessation might promote patients' medical recovery, and the evidence that tobacco use is the most important modifiable cause of premature death.

In summary, the combination of guidelines, insurance coverage, and quality assurance measures will have a strong impact on the institutionalization of tobacco use cessation programs. Mindful of the costs of implementing tobacco use cessation programs, we strongly believe that all healthcare systems need to provide these programs and to be held accountable to their constituents if they fail to do so.

3

Translating Research into Practice: The Example of Staying Free

In the early 1980s, one of the authors (Taylor) along with his colleagues at the Stanford Cardiac Rehabilitation Program identified the need for an inpatient tobacco cessation program. This happened during a home-based exercise study for patients who had suffered a heart attack. Anecdotally, it was noted that many patients quit smoking within the first few weeks following their heart attack. These patients were more likely to remain non-smokers over the long-term than those who did not quit within those first few seemingly critical weeks.

The idea that a heart attack could trigger people to quit smoking and remain abstinent led to the development of a tobacco cessation intervention designed to be initiated at the bedside during hospitalization as soon as possible following a heart attack, and then followed up post-discharge with telephone counseling. The original program was developed to determine whether systematically offering a bedside intervention would encourage more patients to quit smoking immediately following their heart attack, thereby increasing cessation over the spontaneous quit rate that would be evidenced without an intervention. Further, if a bedside intervention did work to increase the number of patients who quit immediately following their heart attack, the question remained as to whether those higher initial quit rates would translate into a higher percentage of patients remaining abstinent over the first year following hospital discharge.

The first randomized clinical trial of the inpatient tobacco cessation program, Staying Free[6], was a huge success. Sixty-one percent of the patients receiving the intervention were biochemically-confirmed non-smokers at one year after hospital discharge compared to 32% among those receiving usual care (Taylor et al., 1990). These one-year confirmed cessation rates and the 29% difference between treatment groups remain among the highest reported in the literature (for a meta-analysis, see France et al., 2001).

Staying Free has now been successfully tested with different patient populations, in different hospitals, with different healthcare systems, with various types of providers, as a stand-alone program in standard practice in a number of different types of hospitals, and even internationally. Testing has included seven

---

[6]Staying Free is the program name used when the intervention runs as a stand-alone program in standard hospital practice—the name has not been used in published research papers.

randomized clinical trials, four with heart patients (Burgess et al., in progress; DeBusk et al., 1994; Sivarajan Froelicher et al., 2004; Taylor et al., 1990) and three with general hospital patients (Houston Miller et al., 1997; Smith et al., submitted; Taylor et al., 1996), and two dissemination projects (Smith et al., 2002; Taylor et al., 2005).

Across studies, Staying Free has resulted in consistently high one-year cessation rates—48%-70% among post-MI patients, and 27-49% among general patients. The program is relatively inexpensive to deliver, appears to be acceptable to the majority of smokers who are hospitalized, and can be extended to hospital employees and their families, work-sites, and communities on a cost-recovery basis. We believe that the success hinges on the synergistic effect of a centralized systems-based case-managed approach, an effective theory-based intervention, and the unique situation created by hospitalization. During hospitalization patients are removed from their daily cues to smoke, surrounded by non-smoking cues, motivated by the saliency of disease, and undergo the worst withdrawal during the first 2-3 days of hospitalization.

In this chapter, we provide an overview of the inpatient tobacco cessation intervention, Staying Free, we have worked with over the last 20 years. The chapter begins with general information about the program—program components, systems-based delivery, and program success. We conclude the chapter with a framework for translating research into practice—i.e., what we believe is required to implement an inpatient tobacco cessation program with a dedicated tobacco cessation counselor. The framework is a translation of the "business of doing business" work that goes beyond the science of the intervention and moves into what is necessary from a practical perspective in order to make an inpatient program a reality in standard practice. Although the focus in this chapter is on Staying Free, the program itself was designed to be similar in principle and application to other tobacco cessation programs.

COMPONENTS OF STAYING FREE INTENSIVE INTERVENTION

Overview

In its original form, Staying Free involves 45-60 minutes of bedside education and relapse prevention counseling during hospitalization provided by a nurse case-manager specially-trained in tobacco cessation. Education and counseling are augmented with take-home patient materials—video, workbook, relaxation audiotape, and pamphlets. Physicians are involved by providing one-minute scripted cessation messages at the bedside. Continuity of care is maintained for three months after hospital discharge through counselor-initiated telephone counseling for relapse prevention.

Education Component of Staying Free

The bedside encounter begins with education. The education component covers the personalized risks of smoking and benefits of quitting tailored to patients' medical conditions, withdrawal, weight gain including how to manage or counteract it with exercise and low-fat snacking, social support, and the importance of creating non-smoking spaces (car, home, and office). Education on nicotine replacement therapy (NRT) and bupropion is provided when requested or indicated, but the medications themselves are not.

Patient Materials Component of Staying Free

Take-home patient materials include an 18-minute relapse prevention video, a companion relapse prevention workbook, and a 15-minute relaxation audiotape. The materials are part of the American Heart Association's Active Partnership for the Health of Your Heart (AHA, 1990), and are available through the AHA.

The video features unequivocal advice from physicians to quit smoking and recommendations to use hospitalization as the opportunity to do so. It also covers the experiential aspects of quitting, and provides ideas for remaining tobacco-free in difficult situations. The workbook includes information on addiction, slips and urges, the importance of adding enjoyable activities to one's day, and suggestions for low-fat snacking. Central to the workbook is a section on preventing relapse, which includes a 14-item questionnaire for rating self-confidence to remain smoke-free in situations that trigger the urge to smoke (Baer et al., 1986). Suggestions for remaining smoke-free in each of the 14 situations are provided. The relaxation audiotape is designed to help patients learn to control anxious feelings and gain more control over their sympathetic nervous system during the cessation process. Pamphlets include information on how to quit, tobacco cessation resources in the community, and information on medical aids to quit smoking if requested (NRT and bupropion). The pamphlets have varied across studies, and have often been provided free of charge by government and non-government agencies with a tobacco cessation mandate.

Counseling Component of Staying Free

Counseling is guided by the 14-item self-efficacy questionnaire (Baer et al., 1986) found in patients' relapse prevention workbooks. The cessation counselor guides patients to rate their confidence (self-efficacy) to resist the urge to smoke in 14 situations that have been identified as being high risk for triggering the urge to smoke (e.g., after a meal, when bored, when emotionally upset, etc.).

After completing the questionnaire, the counselor and patient watch the relapse prevention video, which helps explain the importance of situations in triggering the urge to smoke and provides suggestions for remaining smoke-free when challenging situations arise. Following the video, the counselor and patient use ideas from the film and workbook to develop cognitive, behavioral, and social support coping strategies for situations in which patients have less than 70% confidence to remain abstinent.

Bedside counseling is grounded in Bandura's social cognitive theory (1986), with an emphasis on enhancing self-efficacy to remain smoke-free. Self-efficacy is situation-specific self-confidence—"the conviction that one can successfully execute the behavior required to produce the outcomes" (Bandura, 1977, p. 193). Self-efficacy can be increased by helping patients plan strategies to remain abstinent in advance of encountering situations that might trigger them to smoke. Having preplanned strategies should increase perceived efficacy to remain tobacco-free in each difficult situation, and the higher one's self-efficacy, the greater the likelihood of remaining tobacco-free. (Dr. Bandura was involved in the development of the original Staying Free intervention.)

The counseling paradigm of focusing on difficult situations, developing coping strategies, and enhancing self-efficacy is also guided by Marlatt and Gordon's (1985) relapse prevention model for the addictions. The key to relapse prevention is to prepare for difficult situations in advance so that when difficulty strikes, one can intentionally act to remain tobacco-free rather than react to the heat of the moment and slip back to using tobacco. Each time a coping strategy is successfully implemented and abstinence is protected, self-efficacy will be further strengthened. People who try to remain abstinent in high risk situations without preplanned strategies will have a more difficult time. Their self-efficacy to persevere and remain abstinent in the heat of the moment will be low, they will tend to focus on the rewarding properties of nicotine rather than their desire to remain abstinent, and they will be more likely to break their abstinence, which in turn, will further decrease their self-efficacy to remain abstinent.

Although Staying Free was developed for patients interested in quitting tobacco during their hospital stay, the approach taken with the program is nonetheless consistent with the stages of change theory, part of the more encompassing transtheoretical model of change (Prochaska & DiClemente, 1983). The stages of change theory assumes that individuals are in different stages of readiness to change a health behavior and that interventions need to be adapted to the participants' readiness to change. With Staying Free, we assess readiness to quit using a single item 7-point intention scale ("Do you intend to stay off cigarettes and other tobacco products in the next month?"). If the patient expresses some interest in quitting (a score of 4 or more) the cessation counselor provides the full intervention. If the patient is not interested in quitting, the reasons for their unwillingness are explored. If they remain uninterested, they are encouraged to reduce the number of cigarettes or other tobacco products (Houston Miller & Taylor, 1995, p. 88).

Pharmacotherapy Component of Staying Free

When Staying Free was designed, only limited NRT was available. In recent years, and in later iterations of Staying Free, we began evaluating patients for the need and their interest in using NRT and other prescription agents (e.g., bupropion) based on the assumption that tobacco use is addictive and that patients benefit from NRT. One advantage of including NRT and other prescription agents through an inpatient tobacco cessation program provided by a nurse case-manager is that the potential harmful effects of such agents can be carefully assessed in the context of patients whose medical status has generally been well characterized. Coverage and provision of NRT and other prescription agents, however, depends on the institution and insurance plan—it is not traditionally provided free of charge by hospitals.

Physician Advice Component of Staying Free

Attending physicians are cued by the cessation counselor with a scripted note on patients' medical charts to provide unequivocal advice to their patients to quit smoking. When possible, advice is tailored to patients' medical conditions. Here is the message we have used:

> *I see from your chart that you smoked prior to your hospitalization. Because of the bans on smoking in the hospital, it has probably been difficult for you to not smoke since you've been here. I hope you'll take this opportunity to consider yourself an ex-smoker.*

> *You should realize that the worst period of withdrawal is during the first 2-3 days after quitting, and most patients go through this period during hospitalization.*

> *It is important for you to quit smoking because smoking leads to chronic diseases such as heart attack and lung cancer. Your risk is further increased because* <<smoking cessation nurse puts reason here (e.g., *your blood pressure is high*)>>.

Post-Discharge Telephone Counseling Component of Staying Free

In-hospital education and counseling are augmented with post-discharge telephone counseling calls for continued support. The calls are initiated by the cessation counselor at 2, 7, 21, and 90 days after patients are discharged from the hospital. The counseling calls follow the basic relapse prevention format of the bedside counseling, and take only 5-10 minutes each. They focus on relapse prevention strategies and working through difficulties remaining abstinent. When patients relapse to tobacco use, the calls focus on working with the patient to reinstate abstinence by setting a quit date, creating an environment conducive to quitting, determining what worked and what did not with the last quit attempt, and then creating a new quit plan. The scripts that guide the telephone counseling are published in a monograph (Houston Miller & Taylor, 1995).

Brief Intervention Alternative To the Intensive Intervention

A brief intervention was developed by Stanford Cardiac Rehabilitation Program researchers to serve as a comparison control treatment ("usual care") in the randomized clinical trials of Staying Free. Because of the well-documented harmful effects of using tobacco and the findings that all tobacco cessation interventions work to some degree to help people quit smoking and therefore all interventions serve to decrease health risks to some degree, it was deemed not ethical to provide nothing or a "waiting-list control" as a comparison group in the trials.

The brief intervention was designed to include the minimum components a brief tobacco cessation intervention. It includes advice to quit using tobacco, delivered by both a cessation counselor and the attending physician. The advice is tailored to patients' medical conditions. The brief intervention also includes a pamphlet on how to quit, a pamphlet on tobacco cessation resources in the community, and print information on medical aids to quit smoking if requested (NRT and bupropion). The pamphlets have varied across studies and institutions. If a brief rather than intensive intervention is adopted, the materials do not have to be a drain on resources—they can be a single-page tri-fold pamphlet, and can often be obtained free of charge from government and non-government agencies that have a tobacco cessation mandate.

SYSTEMS-BASED DELIVERY

The key to consistent delivery and program outcomes with Staying Free rests on establishing a hospital infrastructure that involves of a series of systems. Systems are required for identifying patients who use tobacco, screening tobacco users for program eligibility, providing the intervention at the bedside, continuing with telephone support post-discharge, and following up to assess post-discharge tobacco use. Together, these systems create a seamless, predictable, and measurable flow for the program. The program flow is provided in Figure 1.

Figure 1. Flow of Systems-Based Delivery

Tobacco Use Identification
Step 1. Admitting staff ask tobacco use status
Step 2. Tobacco users identified by counselor review of daily census

|

Eligibility Screens
Step 1: Review of daily census meets criteria (e.g., age, unit)
Step 2. Review of patient charts (e.g., medically stable, no substance abuse)
Step 3. Bedside interview

|

Program Recruitment
Baseline data collected for tracking and analyses
If research is being conducted, consent forms completed, assignment to treatment group
Intervention initiated immediately

|

Intensive Bedside Intervention (45-60 min)
Tailored advice, education, relapse prevention
counseling, take-home materials (video, workbook,
relaxation tape, pamphlets)

|

Post-Discharge Counseling (20-40 min total)
Counselor-initiated post-discharge telephone
counseling at 2, 7, 21, and 90 days post discharge

|

Tobacco use status follow-up (15 min total)
Telephone calls at 3, 6, 12 months post-discharge

|

Confirmation of tobacco use status (time varies)
Step 1. Saliva samples collected for confirmation
Step 2. Analysis of samples
(Alternate: proxy confirmation via telephone)

Identification System for Patients Who Use Tobacco

A very simple system was designed as part of Staying Free to identify patients who use tobacco. A single question was added to the admitting forms "Have you used any tobacco products in the last month?". All patients admitted to the hospital are asked this question by hospital admitting staff. A special daily hospital census report with a column added for tobacco use status (yes/no) was developed as the companion piece for easy identification of patients who use tobacco. The tobacco cessation counselor only needs a copy of the daily census in order to quickly identify all patients in the hospital on any given day who, upon admission to the hospital, reported using tobacco in the previous month.

of all possible systems that could be devised for the identification of tobacco use, we believe that this is arguably the simplest, most efficient, least time-consuming, and most consistently accurate. It centralizes the process of identifying tobacco use, and the accuracy is easy to track by comparing the daily census with occasional bed-to-bed fidelity checks (i.e., going bed-to-bed and asking patients if they used tobacco products in the month prior to hospitalization). If accuracy falls short of 90-100% (which is likely—not all patients admitted to the hospital are conscious, coherent, able to communicate, or willing to provide an answer), it is relatively simple to identify barriers to the identification of tobacco use status and find solutions (see Chapter 10).

Screening Systems for Patient Eligibility

Although it is desirable for all hospitalized patients to stop smoking, some degree of targeting is often necessary (see Chapter 6 for a discussion on inclusion and exclusion criteria). The screening systems used in Staying Free all follow from the systems used to identify patients who use tobacco—the single tobacco use question on the admitting forms and the daily census companion piece with a column for tobacco use status.

In our research studies, the first level of screening is to identify patients admitted to units considered ineligible (e.g., obstetric, psychiatric, substance abuse, or pediatric units) and eligible (e.g., medicine, surgery, ICU, CCU, stepdown, gynecology) according to our criteria. This is easily done using the daily hospital census because units are identified on the census.

The second level of screening involves a review of medical charts of patients identified by the census as tobacco users admitted to eligible units. Up to 98.5% of patients who are ineligible for the program by our criteria (e.g., palliative, drug overdose, medically complicated, etc.) can be identified by a chart review. This is a very time-efficient method for counselors and patients compared to having to screen all patients at the bedside.

The third level of screening involves approaching patients, identified as eligible by the chart review, at the bedside after they are medically stabilized. This allows a final check on eligibility including screening for exclusion criteria that could be specific to a given hospital, program, or research study (e.g., willingness to be randomized to a treatment group). This final screen is also used to determine patients' interest in quitting tobacco and receiving help.

Recruitment Systems

If patients meet all eligibility criteria and are interested in enrolling in the program, the cessation counselor describes the program/study, obtains informed consent (when required), and collects baseline data, all of which will take upwards of 20 minutes, depending on the amount of data being collected and the patient's ability to comprehend and communicate (see Chapter 14 for data and measurement). Baseline data are best collected prior to delivering an intervention so as not to bias the information being collected. For research studies, a sealed randomization envelop is opened after the baseline measures are taken, and patients are informed of their group assignment.

Brief and Intensive Intervention Delivery

Both the brief and intensive interventions can be started immediately at the bedside following data collection. The brief intervention will take approximately 5 minutes to deliver, an the intensive will take approximately 45-60 minutes at the bedside and 5-10 minutes for each post-discharge call. Patients receive their post-discharge telephone counseling calls beginning 2 days after they return home from the hospital; calls are scheduled according to discharge dates.

Tobacco Use Status Follow-Up

In our research studies, research staff, blind to treatment conditions, call program participants at 3, 6, and 12 months after hospital discharge to assess tobacco use status. When the program has been put into standard hospital practice, the cessation counselor makes the status calls. The calls usually take less than 5 minutes each. For tobacco use status, we use the National Heart, Lung, and Blood Institute's consensus definition of self-reported 7-day point prevalence (not even a puff for seven consecutive days) and long-term (continuous) abstinence (self-reported 7-day point-prevalence at all follow-ups, 3, 6, and 12 months; Ossip-Klein et al., 1986). In our randomized clinical trials, we also corroborate 7-day point-prevalence status at 12-months by collecting saliva samples for cotinine analyses (< 15 ng/mL indicates confirmed non-smoker) or by asking a designated family member or friend for confirmation.

SUCCESS OF STAYING FREE

Randomized Clinical Trials with Post-Myocardial Infarction Patients

The first randomized trial, conducted between 1986-1989 in four Kaiser Permanente Health Maintenance Organization (HMO) hospitals in Northern California, involved 176 men who had suffered an acute MI. The intensive intervention, introduced to patients one day after transfer from the coronary care unit, about 4 days after admission, significantly increased one-year confirmed (7-day point prevalence) cessation rates by 29% over the brief intervention (usual care). The one-year confirmed rates were 32% for the brief intervention and 61% for the intensive intervention (Taylor et al., 1990).

The second randomized trial with heart patients incorporated the smoking cessation component into a multiple risk factor intervention (MULTIFIT) that included exercise, diet, stress reduction, and medication compliance. It was conducted between 1988-1991 in four Kaiser Permanente HMO hospitals in Northern California (DeBusk et al., 1994) and involved 252 patients who smoked (45% of the 585 patients enrolled in MULTIFIT, 20% of whom were female). The intensive intervention significantly increased one-year confirmed (7-day point prevalence) cessation rates 17% over the brief intervention (usual care). The cessation rates were 70% versus 53%, respectively, and again, remain among the highest one-year confirmed rates in the scientific literature (France et al., 2001). MULTIFIT has now been disseminated as part of cardiac rehabilitation in over 20 Kaiser HMOs in Northern California, Oregon, and Colorado with cessation results similar to the research trials (Smith et al., 1997).

The Women's Initiative for Nonsmoking (WINS), was conducted between 1996-2001 in 10 hospitals in the San Francisco Bay area (Sivarajan Froelicher et al., 2004). It involved 277 women diagnosed with cardiovascular disease. The trial was performed with women only because although men hospitalized with cardiovascular disease show high tobacco cessation rates following an in-hospital intervention with post-discharge telephone counseling, similar data for women were not previously available. The one-year confirmed cessation rates were 48% for the intensive intervention and 42% for the brief intervention (usual care). Although the difference in cessation was not significant, it represents the average difference to be expected between intervention groups according to a meta-analysis (Kottke et al., 1988), and the average time to resumption of smoking for those who relapsed was significantly longer for the intensive intervention patients.

The most recent heart study of Staying Free involved post-MI and post-bypass patients in five cardiac units in a hospital in Western Canada (Burgess et al., in progress). Patients were randomized to receive the intensive or brief intervention following the same protocol as the earlier heart studies with Staying Free. Outcomes are not yet available—data are currently being analyzed.

Randomized Clinical Trials with General Hospital Patients

The success of the randomized trials with post-MI patients prompted the idea to test the generalizability of the program with general hospital patients. It is well-documented that post-MI patients, on average, have the highest cessation rates. So although the inpatient program was extremely successful with post-MI patients, it was not known how well it would work with general hospital patients.

Using the same protocol as the post-MI patient studies, the first randomized clinical trial with general hospital patients was conducted between 1991-1992 in four Kaiser Permanente HMO hospitals in Northern California (Taylor et al., 1996). The study was planned in two phases. The first phase was identical to the post-MI studies—patients were randomly allocated to receive the intensive or brief intervention. It involved 660 general hospital patients (45% female). The intensive intervention significantly increased one-year confirmed cessation 10% over the brief intervention (usual care). The rates were 31% versus 21%, for the intensive intervention and usual care, respectively. These remain among the highest one-year confirmed cessation rates in the scientific literature for general hospital patients (France et al., 2001; Rigotti et al., 2003).

The second phase of the study was designed to expand the scope of the research to compare the efficacy of the intensive and brief interventions with a minimal intervention. The in-hospital portion of the minimal intervention was identical to the intensive intervention; the difference lay in the number of post-discharge telephone counseling calls—the intensive intervention offered four telephone counseling calls at 2, 7, 21, and 90 days after hospital discharge, the minimal intervention offered a single telephone counseling call at 2 days post-discharge.

Phase two of the trial was conducted between 1991-1993 in the same four Kaiser Permanente HMO hospitals (Houston Miller et al., 1997). Patients continued to be randomized to the intensive and brief (usual care) interventions using a balanced randomization procedure. The trial included 2,024 general hospital patients—561 patients received the intensive intervention, 990 received the brief intervention (usual care), and 473 received the minimal intervention. The intensive intervention with 4 post-discharge telephone counseling calls significantly increased one-year cessation by 7% over the brief intervention (27% were confirmed non-smokers versus 20%, respectively). The intensive intervention with 1 call did not significantly increase cessation over usual care (22% were non-smokers versus 20%, respectively), suggesting that multiple calls post-discharge were necessary to increase cessation. The intensive intervention with 4 calls increased cessation over the minimal intervention with 1 call by 5%, but this difference was not significant.

Dissemination Studies with General Hospital Patients

The Chief Executive officer of Stanford University Medical Center approved the implementation of Staying Free as a stand-alone program for patients in 1993, with one full-time nurse hired to administer the program and deliver the intervention to patients. This was the first demonstration project of the program outside of its originating randomized clinical trial structure. Few programs tested in randomized trials are introduced into standard practice or evaluated after the initial trials, so this was an exciting opportunity. It was not clear whether the results from the randomized trials would generalize to standard practice once the tight controls of the study were removed.

Staying Free was implemented following the same systems-based delivery developed and tested in the randomized clinical trials. All patients admitted to Stanford University Medical Center who smoked were offered a smoking cessation program during their hospitalization. Between 1993-1996, 2,091 patients were identified as smokers; 52% of these patients enrolled in the program, 18% wanted to quit on their own, 20% did not want to quit, and 10% were ineligible (Smith et al., 2002). The 12-month self-reported cessation rate (7-day point prevalence) was 35% if patients who were lost-to-follow-up were considered smokers, 49% if not.

Funding was then obtained by the State of California Tobacco Related Disease Research Program (Prop 99) to examine issues of dissemination of Staying Free. The goal was to implement the Staying Free program in at least six hospitals in the San Francisco Bay Area Peninsula and San Jose regions and to compare the effectiveness of the program as implemented in those hospitals with our previous studies. The main objective was to determine if the program could be sustained (institutionalized) once the Stanford research team withdrew from a direct role in helping to manage the project.

Using a nonrandomized, observational design, six hospitals were recruited to participate in the study—a university hospital, a Veterans' Administration (VA), a small and a large community hospital, and a large HMO (Taylor et al., 2005). Having such a wide variety of institutions allowed the examination of dissemination issues in hospitals with different types of funding and patient populations. The research team helped implement the program during the first year of participation (implementation) and then withdrew from active involvement during the second year (institutionalization).

The results were similar to those of the randomized trials. The average 6-month self-reported cessation rates for the six participating hospitals were 26.3% (range = 17.6% to 52.8%) for the implementation phase and 22.7% (range = 12.9% to 48.2%) for the institutionalization phase. The target was 25%. Hospitals with paid professionals providing the program had the best outcomes.

This dissemination study demonstrated the need for inpatient tobacco cessation programs (none of the hospitals had a comprehensive program at that time), and the effectiveness of the Staying Free program when disseminated to a variety of hospitals under a variety of conditions. It also became abundantly clear how many healthcare professionals are eager to provide such services—even on their own time, and how important system-level changes are for programs to succeed.

Translating Success Across Borders

Although Staying Free worked consistently well in research and dissemination studies in Northern California (CA), it was not clear how well it would work in other states or hospital systems, or when performed by research teams other than the original Stanford team. As such, a randomized clinical trial was designed to assess the efficacy of the program with a Canadian population in a Canadian healthcare setting.

At the time the Canadian study was planned, four Stanford-led randomized clinical trials had been completed in HMO settings, and the original dissemination project had been performed in a private hospital, all in the San Francisco Bay area. The HMO and private medical systems differ from the Canadian system. Their catchments tend to be more limited due to the high cost of private medical insurance, with patients tending to be of relatively high socioeconomic status (SES) compared to uninsured individuals. Private insurance also often means that patients are employed by large corporations, and often live in large urban areas (i.e., characteristics of easier to reach individuals).

In contrast to the HMO system, patients in the Canadian hospital system are covered by provincially-funded healthcare insurance. They represent the full spectrum of SES, including those who are unemployed or on social assistance. It was not clear what impact the anticipated difference in SES would have on patients' cessation since lower SES is related to lower cessation (e.g., Siahpush et al., 2005). In addition, the preventive measures encouraged and acculturated in HMOs were not yet part of the Canadian medical system, so it was not clear how patients would respond to the program.

From an ecological perspective (Green et al., 1996), political and social-environmental factors might have also influenced the high cessation rates in the CA studies in ways that could affect the translation of outcomes across geographical boundaries. At the time the Canadian study was designed, CA boasted the lowest smoking prevalence rates in the United States (19%), believed to be due in large part to aggressive government-sponsored anti-tobacco policies and campaigns. In contrast, Ontario, where the study would be performed, had a smoking prevalence rate of about 31% (Health Canada, 1993), many of whom were heavy smokers who found it difficult to quit (COMMIT Research Group, 1995).

The Canadian randomized clinical trial was conducted between 1998-2001 in three community hospitals in Southern Ontario (Smith et al., submitted). It involved 668 general hospital patients (49% female), and tested the efficacy of the brief and intensive intervention with 3 additional post-discharge counseling calls added to the intensive intervention to achieve maximum intensity and test the boundaries of cessation rates. Recruitment analyses showed that the Canadian patients were remarkably similar on baseline characteristics and the primary reason for hospitalization to those in the CA HMO trials, although there was a larger proportion of Caucasians and lower proportion of patients with post-secondary education. Despite the education difference, preliminary analyses showed that the cessation outcomes in the Canadian study were similar to those in the CA study (Smith, 2001).

TRANSLATING RESEARCH INTO PRACTICE

If Staying Free can be translated from HMOs in CA to community hospitals in a universal healthcare system in Canada, we believe that it can be translated to most, if not all, hospitals in the United States and Canada, and even internationally. We also believe that there were three keys to the close replication of Canadian outcomes with the CA outcomes that are important for translating Staying Free into practice.

First, the principal investigator for the Canadian trial was familiar with and well-trained in the systems-based inpatient approach. She had worked with the Stanford research team on the inpatient tobacco cessation program for two years and was able to translate the intervention protocols, administrative components, and details regarding the hospital infrastructure into a new practice setting. Figure 2 provides an overview or blueprint of what we believe these translation factors to be. The rest of this book distills the learning from this translational experience into a straightforward, almost cookbook approach to make it easier for others to introduce Staying Free or a program with similar features.

Second, the CA and Canadian patient populations were very similar on baseline characteristics. The patient populations have also been very similar across the CA studies, so there is a growing realization, or at least a hypothesis, that general hospital patients, or at least those who are eligible by the original Staying Free criteria and willing to enroll in an inpatient tobacco cessation program or study, are likely be similar regardless of geography and medical care systems. So if the program is delivered as intended, with a systems-based approach and case-manager to provide counseling and coordinate the program, it should garner similar results across similar patient populations.

Finally, the nurses in the Canadian trial received the same standardized training the Stanford nurses received. The nurses working with the Canadian trial also had the unique opportunity to capitalize on the experience of the Stanford investigators and research nurses throughout the trial through teleconferences and consults on an as-needed basis. We also offer provider training workshops and are working on a web-based training program to make training more accessible (see Chapter 13 for an outline of the Staying Free training program).

Blueprint for Implementation

In Figure 2 we provide an overview or blueprint of what we believe are the necessary factors for translating our experience with Staying Free from various studies into usable steps for practice. We appreciate the diversity of hospitals, patients, providers, and healthcare systems that require inpatient tobacco cessation programs, so our intent is to provide a heuristic model for translating research into practice and for incorporating tobacco cessation guidelines and quality assurance indicators into practice rather than focusing on specifications for a specific program.

Figure 2. Blueprint for Implementation

Implementing An Inpatient Tobacco Cessation Program		
Phase I: Foundation	**Part 2: Program Development**	**Part 3: Ramp-Up & Delivery**
Build the business case	Clarify counselors & roles	Define policies & procedures & develop protocols & systems
Familiarize with guidelines, quality assurance, insurance	Develop hospital infrastructure	Determine work flow, plan for sustainability
Clarify program administration	Develop intervention	
Define program parameters	Develop training	
Define/estimate target population	Plan program evaluation	
Get buy-in & support	Develop data collection	
Develop the budget & financing	Develop promotion plan	

We have organized the book around this blueprint, with each box representing a chapter in the book. In the next five chapters in Part I of this book, we will provide information on the support structure components that are helpful, if not necessary, to begin the process of implementation. Parts II and III provide the information and work steps necessary to create the work plan for the blueprint presented in Figure 2.

4

Program Administration and Management

Inpatient tobacco cessation programs require a formal structure, someone to be responsible for the administration and management of the program, and a recognized administrative home within the organization. Some inpatient tobacco cessation programs begin as a grass-roots effort and remain loosely organized, championed by a single health care provider within the hospital who is not organizationally or fiscally responsible for the program. Without a formal structure within the organization, however, the program is at high risk of disappearing. And without a person who is organizationally and fiscally responsible, the program will in all likelihood cease to exist if and when the champion leaves or becomes too involved with his or her "real" job to maintain continuity of service for tobacco cessation.

This chapter is dedicated to outlining the administrative framework and management responsibilities for implementing and maintaining an inpatient tobacco cessation program. For hospitals that have a loosely organized program in place, this chapter provides firm grounding for solidifying the program in the organization. For hospitals ramping up to implement a program, this chapter provides insight into the scope of administration and management required for the program. For hospitals contemplating the implementation of a program, this chapter provides a realistic assessment of what is required administratively to make the program successful and sustainable, and provides the starting points for defining administrative responsibilities.

ADMINISTRATIVE FRAMEWORK

One of the first considerations for the administration and management of an inpatient tobacco cessation program is to find an administrative, financial, and physical home within the organizational structure. Administratively, one department has to be responsible for setting up and monitoring the program, and responsible for the actions of the cessation counselors and program outcomes. The program also brings with it financial responsibilities, so it must have a financial home in the organization. There will be costs and possibly reimbursements associated with the program, and quarterly, semi-annual, and/or annual reports will have to be made for fiscal accountability.

Finally, the program will need a physical home. The cessation counselor will need office space, office furniture, access to telecommunications and copying, and privacy (if telephone counseling will be provided), all of which have to be provided by some department. Even when the tobacco cessation program is part of an outside research project and the hospital is simply allowing access to patients (so it carries with it no financial obligations), it will still need an administrative home—a person, department, or committee within the organization, that will have ultimate responsibility for the program, and a physical home for the cessation counselor.

Although tobacco cessation programs are commonly administered through nursing, patient education, or health promotion departments, there is nothing precluding any department from being home to the program. Some hospital-wide tobacco cessation programs have a natural home because they are an outgrowth of a smaller specialty program that has been operating for many years, such as when cardiac units or respiratory medicine develop a tobacco cessation program for their patients run out of their own units by their own providers. In a consortium of hospitals, the tobacco cessation program for all hospitals in the consortium might be run out of one department in one of the hospitals. Depending on the hospital structure and how the program will be paid for, it is also possible for the program to stand autonomously or as part of an affiliated wellness center with its own personnel, policies, procedures, reimbursement, and budget, separate from the parent organization.

It is helpful to develop an organizational chart to determine where the program lies within the organization. This will clarify the chain of command and help stimulate thinking about such issues as program responsibility, accountability and reporting, salary and wage responsibility, vacation and sick leave coverage, department transfer payments, and in unfortunate circumstances, what the possible alternative funding sources will be if budget cut-backs are announced.

Figure 3 provides an example of an organizational chart. The chain of command shows that the Director of Nursing oversees both the Tobacco Cessation Program Director and the Tobacco Cessation Advisory Board, and that there is a Tobacco Cessation Counselor separate from the administrative role of Program Director. In many hospitals, the Director and Counselor will be the same person. Sometimes a new position is created for an inpatient tobacco cessation program. In such a case, the position within the organizational structure might appear directly on the hospital organizational chart. Other times the administrative responsibility for the program simply becomes part of a current staff member's work portfolio. In this case the program responsibility will not be directly represented on the organizational chart, but the chain of responsibility and command should nonetheless be clearly identified. For example, if the program becomes part of a patient education counselor's portfolio, the tobacco cessation program will likely not show up on the organizational chart. However, the chain of responsibility should still be identified. In this case, responsibility would likely lie with the manager or director of Patient Education Services.

Figure 3. Example of Organizational Chart for an Inpatient Tobacco Cessation Program

Knowing where the program responsibility lies on the organizational chart can also serve to stimulate thinking about how the program can contribute in indirect ways to the organization. For example, if the program falls under nursing care, nursing conferences and journals might become important media through which results of the program are disseminated to a broader community, thereby bringing recognition to the department and institution while strengthening the evidence base (and future) of the program.

PROGRAM DIRECTOR

The administration of an inpatient tobacco cessation program benefits from a program director who has knowledge of the clinical practice guidelines for tobacco as well as a strong business and management background. Figure 4 provides an overview of responsibilities involved with implementing, organizing, and managing an inpatient tobacco cessation program. The overview helps to highlight the types of skills a program director will need. Who the program director will be will vary by hospital because the role of the program director will depend on the budget and the organizational structure within any given hospital.

One scenario, more likely to be found in larger hospitals, would be for the program director to be a department head or manager (e.g., Manager of Patient Education or Nursing). The tobacco cessation program would be one part of his or her larger work portfolio. In this case, the work would likely involve only advanced program organization and management, such as budgeting, forecasting, making program and staff needs projections, overseeing program implementation and/or expansion, program planning and modification, managing staff workloads, and doing performance evaluations. Many of the other responsibilities such as marketing, training, and program evaluation would be delegated, in whole or in part, to the appropriate departments such as public relations, finance, research, and human resources. Daily administrative work under this model, such as ordering office supplies and patient materials, would most likely be taken care of by the department secretary. And a tobacco cessation counselor(s) would provide program delivery with little or no administrative responsibilities for the program. This is the basic model we have used in our randomized clinical trials, with all administration and management being taken care of by the research team, and counselors providing the tobacco interventions to patients along with collecting data.

Figure 4. Overview of Program Administration Responsibilities

Program Administration and Management

Initial program set-up & implementation	Ongoing operations and adminstration	Ongoing staff management	Ongoing financial management	Ongoing promotion
Work with IRB, advisory committee, upper managment	Daily tracking and record keeping	Develop position ads and contracts, recruit, interview	Initial and ongoing costing, budgeting and reporting	In-service training
Preliminary work: program definition, forecasting, staffing	Daily office administration including supplies, computers, hook-ups	Hire & train personnel	Establishing baseline budget and annual reports	Notices, pamphlets, brochures, etc
Identify resources: community partnerships funding, reimbursements	Data collection, entry, cleaning, and ongoing data decisions	Continuing education performance planning	Billing and accounts receivable	Media and public relations
Establish program and quality assurance goals and monitoring	Regular program evaluation including development of tools	Scheduling, workload managment, training	Financial forecasting	Publishing: conferences news letters, journals
Develop & document policies, procedures, protocols, and systems	Goal setting/monitoring quality assurance, planning	Supervision, performance evaluations, maintaining personnel files	Insurance reimbursement	
Determine data collection and tools, evaluation planning	Work with advisory committee, IRB, upper managment		Resource allocation, purchasing	
Set up hospital infrastructure and physical space	Prepare reports weekly, monthly, quarterly, annually			
Project management and problem solving				

In other hospitals, especially smaller hospitals, the program director might also be the tobacco cessation counselor and have additional roles in the hospital system (e.g., respiratory therapist in a rehabilitation program). In this scenario, one full or part-time person would be solely responsible for all administrative aspects of the program, including advanced program organization and management (budgeting, projections, planning, etc.), daily office administration (ordering supplies, etc.), delivering the program to patients, and making the one-year tobacco use status calls to patients. Program evaluation might be delegated to the research department or an outside consultant because evaluation requires specialized skills involving databases and statistical analyses. This is the basic model we have used when Staying Free has been put into standard practice.

CHECKLIST OF RESPONSIBILITIES FOR PROGRAM IMPLEMENTATION

Regardless of how the program director position is structured, and whether the program director is also the tobacco cessation counselor delivering the program, there are administrative and management responsibilities that are important to the success of the program. The following checklists provide a summary of the administrative and management tasks involved in setting up an inpatient tobacco cessation program. Although the lists are quite detailed, they are nonetheless meant to be generic and provide a summary only. The checklists are not exhaustive of the work that needs to be done in any one hospital because each hospital will differ to some degree in the program that is implemented, and each will have its own requirements. The checklists also include many tasks that might not be relevant to all hospitals. For example, developing protocols for saliva collection to bio-chemically verify tobacco use status might be necessary for research studies but not stand-alone programs in standard practice.

The checklists correspond to the first column of Figure 4 (Initial program set-up & implementation). The other columns in Figure 4 are important for the ongoing management of the program as the headings indicate. However, they represent basic management duties and skills involved in most management positions and most programs, so they will not be detailed here. What is important to note about these other columns is that the types of tasks involved in the ongoing management of the program can help highlight the background experience and skills required of a program director. For some readers, the checklists might make more sense after the other chapters in this book have been read, at which point the checklists can be used as the starting points for developing and implementing the program.

Checklist 1: Working with Committees

Work that involves working with steering, advisory, and community committees and upper management can include, but is not limited to the tasks listed below (see Chapter 7 for the role of advisory committees).

☐ Form an advisory committee for the inpatient tobacco cessation program with an identified purpose statement and terms of reference.
☐ Develop meeting agendas and schedule meetings.
☐ Chair meetings.
☐ Take minutes at the meetings and create a searchable filing system for minutes and reports.
☐ Report to committees formally and informally.
☐ Follow-up on committee requests for information.
☐ Prepare regular updates for committees and management.

Checklist 2: Preliminary Work Prior to Implementation

The preliminary work prior to implementation involves clarifying exactly what the program will look like, what it will include, and what it will entail, as well as how it will be paid for and the budget that it will depend on.

2.1 Program Definition and Components

☐ Define primary aims and values of the inpatient tobacco cessation program.
☐ Decide on program components (e.g., identification of tobacco use, brief or intensive intervention, post-discharge counseling, etc.), and document rationale for choices.
☐ Decide on program provider(s), document rationale, and clarify the extent of responsibilities (e.g., administration, meetings, patient care, reporting etc.).
☐ Define the eligible patient populations and provide rationale (e.g., patients 18 years of age and older who used tobacco in the month prior to hospitalization).
☐ Define exclusion criteria and provide rationale (e.g., psychiatric, substance abuse, etc.).
☐ Determine whether a stepped-implementation will be followed, such as beginning with one or two hospital units or with a narrowly defined patient population (e.g., cardiovascular patients), and if so, clarify the timeline for expansion. Document rationale for choices.

2.2 Forecasting

☐ Estimate the amount of time each intervention component will take to complete for each patient (e.g., if four post-discharge counseling calls will be made for each patient at an estimated time of 10 minutes each, plus an additional 5 minutes per patient for multiple attempts to contact patients, leaving messages, and tracking patients lost-to-follow up, the estimate would be 45 minutes per patient for discharge calls).

☐ Using inclusion criteria and annual patient flow data, estimate the annual enrollment into the program and retention (retention is only important if post-discharge counseling is planned so that resources can be estimated according to caseloads).

☐ Estimate the total time it will take per patient to provide tobacco services according to the estimated annual enrollment.

☐ Establish a baseline estimate for providers' caseloads based on estimated time it will take to provide the services given the program choices made.

☐ Based on the patient population, estimate the annual projected cessation rates. Stratify these rates by unit or disease category if it will be helpful for overall projections. This is especially important for plans that will involve a stepped roll-out, beginning, for example, with cardiac patients and then moving gradually to include all units because cessation will vary by disease category and therefore by hospital unit. If the program starts with those most likely to quit (i.e., cardiovascular patients), it is important that administration does not expect all patient groups to have similarly high cessation rates.

☐ Make advanced forecasts and projections when required or requested. These can be done with the help of the research department, consultant, or in part, using a return on investment calculator (see Chapter 8), and can include:

   o   the cost per patient to provide the program
   o   the cost per extra quitter by providing the program
   o   the cost per quality year life saved
   o   potential cost recovery with program reimbursement choices
   o   potential cost savings to the hospital due to projected decreased healing time and hospital stays, decreased intra- and post-operative complications, decreased admissions to ICU following surgery, and decreased hospitalizations.

2.3 Patient Materials

☐ Explore options for patient materials and provide detailed costs including taxes. Explore options such as paying for copyright and printing/taping one's own materials as well as purchasing the finished products. There might be opportunities to cost share with other programs in the community.

Checklist 3: Community Resources

It is helpful to identify community resources that might be available to augment or support the inpatient tobacco cessation program. There might also be partnering opportunities in the community that should be explored. A relatively complete account of what to look for in terms of community resources is covered in Chapter 7.

Checklist 4: Resources and Financial Management

The initial set-up of financial management will be multifaceted, as will ongoing financial management.

☐ Decide on an appropriate accounting program that will allow easy tracking of expenses and income, and that will allow effortless reporting.

☐ Develop a baseline budget by costing out the program choice options including wages and benefits, possible overtime and vacation time, office supplies, patient materials, annual evaluation, etc.

☐ Determine how to pay for the program, including the following:

    o   Assess how much the hospital operating budget will likely have to contribute to the annual budget for administration and management, and provide justification for each item.

    o   Explore reimbursement strategies and working with third party payers. Clarify what clinicians can bill under insurance codes.

    o   Determine what clinicians, if any, have tobacco cessation counseling fall under their regular staff responsibilities and will therefore be covered by their regular wages and benefits without extra cost to the tobacco cessation program.

    o   Explore partnering possibilities with government agencies, non-government agencies, organizations, and businesses.

☐ Make the initial financial forecasts relative to projected patient volumes, including costs, revenues, and anticipating unforeseen costs such as equipment failure or large fluctuations in patient volumes.

☐ Make initial projections and assessments for equipment needs and maintenance, and patient materials.

Checklist 5: Goal Setting and Quality Assurance

Goal setting and achievement are important aspects of program administration. The program director will be responsible for developing immediate, mid-term, and long-term goals consistent with the vision and mandate of the program. The goals will need to be specific, measurable, attainable, and reasonable. Evaluation will be an important aspect of the program director's role in order to provide feedback and evidence of goal attainment, and to use for setting new goals.

5.1 Forecasting

☐ Make initial quarterly, semi-annual, and annual projections for program enrollment and retention.

☐ Make initial quarterly, semi-annual, and annual projections for staffing needs, vacation scheduling, and sick-day coverage based on enrollment and retention projections.

5.2 Goal Setting

☐ Determine what might be a realistic increase for enrollment and retention for each time period (e.g., no projected increases for the first year to allow a baseline to be set and to allow for learning curves and bugs in the systems and protocols).

☐ Set quarterly, semi-annual, annual, and long-term (5 year) goals for all aspects of the program based on initial projections, including:
  o Clinical outcomes (patient recruitment, retention, cessation)
  o Delivery (training, fidelity)
  o Program administration
  o Staff (recruitment and retention, training, continuing education)
  o Marketing and promotion including in-service training for hospital staff and dissemination of information
  o Budget and budget items
  o Program modification and expansion

5.3 Goal Monitoring and Evaluation

☐ Develop monitoring systems to evaluate goal achievement.
☐ Develop an evaluation plan for goals that includes process, impact, and outcomes.
☐ Monitor, report, and adjust quarterly, semi-annual, annual, and long-term (5 year) goals for all aspects of the program—clinical outcomes (patient recruitment, retention, cessation), delivery (training, fidelity), program administration, staff (recruitment and retention, continuing education), marketing and promotion (including in-service training), and program expansion.

5.4 Quality Assurance

☐ Determine and document quality assurance indicators.
☐ Develop monitoring systems to ensure quality assurance.

Checklist 6: Policies, Procedures, Protocols, and Systems

The work involved with policies, procedures, protocols, and systems involves the discovery/decision process and then final documentation. Additional checklists for documentation are included in Chapter 16 in the final steps for ramping-up for delivery.

6.1 Operations Procedures and Protocols

- ☐ Detail patient identification protocol.
- ☐ Determine and detail referral systems to the cessation program. This will involve meetings with the various departments and units.
- ☐ Detail screening protocols.
- ☐ Detail intervention protocols.
- ☐ Detail procedures for daily recording and monitoring of patient interactions including daily work logs for patient identification, screening, and intervention and charting.
- ☐ Detail protocols for clinical consultation assistance for challenging patient cases, including medical queries about patient eligibility.
- ☐ Determine computer and hard copy storage of patient data and records to protect confidentiality of information.
- ☐ Develop schedules for fidelity checks to ensure quality assurance goals are met on an ongoing basis.
- ☐ Develop policies and procedures for personnel such as daily hours, ensuring caseload coverage, vacation scheduling, coffee breaks and lunches, overtime, confidentiality of patient information, etc.
- ☐ Develop scheduling guidelines for staff and vacation coverage.
- ☐ Develop procedures for the various types of required reporting.
- ☐ Develop protocols and monitoring systems for keeping patients' physicians apprised of tobacco cessation encounters.
- ☐ Develop procedures for collection and storage of saliva, urine, or blood for cotinine analysis, covering issues such as barriers to infection, awareness and disposal of potential infectious materials and sources, hand washing, and patient comfort.

6.2 Forecasting

- ☐ Create a system for making ongoing quarterly, semi-annual, and annual projections for program enrollment and retention.
- ☐ Create a system for making ongoing quarterly, semi-annual, and annual projections for staffing needs, vacation scheduling, and coverage based on enrollment and retention projections.

6.3 Staffing Procedures and Protocols

- ☐ Determine hospital requirements for written job descriptions and position advertisements including policies for internal and external postings.

☐ Determine qualifications for the tobacco cessation counselor.

☐ Determine salary and benefit ranges to meet the qualifications of the tobacco cessation counselor.

☐ Determine hospital policies for salary increases (merit and cost-of-living).

☐ Determine hospital policies for hiring, job-sharing, probation, discipline, and termination.

☐ Write job descriptions and advertise positions according to hospital protocol. Ongoing work will include updating and/or modifying job descriptions, and advertising as needed.

☐ Develop interview questions and protocol.

☐ Determine hospital orientation procedures.

☐ Develop initial training.

☐ Develop a plan to recruit and interview staff.

☐ Develop a plan to orient and train new staff.

☐ Develop a plan for providing or making accessible continuing education.

☐ Develop initial performance objectives.

☐ Develop performance evaluations.

☐ Determine schedule for case meetings.

☐ Determine schedule for performance evaluations.

☐ Develop a plan to schedule staff and manage workloads based on enrollment and retention projections.

☐ Develop a plan to create and keep up-to-date personnel files that include renewal of certifications and licenses, resumes, synopses and attendance for training programs and other education meetings, and performance objectives and evaluations.

☐ Develop a plan to ensure confidential storage of personnel records.

☐ Develop a plan to ensure appropriate supervision and availability of clinical consultation for cessation staff.

Checklist 7: Data Collection and Evaluation

☐ Determine data needed to meet institutional (and scientific) requirements for program evaluation and outcome assessment.

☐ Determine what data already exist and how they can be incorporated in the program proposal and ongoing program reporting.

☐ Research and design/buy/borrow instruments to collect the required data.

☐ Pilot test the data collection instruments for comprehensibility, ease of administration, response burden in terms of time to administer and ease of answering, and completeness and adequacy of data collected (e.g., some data, such as dates and frequencies, are difficult for patients to provide).

- ☐ Determine whether the data will be collected by directly inputting information into a computer (laptop or handheld for bedside collection) or by pen and paper.
- ☐ If data will be collected by pen and paper, develop the hard copy forms, design a computer database for long-term storage and analyses of the data, and determine who will enter the data into a computer for storage and analyses. Also determine how the hard copy data will be stored and the length of time the hard copy data will be kept (there are regulations around this depending on how the data will be used).
- ☐ If data will be collected by inputting information directly into a computer:
  - ○ Research whether a laptop or handheld will be used and what the associated costs, pros, and cons are for each.
  - ○ Determine what database software programs are available and what software programs will be required for backup, virus protection, confidentiality of patient information, and firewalls (if the computer will be connected to the internet).
  - ○ Determine what will be involved in ensuring a daily backup of data.
  - ○ Determine who will be responsible for trouble-shooting data-related problems with the computer.
  - ○ Determine who will be responsible for updating hardware and software and when.
  - ○ Determine whether the data will be stored on a desktop computer or whether it will be web-based to allow entry from multiple sites.
  - ○ If data storage will be on a desktop, determine what desktop computer will provide storage of the data from the handheld or laptop computers.
  - ○ Determine what procedures will be used for downloading the data for analyses.
  - ○ Determine frequency of downloading data from the laptop or handheld to a desktop for storage, analyses, and backup.
  - ○ Detail what will be involved in ensuring a daily backup of data, including procedures, software, and personnel.
  - ○ Determine who will have access to the patient-related data and how data will be password protected.
  - ○ Determine what hook-ups or connections are required for the computer, such as internet, networking within the organization, and connecting with electronic patient records.
  - ○ Design a database for storage of patient-related data.
- ☐ If the computer will have to be purchased, determine the requirements including software and backup.

☐ Design and schedule fidelity checks for data accuracy and completeness in the database.

☐ Develop a monitoring system for data collection for such things as identifying questions that are not providing adequate data, and adding questions to fill gaps in the information provided by patients.

☐ Develop a full evaluation plan including process, impact, and outcome.

☐ Develop an evaluation schedule (minimally on an annual basis) and prototype the reports.

Checklist 8: Set Up Hospital Infrastructure and Physical Space

☐ Determine what has to be done to set up the hospital infrastructure to support program choices (e.g., centralized system for identifying tobacco use).

☐ Determine who will need to be involved to set up each component of the program (e.g., information technology [IT] department for access to electronic records).

☐ Work with hospital administration, admitting department, and IT department to get a tobacco use question added to admitting records and get tobacco status added to the daily census.

☐ Work with the admitting or other department to set up printing of the daily hospital census.

☐ Work with the pharmacist to add pharmacotherapy to the hospital formulary.

☐ Work with administration for access to patient records for screening purposes. This might involve the IT department in the case of electronic records.

☐ If hard copy medical charts are used, work with each unit to establish chart sharing and best times for access.

☐ If equipment such as computers, printers, photocopiers, and freezer storage will be shared with other departments or units, set up access procedures.

☐ If equipment such as computers, printers, photocopiers, and freezer storage will be purchased, work with purchasing and engineering (for clearance on electronics).

☐ Set up telephone and internet hook-up for the cessation office.

☐ Develop adequate referral systems within the hospital to the cessation program and develop monitoring systems to ensure they are maintained.

Checklist 9: Marketing and Promotion

Although not included in column 1 of Figure 4 under Initial Program Set-up & Implementation, the inpatient tobacco cessation program will need at least minimal fanfare to announce its availability and to help create a presence with staff, patients, community, and media.

- [ ] Develop announcements and short information pieces for hospital, community, and industry newsletters.
- [ ] Develop materials, procedures, standardized content, and scheduling for in-service training.
- [ ] Provide regularly scheduled in-service training to hospital staff.
- [ ] Develop letterhead and logo if appropriate.
- [ ] Develop a media kit. Send information out to local media and prepare for interviews.
- [ ] Make community presentations to increase awareness, and depending on the funding structure, explore ways to expand the program to the community to help recover costs.
- [ ] Answer inquiries or requests for information from patients, community, and staff.
- [ ] Develop a community outreach and public relations plan. This can be done in conjunction with or even by the advisory committee.

Checklist 10: Project Management

- [ ] Clarify what needs to be done for implementation and create a timeline. It helps to separate the project into phases and then identify the components within each phase. Anything that has to be ordered (e.g., patient materials and equipment) should be done as soon as possible.
- [ ] Create milestones for implementation and a timeline to keep implementation on track and to provide progress data for meetings.
- [ ] Identify staff and departments that will be involved in implementation.
- [ ] Meet with everyone involved in the implementation to verify availability to work on the project and ensure that the work can get done within the estimates in the timeline. If not, make adjustments as needed.
- [ ] Identify potential bottlenecks in the project and address them as soon as possible to prevent delays in implementation.

PROJECT MANAGEMENT: IDENTIFYING BOTTLENECKS IN PROGRAM IMPLEMENTATION

Before leaving the topic of project administration and management, we would like to provide some insight into potential bottlenecks that might surface during implementation. Bottlenecks are situations and events that impede the flow of the project and need to be managed. Some of the most common and noteworthy bottlenecks are signatures and approvals from review boards, regulatory agencies, insurance companies, and department heads; equipment issues; holidays, shutdowns, vacations, and part-time personnel; purchasing and back-orders; and, daily interruptions (Zeldman, 1999). Many of these potential bottlenecks can be identified and managed at the start of program implementation.

Signatures and Approvals

Some hospitals might require numerous signatures of approval throughout the implementation process. It is important to find out exactly what will require approval (e.g., installation of telephone or internet service, equipment purchases, etc.), the individuals or committees responsible for the approvals (e.g., telecommunications department, purchasing manager), submission deadlines or cut-offs, and traditional turn-around time for approvals or signatures taking into consideration potential bottleneck times (e.g., times when departments might be working with reduced staff due to vacations or peak times such as year end for finance).

Some of the more common approvals include:

1. Chief of Staff for physician support of the project and/or for blanket approval to approach patients.
2. Information technology (IT) department to agree to add projects to their project list, such as setting up computer networking for the inpatient tobacco cessation project, computer and software set-up and maintenance, writing software or creating databases, setting up high speed internet access, adding a tobacco use status question to the admitting records, and/or adding tobacco use status to the daily hospital census.
3. Department heads for staff time, such as the IT staff who will do the actual work, or personnel who will attend in-service training for the program such as admitting staff and nurses.
4. Finance for setting up an account for the program, and agreeing to add the project to their project list and assign a project finance administrator.
5. Telecommunications for connecting telephone lines and providing equipment.
6. Pharmacy for agreement to dispense pharmacotherapy cessation aids, and/or to agree to provide education for patients on pharmacotherapy use.
7. Labs to agree to freezer storage if saliva samples will be collected to confirm tobacco use status.

It is also helpful to find out what, if anything, will help move the project through the various approvals quickly and efficiently. For example, the purchasing department might require signatures from finance and a department head—that means having the requisite signatures before submitting the documents to purchasing will help expedite the process; otherwise the documents might sit in someone's pending box for a longer than desired time.

Internal Review Boards and Regulatory Agencies

Some, but not all, projects will require approval through internal review boards or regulatory agencies. Regulatory bodies, such as internal review boards (IRB) for ethics clearance have deadlines and can have upwards of one to three month turn-around times. Original submissions are often returned with requests for revisions that can take weeks to months to revise and move through clearance. It is important to ensure that the information required and the format it is required in are clearly understood and provided or it could cost an extra month of time. It is also important to be clear about when the submission and meeting dates are, as well as what the turn-around procedures require if revisions are requested.

Some IRBs have staff that will meet with applicants prior to submitting a proposal for formal review to ensure that the required information is provided in sufficient detail. If this option exists, it is a bonus and definitely something to be taken advantage of. It is also helpful to find out if the IRB requires someone present at the review meeting to represent the inpatient tobacco cessation program and to determine who the best person would be to attend (e.g., a physician championing the program).

Rather than, or in addition to an IRB review, some projects might have to have a proposal reviewed by the Board of Directors, either for funding or program approval. It is important to find out when the Board meets, exactly what the Board is looking for in a proposal, as well as historically, what helps move a proposal forward with the given Board and what hinders it. If possible, it is helpful to run the proposal by someone who has successfully presented to the Board and have them critique it and/or provide insight into the process of going before the Board.

Equipment

If electrical equipment such as computers, VCRs, DVDs, televisions, or telephones will be purchased for the program, they will most likely require approval from the engineering department to ensure they meet hospital standards and will not interfere with hospital systems. It is important to find out what the process entails and how much time it takes, and then plan for it.

If equipment, such as copiers, printers, computers, VCRs, DVDs, televisions, and/or LCD projects, are going to be shared with others in the hospital, it is necessary to determine what the booking regulations are, how equipment use is charged, if there is a backlog in availability or any other predictable delays, and what the back-up systems are in case of equipment failure. For example, it is more efficient, especially on tight schedules, to find out in advance that should the copier in 9 East be broken that there is an agreement with 10 East but not 8 East to use their equipment, and that large print jobs need to be sent out to a print shop, which can take up to 2 days instead of the 1 hour it would take to stand in front of the machine and make the copies.

Holidays, Shutdowns, Vacations, and Part-Time Personnel

It is important to project forward in time to determine what possible interruptions might exist for a particular project component. For example, it might turn out that the IT department is needed in January to add the tobacco use question to the admitting records but the IT department takes an extended holiday between Christmas and New Year's thereby creating a backlog of work in January that they do not traditionally clear until February. If not adequately planned for, perhaps by putting in a request early enough, the tobacco cessation project might face a delay of over a month for that one small component. Or the IRB might shut down for the summer, or the Chief of Staff might be on vacation or sabbatical when his or her signature is needed for the information letters that are scheduled to go to physicians, or the IT person needed to work on the database software is only part-time so a month's worth of work takes two or more months to complete.

Back Order of Materials and Equipment

Some materials or equipment required for the project might be temporarily out of stock or end up being on back order. It is important to identify all purchases early in the planning stage, especially patient materials, and send out purchase orders with requests for guaranteed delivery dates. The sooner materials are ordered, the sooner problems will become apparent and the larger the window will be for taking corrective action such as finding an alternative supplier.

Lining up alternative suppliers is a good precaution to take even if things are moving smoothly—and it helps to do it in the planning stages rather than when a crisis hits. Current suppliers will often recommend a replacement for their services should there be a delay in an order. Many institutions require a minimum of three cost estimates for purchases—it is a good idea to retain the information from the companies not chosen and keep the information in the purchasing files as potential backup suppliers—their initial quotes serve as estimates that will likely be honored if the need arises.

Interruptions

Interruptions are the most difficult events to plan for effectively, yet they can prove to be one of the biggest bottlenecks that will be encountered during implementation because they often happen on a daily basis and are cumulative over the life of the project.

The major interruptions include:
    a.   Telephone calls received and placed, email, internet searches, and mail.
    b.   office drop-ins and hallway conversations.
    c.   Meetings, especially ones that are not absolutely necessary to attend.

Interruptions will happen during the implementation of a program, so one of the best offences is to build interruptions into the implementation scheduling. Enhancing time estimates for work completion is really about planning *reality in calendar time* rather than *effort* in an ideal world of unrestricted concentrated work. For example, various estimates suggest that, on average, most employees spend about 2 hours a day on email. Two hours out of an 8 hr. day is 25% of a day's work, which means that if email is not scheduled into the implementation plan in terms of time estimates, as well as monitored/managed, implementation will be behind schedule 2 hours a day for every day of implementation or one week each month just due to email alone. Add to email time, telephone calls that are self-initiated and calls received or returned (say 1 hr. a day), a couple of 15 minute hallway conversations, responding adequately to mail and deliveries (say 30 minutes to be conservative), and the result is quality project time is down to a 4.5 hour day, not taking into account the two one-hour meetings that can pop up on a regular basis.

It is important to think strategically in order to minimize the amount of time these daily administrative activities take and find ways of doing them efficiently. Time management books are a great place to look for ideas. Some traditional time management strategies include scheduling specific times throughout the day and capping the amount of time allotted for phone calls and email instead of letting them be an ongoing interruption, handling mail (and email) only once, and clarifying with superiors what meetings are absolutely necessary to attend and what ones can be skipped. Another time management strategy is to obtain permission to attend only the portions of meetings that concern the tobacco cessation program directly. For those who work in a satellite office, it is sometimes possible to have telephone meetings rather than face-to-face meetings in order to save travel time, at least for some meetings.

The bottom line from a time perspective in project management is that it is critical to create a list of all possible bottlenecks and gather information about them at the beginning of the project. When potential bottlenecks are identified, such as deadlines for ethics proposals submission, they should be clearly marked on the project calendar to serve as continual reminders and prompts, and then a plan created to minimize each potential bottleneck. It also helps to track task times to get an accurate assessment of how long each task takes, and to schedule reality in calendar time not just the amount of effort a task will take.

5

Defining the Program Parameters

The program parameters make up the big picture of the inpatient tobacco cessation program. They include the primary aims, scope, objectives, values, and quality assurance indicators. Part of the process of defining the parameters could also include developing a vision for where the program will be in the future and the schedule for implementation.

Although this book describes how to implement an inpatient tobacco cessation program that meets clinical practice guidelines, each hospital setting will need to individualize its program and clarify the parameters. If possible and feasible, involving a variety of individuals in defining the parameters will help ensure the program's success. It is especially important to involve the program champions and what they perceive to be the parameters because they will be the most important advocates for the program. Decisions about the specific components and details of the program (e.g., intensity of the intervention, who will deliver the program, etc.) can be flushed out more easily after the parameters of the program have been clarified.

The program parameters must align with the hospital's mission, goals, and values because the institution will ultimately need to approve the program. often advocates for tobacco cessation have broader goals than institutions do. Administration for an institution might, for example, perceive tobacco treatment simply as a small part of patient education already being taken care of by the health education department, and thus will not see a need to spend any more effort or resources developing a systems-based approach.

Ideas for defining the parameters can come from a variety of sources. The USDHHS guideline (Fiore et al., 2000) and quality assurance indicators, such as those put out by the Joint Commission on Accreditation of Healthcare Organizations (JCAHO, 2005), are some of the best places to start to define the parameters of the program. In addition, ideas for parameters can come from published books and articles, word-of-mouth or personal experience with other hospital tobacco cessation programs, conference presentations and workshops, needs or desires stated by patients, providers and/or administration, hospital policies and requirements, and community tobacco cessation programs.

This chapter introduces various program parameters that should be considered when developing an inpatient tobacco cessation program. It provides suggestions for defining the various parameters and highlights issues to consider.

WHAT ARE THE PRIMARY AIMS OF THE PROJECT?

The primary aims of the project are the underlying reasons for the inpatient tobacco cessation program to exist. The primary aims answer the question "Why?". Why does the program exist? The following are some common reasons why an inpatient tobacco cessation program would exist within a hospital:

> To be compliant with the Treating Tobacco Use and Dependency Clinical Practice Guideline (Fiore et al., 2000).

> To create a needed expansion of the cardiac rehabilitation program in order to decrease patient morbidity and mortality.

> To enhance the quality of patient care hospital-wide.

> To be compliant with quality assurance indicator measures like JCAHO.

> To create a new potential stream of revenue.

> To improve the financial bottom line by decreasing post-surgical recovery time and/or future utilization.

> To decrease medical care expenditures through increasing tobacco cessation.

> To inform science through research (efficacy, effectiveness, and/or process).

> To improve the public's awareness of the hospital's mission to provide health promotion and disease prevention services.

> To contribute to state and provincial population-based tobacco control initiatives.

> To supplement a 100% smoke-free grounds policy by helping patients and staff to quit.

Programs funded from sources outside of the hospital, including funding in part or whole through health insurance coverage of tobacco cessation services, might have different expectations and aims than those funded solely through the hospital's operating budget. For example, if a program is funded through the hospital's operating budget, the primary aim might be to meet JCAHO (2005) requirements for adult smoking cessation advice and counseling performance measures for specific patient groups. In this case, providing printed materials handed out by unit staff and collecting the requisite data might be perceived by hospital administration as being sufficient to meet JCAHO requirements and therefore, meet the primary aims of the program.

In contrast, when health insurance plans and third party payors cover the costs of tobacco cessation services, one of their primary aims of coverage is to receive a return on investment within three to five years, measured as reduced medical care expenditures for quitters (Manley et al., 2003; McPhillips-Tangum et al., 2004; Warner et al., 2004). In order to reduce medical expenditures, cessation rates need to be maximized (and assessed), which in turn means that to meet the primary aims, intensive interventions including pharmacotherapy and frequent relapse prevention counseling would be the best choice, and data collection would have to include various indicators of medical expenditures and cessation (e.g., frequency of hospitalization, number of hospital days, etc.).

WHAT IS THE SCOPE OF THE PROGRAM?

Whereas the primary aims of the project answer the question "Why does the program exist?", the scope of the program clarifies the program's boundaries. "How far will the program extend?" This can either be the initial vision for the program or a reassessment of an ongoing program. The boundaries of the program will define the amount of developmental work and planning required to implement the program. The scope does not include the specific components of what the program will include, such as following the "5 As" as recommended in the USDHSS guideline (Fiore et al., 2000). Specific components are decided after the boundaries of the program have been clearly delineated. An excellent example of how the scope of a project will dictate the planning (and eventually implementation) work that needs to be done is provided by the Calgary Health Region when the hospitals went 100% smoke-free grounds (CHR, 2000; 2004).

Questions that can help define the scope of the project include:

> Will the program be offered to all patients or will some patients be considered ineligible? For example, in our research studies we have excluded patients admitted to psychiatric and substance abuse units because they tend to need specialized programs. If the program will be offered to all patients, consideration will need to be given in the planning stages to the special needs of some patient groups, such as

those with psychiatric disorders. This might involve additional developmental work such as literature reviews and environmental scans to clarify the best practices, challenges, and issues for each patient population.

> Will the program be extended to hospital employees or to the community? For example, when Staying Free was disseminated into standard practice at Stanford University Medical Center, it was offered to hospital employees as part of the employee health improvement program. That required meetings and negotiations with the employee health improvement program to establish what services would be provided and how they would be compensated.

> Will the program be a stand-alone service or merge with other programs in the hospital such as cardiac rehabilitation? For example, MULTIFIT, the cardiac rehabilitation program developed at Stanford Cardiac Rehabilitation Program (DeBusk et al., 1994) and disseminated into over 20 hospitals in Northern California, Oregon, and Colorado, includes Staying Free as part of a multiple risk factor intervention program for post-MI patients. A multiple risk factor intervention is of substantial broader scope than a tobacco cessation program alone.

> If the hospital is part of a consortium of hospitals and clinics, will the program be offered in all hospitals and clinics?

> Will data be systematically collected? If so, to what extent? That is, will data only be collected on program participants or will data on all inpatients who report using tobacco prior to hospitalization be tracked and used as a measure of the reach of the program (as required by JCAHO [n.d.[c-d]] for AMI, heart failure, and pneumonia patients)? Systematically collecting data on all patients who use tobacco, regardless of whether they participate in the tobacco cessation program or not, is a project of substantially wider scope than one that will only collect data on those who enroll in the program.

> How will the data be used? Will outcomes be reported internally, will data be aggregated and provided to healthcare plans, and/or will papers be submitted for scientific publication? Collecting data for scientific publication will usually result in a project of greater scope than internal reporting, as specific criteria will have to be met in

order for the data to be publishable, such as that required by the CONSORT guidelines (Altman et al., 2001).[7]

➢ Will a dedicated position for a tobacco cessation counselor be created for the program or will all clinicians be expected to provide tobacco cessation services to their own patients? Paradoxically, the latter is a project with a broader scope because it entails ongoing training of the hundreds of clinicians who are expected to intervene with their patients for tobacco use.

➢ If all clinicians will be expected to intervene, who will be trained—only physicians, nurses, and respiratory therapists or all clinicians? Will CME credits be offered? offering CME credits broadens the scope of the project.

➢ Will staff be trained on an ongoing basis or will there be one-time startup money for training? On-going training is a project with a larger scope than a one-time training because it will entail developing standardized training, on-going scheduling, continuous information updating, possibly working with continuing education accreditation and credits (CME), etc.

➢ Will the program involve changing any hospital policies? Sometimes when a hospital implements an inpatient tobacco cessation program, a number of issues surrounding tobacco surface including ways in which staff facilitate smoking, such as escorting special patient populations outside to have a cigarette (e.g., forensic, palliative care, and psychiatric patients), have to be examined and new policies might have to be developed. Policy changes, which result from examining the issues, can broaden the scope of the project substantially, and require a number of individuals and departments, such as the legal department, to be involved.

Although it might be difficult to define the full scope of the program until after some of the details are worked out (e.g., who will deliver the program, Chapter 9), setting the initial boundaries of the program provides a starting point for defining specific objectives and values. Ultimately, clarifying the boundaries of

---

[7] Although the CONSORT guidelines were written specifically for randomized trials, many of the recommendations apply to non-randomized research as well. For example, more scientific journals and reviewers are requesting information on the reach of a program, which involves collecting data on all patients assessed for eligibility, the number who were excluded or refused, the number who enrolled in the program, and the number available for follow-up.

the project will help clarify what resources and effort will be required and considered reasonable for start-up, delivery, and maintenance.

Institutional and staff concerns and expectations need to be considered in defining the scope of the project as well. For example, institutional expectations for reporting, in-services, mode of delivery, budget, and training will all play a part in defining the scope. Attending physicians might have expectations that can affect the scope, such as requesting letters informing them of their patients' enrollment. Pharmacy might have expectations for distribution of pharmacotherapy, including forms to be signed. There will likely be staff concerns and expectations from the various departments and units that can range from the desire to have their patients included as eligible for the program to the amount of training and disruption they consider reasonable to bring the program onboard. Some expectations will be apparent at the outset, possibly due to internal surveys or informal or formal meetings, whereas others will surface later in the process. Some expectations will affect the scope of the project, others might only affect specific components of the actual program.

PROGRAM OBJECTIVES

Whereas the primary aim of the program clarifies why the project exists, and the scope clarifies the boundaries, the objectives clarify measurable results or outcomes. Objectives will follow, in large part, from the primary aims and scope.

Objectives might include:

➤ Create a systems-based approach to identify all patients admitted to the hospital who use tobacco.

➤ Create a stepped-care systems-based tobacco cessation intervention, with brief interventions provided by staff nurses and an intensive intervention delivered by a dedicated tobacco cessation counselor.

➤ Implement the program in incremental steps, increasing enrollment by 10% each year.

➤ Collect process, impact, and outcome data.

➤ Publish annual outcomes.

➤ Decrease the rate of post-operative complications among smokers by providing tobacco cessation services.

Objectives become goals by breaking them down into achievable steps, adding specific numeric targets where applicable, and by adding specific dates of completion. For example, an objective of enrolling 10% of all tobacco users admitted to the hospital is measurable, but it is only a starting point because 10% of tobacco users must be defined in terms of actual numbers of patients (i.e., is 10% equal to 100 patients or 1,000 patients?) and a date of completion must be provided in order to determine when the target is to be reached.

Objectives can be flushed out for a research project by providing testable hypotheses. For example, if one of the objectives is to analyze one year cessation data, a hypothesis might be: 30% of patients receiving the intensive intervention will be confirmed non-smokers one year after discharge compared to 20% of patients receiving usual care.

WHAT VALUES WILL GUIDE THE PROGRAM?

"Make sure that those who leave us, voluntarily or involuntarily, can testify to having learned a lot, having had a special experience, and having made fast friends while they were here. (Ye shall be known by your alumni!). Tom Peters, Pursuit of Wow! (1994).

Values are what we believe in, what guides our work and our actions. Values are more emotional than cognitive. It might seem odd to consider values for an inpatient tobacco cessation program, but they are important because they direct those involved to think about the experiential aspects of the program for providers, patients, patients' families, and hospital staff. Clarifying the program values also helps to inform decision-making about the program and delivery.

The values that guide the program will determine how people—staff and patients, remember the program, how they felt about what was done and said. If they felt good about their experiences with the program, they will be the greatest program advocates. If they have a terrible experience, they can kill a program.

Values can be thought of as the general rules to work by. Some examples of values for a program include:

> ➢   Provide the best intervention time and resources allow.

> ➢   Promptly respond to all correspondence and questions.

> ➢   Always be calm and show patients they are the number one priority.

>   Respect the dignity of all patients.

>   Be patient, kind, and non-judgmental with all patients.

>   Learn from every patient.

>   Respect hospital staff and patients' families.

>   When in doubt, ask.

>   Create a collegial and light-hearted, yet professional work environment.

>   Ground the program and training in evidence.

HOW WILL QUALITY ASSURANCE BE DETERMINED?

Quality assurance can be determined by using external standardized quality assurance indicators for hospitals and healthcare plans or by using internal standards. It is important to identify as many quality assurance indicators as possible in the big picture planning stage. Measurement of the indicators will determine to a large degree the components of the program that are developed for any given hospital, the data that must be collected, and the resources and costs involved.

External Quality Assurance Standards

External quality assurance standards are published in the form of performance measures by various organizations. For example, JCAHO (2005) has clear performance indicators for tobacco use and cessation services that must be assessed using standardized measures. The JCAHO measures are provided in this section as examples to highlight how quality assurance indicators from regulatory agencies dictate the parameters of a program and clarify what must be considered in the design phase. If a hospital is already participating in an external quality assurance program, data collection systems might exist that can be tapped into by the tobacco cessation program and used in many ways, such as the identification of the patient population and forecasting caseloads. There might also be the potential to share costs for data collection and evaluation.

Joint Commission on Accreditation of Healthcare Organizations (JCAHO).
JCAHO is an American standards-setting and accrediting body in healthcare. Accreditation is a distinction given to an organization when its performance meets or exceeds the JCAHO's standards and quality expectations. The JCAHO

(n.d.$^{c-e}$) quality assurance measures include the identification, documentation, and provision of tobacco cessation services for patients admitted to the hospital with an acute myocardial infarction (AMI), heart failure (HF), and community-acquired pneumonia.

The specified data that must be collected as measures of quality assurance include the number of patients in the JCAHO-identified patient groups who have a history of smoking within one year of admission (used as the denominator) and the number of patients who receive smoking cessation advice or counseling during the hospital stay (used as the numerator). The outcome is represented as a ratio (numerator/denominator), and quality improvement is noted as an increase in the rate over time. Other data that must be collected and reported include admission date, adult smoking history, birth-date, comfort measure only, discharge status, ICD-9-CD principal diagnosis code, ICD-9-CM other diagnosis codes, pneumonia, AMI, or HF working diagnosis on admission, and transfer from another emergency department. Improvement in the compliance rate of data collection is another measure of quality assurance.

Internal Quality Assurance

In addition to external quality assurance indicators set by various agencies like JCAHO, performance indicators can be individualized for each program using internal standards. For example, the RE-AIM framework (Reach, Efficacy/effectiveness, Adoption, Implementation, Maintenance; Glasgow et al., 2004) provides dimensions and template questions for evaluating health education initiatives such as the percentage of potentially eligible participants who were excluded and who took part in the program, attrition rates, the fidelity with which the various program components are delivered, and the extent to which the different intervention components are institutionalized or continue over time. The data suggested by the RE-AIM framework can benchmark measures at pre-determined points in time, such implementation and after the first year, with the data collected at each point being used to set quality assurance improvement goals over time.

Other internal quality assurance measures, as well as external quality assurance measures, can be more general and relevant to general hospital policies and hospital quality assurance measures, such as ensuring tobacco cessation counselors are aware of any hazardous waste materials present in their work areas, and ensuring that they know where the barriers to infection are in the department. Program-specific quality assurance measures can include the availability of clinical consultants for questions regarding patient cases, documentation of all counseling in patients' charts including plans for follow-up, and evaluation of progress and long-term cessation. However, whereas the external quality assurance standards are big picture items and help define the parameters of the program due to reporting requirements, the more individualized quality assurance measures, such as those just mentioned, are more detail-oriented and might be more easily identified and/or clarified during the work involved in defining the program components, clarifying what data will be collected, goal setting, designing the evaluation, and/or defining policies and procedures.

6

Defining the Target Population and Forecasting Enrollment

Accurately defining the target population for an inpatient tobacco cessation program is necessary in order to establish the need for the program and to forecast enrollment. In turn, quantifying program need and enrollment is necessary for making the business case for the program, estimating counselor caseloads and the resources required to meet caseload demands, establishing the budget, and informing strategies for future growth and development of the program. The size and nature of the target population will also help define the type of program components that will be included.

We begin this chapter on the topic of defining the target patient population by defining inclusion and exclusion criteria. The chapter then moves onto estimating age-adjusted tobacco use prevalence and program enrollment.

INCLUSION CRITERIA

Inclusion criteria define the most inclusive group of patients that will be considered for the inpatient tobacco cessation program. Reasons to restrict whether patients will be considered for a program include limited resources, feasibility issues (e.g., short stays in some units such as obstetrics), ethical issues (e.g., palliative care units), background and training of the cessation counselors (e.g., counselors might not be trained to work with special populations such as psychiatric patients), or concern over potential disruption to care (e.g., ICU).

Inclusion criteria will differ among hospitals according to the primary aims, scope, and objectives of the inpatient tobacco cessation program. For example, if the primary aim is to determine program efficacy through a randomized clinical trial, the inclusion criteria will need to tightly define the target population in order to draw appropriate conclusions from the data. If the primary aim is to provide a program to all patients, staff, and their families, the inclusion criteria will be more generous and quite broad. If the primary aim of a program is to be compliant with the USDHHS guideline for treating tobacco use and dependence (Fiore et al., 2000), the inclusion criteria for the target population will technically be all hospitalized patients who use tobacco. If the primary aim is to be compliant with JCAHO (2005) performance measures of adult tobacco cessation advice and counseling, the inclusion criteria will include patients discharged with an ICD-9-CM[8] principal or other diagnosis code of acute myocardial infarction, heart failure, or pneumonia, who are 18 years of age and older, and who have a history of smoking cigarettes anytime during the year prior to hospital arrival.

Inclusion Criteria: the Example of Staying Free

In our inpatient research studies with general hospital patients, the most inclusive group of patients considered eligible for the program include patients who are admitted to the hospital who are 18 years of age and older and who have used any tobacco products in the previous month (Houston Miller et al., 1997; Smith et al., 2002; Smith et al., submitted; Taylor et al., 1996; Taylor et al., 2005). The rationale for each of our inclusion criteria follow.

Patients who are admitted to the hospital. Patients not actually admitted to the hospital, such as day surgery, emergency, outpatient clinics, and short-term holding patients, have not been included in our research studies as there is not sufficient time to approach these patients with the intensive intervention we have used. However, brief interventions with a different approach than we have used can be designed to target patient subgroups such as pre-surgical patients and those admitted to the emergency department or 24-hr observation units (Bock et al., 2000; Boudreaux et al., 2004; Ratner et al., 2004).

18 years of age and older. It can be difficult ethically to work with minors and protect their privacy, especially if their parents do not know they smoke. In research trials, parents usually need to sign the informed consent, at least for children under 16 years old. Depending on hospital policies and how the tobacco cessation services are being funded, a program in standard practice might not require parental approval. However if tobacco cessation services are covered through a healthcare plan, parents of pediatric patients who use tobacco cessation services are likely to find out through reporting mechanisms, which might be a deterrent for some under-aged smokers. Some funding agencies and internal review boards require a justifiable rationale for excluding children if the treatment would benefit them.

Used tobacco products in the last month. Assessing tobacco use for the previous 30 days ensures that those patients who recently quit tobacco and who might be at high risk of relapsing, as well as those who quit tobacco for a

---

[1] ICD-9-CM codes are discharge diagnosis codes. Although JCAHO requires reporting of performance measure outcomes using the discharge diagnoses codes, only admitting criteria such as hospital unit or primary reason for hospitalization provide a feasible approach for providing actual point of care service based on diagnoses, despite the short-comings that admitting reasons are not diagnoses.

planned hospitalization and only have short-term cessation in mind, (i.e., to get through the hospitalization) are approached with the opportunity to enroll in a tobacco cessation program that will help them prevent relapse in the long-term. Although the JCAHO (2005) criteria include patients with a history of smoking in the year prior to hospital arrival, we have found, anecdotally, that patients who quit tobacco for any amount of time prior to hospitalization do not perceive a personal need for a tobacco cessation/relapse prevention program because they consider themselves to be non-smokers. If cessation data will be collected as part of the program, it is important to consider that including patients who quit prior to hospitalization, especially those who have quit for more than a few days or weeks, will serve to artificially inflate at least initial cessation outcomes, and potentially long-term cessation rates if the patients who quit prior to hospitalization remain tobacco-free.

EXCLUSION CRITERIA

Although it might be desirable for all hospitalized patients who use tobacco to stop using, some degree of targeting and exclusion might be necessary. The degree of targeting will depend on the primary aims and scope that define the program as well as on the feasibility of program delivery, resources available, and the ethics guiding the program. Exclusion criteria will be more tightly defined if the primary aim of the program is a research trial in which cessation is a primary outcome. In contrast, if the primary aim is to evaluate the implementation process, with little need to measure cessation, it might be desirable to include all (or most) patients who use tobacco in an attempt to gather information on the facilitating and hindering factors to implementation with various patient groups or hospital units.

Whereas the USDHSS guideline does not specify exclusion criteria (Fiore et al., 2000), the JCAHO (2005) performance measures of adult tobacco cessation advice and counseling do have exclusion criteria. The JCAHO exclusion criteria are presented in Table 4 as an example of potential considerations for exclusions in practice that might not be evident in the general recommendation that all patients who use tobacco should be approached and offered cessation services on every encounter.

Research calls for tighter exclusion criteria than programs in standard practice. The exclusion criteria we have used in our research studies of Staying Free can be grouped into those related to patients' medical conditions, those related to the feasibility of program delivery, and those that are specific to the research study. Our rationale for these exclusion criteria follow in order to highlight some of the considerations that might arise.

Table 4. JCAHO (2005) Exclusion Criteria for Adult Tobacco Cessation Advice and Counseling

Excluded Populations	AMI Patients	HF Patients	Pneumonia Patients
Patients received in transfer from another hospital's ER			x
Patients who had no working diagnosis of pneumonia at the time of admission			x
Patients receiving *Comfort Measures Only*			x
Patients who expired in the hospital	x	x	x
Patients who left against medical advice	x	x	x
Patients discharged to hospice	x	x	x
Patients who transferred to another acute care or federal hospital	x	x	x
Patients less than 18 years of age	x	x	x

AMI = Acute myocardial infarction
HF = heart failure

Staying Free Exclusion Criteria Based On Patients' Medical Conditions

Staying Free exclusion criteria related to patients' medical conditions have included patients who are in the terminal stages of illness, medically unstable or confused, are admitted for substance abuse, psychiatric disorders, or obstetrics, and/or whose physician has refused an individual patient's participation.

Patients Who are in the Terminal Stages of Illness, Medically Complicated, or Confused. If patients are terminally ill, we do not approach them to suggest that they stop using tobacco. We have felt that to do so would be insensitive and unethical. Patients who are medically complicated, defined as medically unstable or unconscious, are not capable of participating in an intensive tobacco cessation program. We have also found it inappropriate to intervene with patients who are confused, which can include cognitive deficits, dementia, and being disoriented.

Substance Abuse Admissions. A high percentage of individuals with substance abuse disorders smoke, they tend to be highly addicted, and they might need help to quit (Orleans & Hutchinson, 1993). Most experts now agree that tobacco cessation can and should be dealt with simultaneously with drug and alcohol abuse (Hoffman & Slade, 1993, Hurt et al., 1994). The rationale for excluding patients hospitalized for substance abuse from our research trials was based on the primary aims of the trials, which were to test the efficacy of an inpatient tobacco cessation intervention in a population of general hospital patients. In practice, patients admitted for substance abuse can be a particularly refractory group that might require special services beyond that which is being offered or that tobacco cessation counselors are trained to deliver. This population might require special treatment to help them quit and practitioners might require special training in dealing with dual addiction issues. The issues that surface when dealing with this population can get quite complex, such as when patients are admitted to the hospital for drug overdoses.

Psychiatric Admissions. A high percentage of psychiatric patients use tobacco products, with the prevalence averaging about 54% and reaching into the high 80%'s depending on the disorder (Hughes et al., 1986). The rationale for excluding psychiatric patients from our research studies was based on the fact that these populations might require special treatment and that it is difficult to design cessation programs taking into account the various cognitive and social deficits of some patients, such as those with schizophrenia (Esterberg & Compton, 2005). Research has found treatments effective in helping smokers in this population abstain from tobacco, although there have been no studies with chronically ill inpatients (Lyon, 1999).

The American Public Health Association (2003) has published a policy statement urging mental health and substance abuse treatment professionals and facilities to implement integrated cessation plans. However, cessation counselors trained only to work with general hospital patients need to be aware of the special needs of the various psychiatric populations when providing tobacco cessation interventions. For example, there is evidence that smoking increases the metabolism of some psychiatric medications, resulting in increased dosing requirements for some smokers; quitting can increase the blood levels of psychiatric medications, lead to exacerbations of symptoms, and might result in problematic side effects such as an increase in anxiety and depression (Dalack & Meador-Woodruff, 1996; Hughes, 1993; Lyon, 1999).

Obstetrical Patients. We are not aware of any programs that have focused on inpatient obstetrical patients (many are available for pre- and post-natal women). Our reason for excluding these patients was based, in part, on the feasibility of delivery—their hospital stay is usually less than 36 hours, which is too short a time to intervene with a tobacco cessation program, and in part on practical reasons—women tend to have other priorities during hospitalization following delivery. Even if intervention was possible within their brief hospital stay, postpartum women tend to be a refractory group that might require special intervention. Many are not highly motivated to quit if they did not quit during their pregnancy, and those who do quit during pregnancy have a high degree of relapse (McBride & Pirie, 1990), with many intending to quit only for the pregnancy. Nonetheless, this is an important target group for cessation given the very strong impact of parental smoking on children's growth and development. Therefore creating alternatives for this population, possibly in conjunction with physician/nurse involvement at well-baby visits, should be a high priority.

MD Refusal. In our studies we have received blanket agreement from all physicians to approach patients at the bedside to offer them the inpatient tobacco cessation program. The blanket approval has been organized through a memo from the Chief of Staff to all physicians. Physicians are to request non-participation for specific patients they deem unfit for the program. We have only had two cases in the past ten years of physicians refusing their patients' participation in a tobacco cessation program.

Staying Free Exclusion Criteria Based On Feasibility of Program Delivery

The feasibility of delivery has helped to determine the exclusion criteria in our work with Staying Free. Exclusion criteria related to feasibility of program delivery have included patients hospitalized for less than 36 hours or who have language or communication barriers. of greatest concern to feasibility of program delivery is lack of time. Many hospitals have patient management teams designed to ensure patients move as quickly and as efficiently as possible through the system. This can mean relatively short hospital stays, which in turn can pose feasibility challenges relative to patient access because patients are usually busy during a short stay.

Hospital Stay Less than 36 Hours. For research studies, the 36-hour restriction helps ensure sufficient time for the intervention to be delivered, allowing for times when patients are unavailable. Time consideration in terms of patient availability needs to be given to sleeping, bathing, visiting, undergoing procedures or various therapies, patient consultation with providers, patients not in their rooms, and transient conditions that limit concentration or desire to participate (e.g., disoriented, drowsy, or experiencing physical discomfort). Some patients are admitted late on Friday (or on the weekend) and discharged prior to the cessation provider's shift on Monday. Even if a brief intervention is being provided, time limitations might make it difficult to find the patient available to even drop off materials in a meaningful way. Also, many of the factors that help patients quit and remain tobacco-free during hospitalization are not present during stays of less than 36 hours. That might mean that patients with short stays might not be as motivated as those with longer stays or might have more trouble remaining tobacco-free post-discharge.

Language Barriers. In our earlier research studies, tobacco cessation materials were only offered in English and the cessation nurses only spoke English. In our more recent studies, we continue to develop programs for non-English speaking populations. At Stanford we have developed programs for Spanish and Vietnamese speaking populations, and work with counselors who are bilingual or multilingual. In assessing the target populations it is important to determine what languages are spoken, and efforts should be made to address various languages. At a minimum, Canadian programs might want to offer French and Aboriginal versions and American programs might want to offer a Spanish version. The choice is dependent on patient demographics, program resources, and the personnel available. In some settings, bilingual or multilingual nurses might be required and print materials might have to be translated into various languages (Sivarajan Froelicher et al., 2004).

Communication Difficulties. Some patients might have hearing or speech difficulties, disorders such as aphasia, or even temporary conditions such as having their jaw wired shut. All of these can make intervening on tobacco use difficult if not impossible and need to be considered.

Staying Free Research-Specific Exclusion Criteria

Research-specific exclusion criteria for Staying Free have included patients who are involved in a concurrent tobacco cessation trial, who do not have a telephone for telephone counseling and follow-up, who live outside of the geographical area, who are transferred to another institution, or who are unwilling to participate. Idiosyncratic factors that might exclude a patient from a research trial can surface during the course of a study. For example, some patients might be violent, abusive, or incoherent when approached making it impossible to provide cessation counseling; these patients would likely fall under "other" exclusion criteria in a research trial but might not pose a concern for a tobacco cessation program in standard practice in which tightly controlled data are not being collected.

Patients Involved in a Concurrent Trial that Includes Tobacco Cessation. This is only a necessary and meaningful exclusion criterion in research studies in which cessation is a primary outcome used to measure the efficacy or effectiveness of the program. In the broadest sense, this criterion also includes a patient who is re-admitted to the hospital and who is already enrolled in the study. In this case, readmissions serve to inflate the ineligibility statistics.

Patients Who Do Not Have a Phone. This is only an exclusion consideration if post-discharge counseling will be provided and/or if tobacco use status post-discharge will be measured via telephone contact. This exclusion criterion can include patients who are incarcerated or who live in an institution or even a trailer park in which they do not have their own phone or easy access to a communal phone. of special note, patients who only have a cell phone can be difficult to contact because cell phones often require only an infusion of cash with no credit rating required, so some patients who do not have the credit rating for regular landline service might show a pattern of on/off cell phone service (on when cash is available, off when it is not).

Patients Who Live Outside the Geographical Location. All hospitals admit patients from out of province/state and even country. Depending on the telephone billing plan and the degree of post-discharge counseling and follow-up, counselor-initiated telephone calls outside the hospital's telephone exchange area can add unpredictable variable costs to the program, so some decision as to geography should be determined, even if just to allow budget estimates for long-distance. There are also other geographical considerations for research studies— patients who live outside the calling area might not be able or willing to return to the hospital for biochemical verification of tobacco use status, they might be more difficult to track if they do move, and insurance coverage might shift, which could pose a challenge if the tobacco cessation program is supported through insurance coverage.

Patients Who Are Transferred to Another Institution. This is not as much an exclusion criterion as a consideration for maintaining complete records in a research trial. A patient might be eligible for the program and assigned to a treatment condition but is transferred to another hospital before counseling begins or is transferred after counseling but is unreachable for further counseling or follow-up.

Patients Unwilling to Quit. From a public health perspective it is desirable to provide treatment to as many people as possible. The USDHHS guideline recommendations include offering a motivational intervention based on the "5 Rs" for patients unwilling to make a quit attempt (Fiore et al., 2000). However, if data are being collected either for internal or external reporting purposes, it is important to note that there might be many holes in the data if patients unwilling to quit or even engage with the cessation provider for a brief motivational interview are also unwilling to provide any personal information (e.g., baseline demographic or smoking history) or receive post-discharge contact to provide tobacco use status.

FORECASTING EXCLUSION NUMBERS

Exclusion criteria are usually broad enough that patients can be screened for eligibility by reviewing their medical charts. In one of our studies, 98.5% of patients considered ineligible for the tobacco cessation program could be determined from admitting records and patient charts without having to approach patients at the bedside. This is good news from a time and effort perspective. It also enhances the ability to make relatively accurate forecasts for program enrollment before the program begins by doing a one to two week chart review.

The data in Table 5 show the percentage of patients by exclusion criteria for our dissemination hospital study using the exclusion criteria described in the previous section (Smith et al., 2002). The percentages are based on patients identified as eligible for enrollment. If all hospitalized patients are considered, including those who are medically unstable, confused, who have short admissions, or who expired during hospitalization, the percentage of those ineligible would be greater, likely over 50%-60% (Smith et al., submitted).

Table 5. Forecasting Exclusion (Smith et al., 2002)

Status	% of Eligible Tobacco Users
Enrolled into program	52%
Ineligible	10%
Refused program	18%
Did not want to quit	20%

It is helpful to explore from a forecasting perspective, if possible, what proportion of hospital stays are less than 36 hours (the data might or might not be available). A one to two week chart review might provide some insight as to the percentage of patients that would be considered medically complicated as well as the average hospital stay of patients who might be considered eligible for an inpatient tobacco cessation program. Since these are the major reasons for exclusion, estimating how they will affect individual hospitals might serve to enhance forecasting accuracy.

In the one study in which we were able to track eligibility of all patients admitted to the hospital, the ineligibility was over 50% (Smith et al., submitted). The majority of patients considered ineligible were those who had short hospital stays (feasibility criteria) and those who were medically complicated or confused (medical criteria). Both are factors of hospitalization and will vary depending on the hospital, patient population, and the hospital system. The high exclusion rates for medically complicated and short stays are consistent with hospital statistics that show inpatient admissions are decreasing due to advancements in medical technologies and there is a shift towards day and outpatient treatments (Canadian Institute for Health Information, n.d.), suggesting that those who are hospitalized for more extended periods of time will tend to be quite ill or require major procedures/surgeries not available on an outpatient basis. These factors might mean that innovative approaches to providing inpatient tobacco cessation programs might need to further evolve to address the changing environment.

ESTIMATING TOBACCO USE PREVALENCE

Estimating tobacco use prevalence in a hospital population is not as simple as projecting the population tobacco use prevalence onto the hospital population. Even though people who use tobacco are more likely to be hospitalized than those who do not, paradoxically, tobacco use prevalence might be lower in the hospital than it is in the general population. This is because the age distribution in the hospital tends to be skewed by a larger proportion of older patients and the fact that tobacco use prevalence decreases with age. Therefore, age is one of the most important factors in estimating tobacco use prevalence among hospitalized patients. In this next section, we provide an algorithm to estimate tobacco use prevalence taking age into consideration.

Figure 5 provides an example of how to calculate tobacco use prevalence. The algorithm is based on our Canadian trial but the numbers are for example only (Smith & Corso, submitted). These data can be collected using daily hospital admissions over a given period of time or estimated using data from each participating hospital's medical records.

Figure 5 shows that the overall tobacco use prevalence is 21% (1,750/8,400)—16% for patients 45 years and older, and 37% for patients less than 45 years. A 21% tobacco use prevalence rate is substantially lower than the overall population prevalence at the time of the study, which was 31% (and estimated conservatively at 25% for the study). The lower than estimated tobacco use prevalence in this example shows the importance of considering age when estimating tobacco use prevalence. In this example, patients 45 yr. of age and older more heavily weighted the average tobacco use rate—they represented 77% of all patients eligible to screen for the program. Because age is such an important factor in estimating the size of the target population, we have provided the steps for estimating tobacco use prevalence using an age-adjusted method.

A Step by Step Approach for Estimating Tobacco Use Prevalence

Step 1: Separate annual hospital admissions into units eligible and ineligible to screen. To begin the age-adjusted estimate of tobacco use prevalence, the annual patient flow data from the participating hospitals need to be separated into units that are eligible to be screened (e.g., surgical, medical, ICU, etc.) and those deemed ineligible to be screened (e.g., psychiatric, obstetric, substance abuse) based inclusion/exclusion criteria. If tobacco use prevalence is being estimated for more than one hospital, it is essential to keep the data separate for each hospital because the size of the units ineligible to screen will differ across hospitals. For example, one hospital might have an usually large obstetric unit and another hospital might not even have an obstetric unit, meaning that the percentage of patients eligible to be screened from all new admissions will differ across the two hospitals.

Figure 5. Estimating Tobacco Use Prevalence

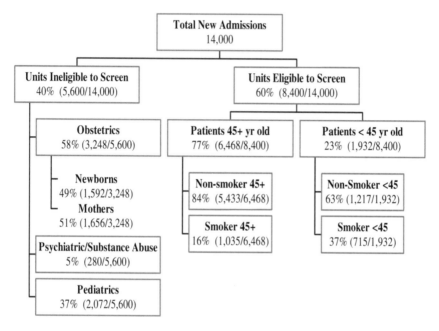

The units not eligible to be screened might provide important future opportunities for program expansion. Therefore, it is helpful to provide the number of patients in each of the units not eligible to be screened. Tobacco use prevalence can also be estimated for these groups using the age-specific methods that follow in Steps 2 and 3, in combination with published tobacco prevalence data for each of the special populations (i.e., substance abuse, pediatrics, obstetrics, and psychiatric).

If quarterly or semi-annual admissions are available, separate flow charts for each quarter or half-year can be created to allow more accurate estimates for staffing, resource allocation, and goal setting for enrollment. Separating the data into quarterly or semi-annual admissions is also helpful for estimating enrollment in research trials involving less than full year recruitment because patient flow can vary by season.

Step 2: Define age cohorts. In order to estimate age-adjusted tobacco use prevalence, the number of patients eligible to be screened must be divided into age cohorts. Age can usually be obtained from the hospital admission records. We have used two age cohorts, with 45 years of age as the breakpoint (Figure 5). Although tobacco use prevalence in the population decreases more at age 55 than 45, the breakpoint of 45 was based on one of our earlier studies that showed patients less than 45 years of age who had less than 100% confidence to quit smoking did not respond to the intensive intervention (Smith et al., 2002).

If age data are not available from medical records, the percentage of patients in each age cohort can be estimated using a lower bound of 60% of patients expected to be 45 yr. and older and 40% estimated to be less than 45 yr. (following from the Stanford studies in Health Maintenance Organizations and private hospitals) and an upper bound estimate of 80% expected to be 45 yr. and older and 20% estimated to be less than 45 yr. (based on the Canadian study in a universal healthcare system). It might be desirable to use more than two age cohorts. For example, following population tobacco prevalence trends, it might be helpful to break the age cohorts at 18-24, 25-44, 45-64, and 65 and older, even if only as a check for a two-group age break to see if it makes a difference in estimates.

Step 3: Calculate age-adjusted tobacco use prevalence. Once the admission data have been separated into age cohorts within the units eligible to be screened, the age-adjusted tobacco use prevalence can be estimated, either using hospital-specific tobacco use data if they are available or by using published regional and state/provincial age-specific tobacco use prevalence rates. Many, if not most, hospitals do not yet systematically collect tobacco use status data, so tobacco use prevalence will likely have to be estimated using published statistics.

We have found that regional and state/provincial age-specific tobacco use prevalence rates are relatively accurate estimates for the hospital population as long as the hospital population is separated into age cohorts (as per Figure 5) and age-adjusted tobacco prevalence rates are used. The closer to "home" the published prevalence rates are, the more accurate they will be—that is, regional rates will be more accurate than provincial/state or federal rates. Prevalence data can be found through local health departments or on municipal, state/provincial, or federal government websites (e.g., http://www.hc-sc.gc.ca/hecs-sesc/tobacco /research/ctums/2002/summary.html in Canada, and http://www.cdc.gov/nchs/ fastats/smoking.htm in the United States).

The age-adjusted calculations demonstrate the role played in the estimation of tobacco use prevalence by the relative number of older patients in any given hospital and their average age (see Talking to Counselors below). The smaller the age categories used in the tobacco use prevalence calculations (e.g., 18-24, 25-35, 35-45, 45-55, 55+), the more accurate the tobacco use prevalence estimates will likely be.

Talking to Counselors

Linda Corso, BScN, MA, recruitment nurse for the Canadian multi-site general hospital inpatient trial, and co-founder and principal of InfoFinders, a healthcare information search company (infofinder2@ rogers.com).

Q: What are the most important things you learned about estimating tobacco use prevalence?

A: The relationship of age to smoking status was a real eye-opener. In the beginning of our cessation trial, our recruitment fell substantially short of projected—there just didn't seem to be many smokers. Along with our PI we devised a system to track what was going on and found that about 75% of our patients were over 45 years of age and their average age was hovering around 70. When we realized that the provincial tobacco use prevalence for that age group was about 13% (not 25% as projected for the project), it all made sense and we felt a lot better about our job performance. It wasn't that there weren't any smokers, it was that we had an older population so fewer smokers should be expected.

Estimating Tobacco Use Prevalence Through a Pilot Study

If annual hospital admission data are not available, a pilot study can be designed to estimate tobacco use prevalence for the target population. The pilot data collected must be sufficient to clearly identify those patients who meet inclusion criteria such as age and unit requirements. Exclusion criteria are not relevant at the level of estimating tobacco use prevalence—they are relevant further along the process, when estimating enrollment.

In our most recent dissemination study (Taylor et al., 2005), we hired a research assistant to collect pre-admission tobacco use data in six different hospitals in Northern California. For 14 consecutive days, the research assistant interviewed every patient admitted the hospitals about their use of tobacco products in the 30 days prior to their hospitalization. Our findings are presented in Table 6.

Although these prevalence data are not age-adjusted, they do provide an overall estimate of the tobacco use prevalence at each hospital. There were large differences in tobacco use prevalence across the different hospitals. The prevalence rates of tobacco use were relatively low. for all but the Veterans Administration (VA) hospital, reflecting the lower overall rates in California. The higher prevalence rates for the VA are consistent with data that show veterans tend to have higher tobacco use rates (Enstrom, 1999), and might reflect, among other factors, higher rates of psychiatric co-morbidities and substance abuse.

Table 6. Tobacco Use Prevalence in Six Hospitals

Hospital	Total # Admits	Total # Surveyed	Total % Surveyed	# Tobacco Users	% Tobacco Users
Veterans Admin	136	132	97%	39	30%
County	707	596	84%	90	15%
Small Community	248	217	88%	22	10%
Large Community	288	233	81%	27	12%
University	605	313	52%	26	8%
HMO	616	446	72%	57	13%
Total	2600	1937	74%	261	13%

FORECASTING ENROLLMENT

Estimating enrollment is important for estimating counselors' caseloads. Caseload estimations, in turn, are important for estimating staffing and resource needs. If a brief bedside intervention without post discharge follow-up will be provided to *all* hospital patients, estimating enrollment is not relevant— estimating tobacco use prevalence and adjusting for eligibility will suffice as the main factors affecting tobacco counseling caseloads. However, if a more intensive bedside intervention and/or post discharge counseling will be provided, it is important to estimate the number of patients who might be interested in accepting such services in order to calculate counselors' caseloads.

Enrollment might be affected by many factors, including patient and counselor characteristics, hospital specialties, and sociopolitical factors. However, one of the most relevant factors in estimating actual enrollment is ensuring that the starting point for estimating, annual admissions, is correct (see Talking to Counselors below). Nonetheless, it is possible to estimate (even if roughly) the number of patients who will enroll in an inpatient tobacco cessation program by using data from previous studies.

Talking to Counselors

Linda Corso, BScN, MA, recruitment nurse for the Canadian multi-site general hospital inpatient trial, and co-founder and principal of InfoFinders, a healthcare information search company (infofinder2@rogers.com).

Q: What are the most important things you learned about estimating the patient enrollment?

A: What was most striking was how difficult it is to get an accurate record of the starting point—that is, all new admissions to the hospital. In Ontario, the statistical Management Information System might count the same patient twice. A patient might be admitted to a medical unit for a short acute stay, discharged on paper, and readmitted on paper to a rehab unit. Although this counts as two new admissions for the hospital, it should not really count as two admissions on the tobacco cessation tracking log because a patient who is either not eligible for the program or refuses the program will be counted twice and patients who do enroll in the program will automatically become ineligible for the second admission thereby inflating the ineligibility rate. This is also true of frequent readmissions for the same patients throughout any given period of time. And in Canada, at least, our readmission rate is quite high.

Table 7 provides data from three of our general hospital studies. Our enrollment has ranged from 34% to 52% among identified tobacco users who meet eligibility criteria. Among the 48% to 66% who did not enroll, just over half did not want to quit, with the remainder refusing participation for a variety of reasons including reasons such as wanting to quit on their own, not wanting to be in a study, or for personal reasons.

Table 7. Enrollment Statistics the Randomized Trials of Staying Free

	Hospitals		
	Stanford Medical[a]	Kaiser Permanente[b]	Canadian Community[c]
Number of Sites	1	4	3
Enrollment Period	2 yr	2 yr	1.3 yr
Eligible Smokers	1871	1553	1945
Enrolled	52% (1,077)	42% (660)	34% (668)
Did not enroll	48% (794)	58% (893)	66% (1,277)

[a] Smith et al., 2002; [b] Houston Miller et al., 1997; [c] Smith et al., submitted

To estimate enrollment, we suggest creating a flow diagram similar to Figure 6 (data in Figure 6 are for example only), and keep the estimates conservative (see Table 7). Figure 6 separates data for the age categories, and provides a realistic estimate that approximately 50% of identified smokers will be eligible to receive an intensive bedside intervention. Beyond the point of estimating tobacco use prevalence, our data suggest that age does not seem to matter relative to reach statistics (e.g., enrollment, refusal, dropout etc.). Differences by hospital at this level of calculation are difficult to estimate. Differences will likely result from how tightly systems can be designed for consistent recruitment, program delivery, and follow-up, and from who runs the systems rather than the patient population.

Figure 6. Enrollment and Program Completion by Age Category

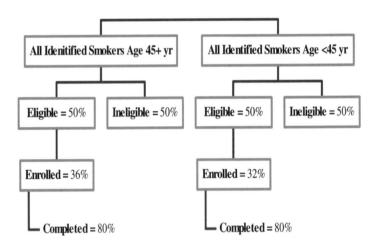

Despite potentially large numbers of patients who might be excluded due to not meeting eligibility, the examples in Figure 6 and Table 7 shows that the reach of an inpatient tobacco cessation program still exceeds that for outpatient programs and for programs targeted at the general population, both of which run at <1% enrollment of targeted smokers (e.g., Smith et al., 2004). It is important that hospital and program administrators and tobacco cessation counselors have realistic expectations for an inpatient tobacco cessation program—consideration must be given to inclusion and exclusion criteria, and not all patients will be eligible, want to quit, or want help quitting.

7

Champions, Advisory Committees, Stakeholders, and Community Resources

The adoption, implementation, and sustainability of an inpatient tobacco cessation program in standard hospital practice requires a strong multilevel support structure within the hospital. Even when the proposed program offers visible benefits to patients, quality of care, and staff, the initial reactions to the program might be resistant or even negative. Less than positive reactions can result from territory-protection issues, struggles for limited resources, concerns about additional work volume, competition over what programs get the spotlight, defensive interpretations that a new program means providers are not currently doing an adequate job, cross-discipline conflicts, low morale, new-initiative burnout (flavor of the month), and/or cynicism ("we've tried that before and it didn't work"). Change of any sort is often difficult and uncomfortable because it disrupts the status quo, breaks up routines, often leaves people feeling inefficacious, and is unsettling.

This chapter helps to identify what supports might aid with program adoption, implementation, and maintenance. It is essential to think through who might be affected by the change, what the far-reaching implications might be that could foster support or opposition, and what will be required to gain buy-in and smooth the way for implementation. For example, support and acceptance of the program goals and methods will need to come from upper management, as well as from all departments that will be affected by the program. A program champion is useful (usually necessary), and an oversight committee or advisory board is helpful. Stakeholders and their needs must be identified and attended to. Community resources can also play a role in supporting the program, so an inventory of what exists is suggested and some degree of networking is advisable.

PROGRAM CHAMPIONS

Through our years of work with Staying Free, it has become abundantly clear that every inpatient tobacco cessation program benefits from having a champion. A champion is a person inside the organization who has a fierce desire to provide or improve tobacco cessation services in the inpatient setting. In our experience, physicians and nurses have usually been program champions, although we have had psychologists, ministers, patients, and administrators take this role. There may be more than one champion in a hospital. Sometimes members of the tobacco control or wellness committees collectively are the champions.

In addition to desire, a champion (or champions) should have influential control, be willing to lobby for a program at all levels of management and staff, and be willing to negotiate to make it happen. And because influential control is an essential component, it is almost essential that at least one program champion in a hospital be a physician.

It is also ideal to have a champion in each department to help bring each department onboard. We have been impressed with how many healthcare professionals feel very strongly about tobacco cessation and are willing to spend extra time and effort to provide an opportunity for their patients to quit. A program can be seriously sabotaged if any given department or departments do not buy-in, or worse, try to make sure that the program does not happen.

How to Find a Physician Willing to Champion an Inpatient Tobacco Cessation Program

A potential physician champion might be apparent because he or she writes editorials or journal articles on tobacco cessation, is trying to push for the implementation of clinical practice guideline for treating tobacco use and dependence, teaches courses in tobacco cessation or lifestyle change, sits on the wellness or tobacco control committees at the hospital, runs a research program or outpatient clinic in tobacco dependence, is an advocate for behavioral medicine, or is in charge of or participates in lifestyle and health promotion programs in the hospital. Cardiac rehabilitation personnel usually have a fierce commitment to tobacco cessation. If a champion is not apparent, it can be helpful to ask around the hospital to find out what physicians counsel their patients on lifestyle factors, especially tobacco.

Physicians who are involved on tobacco control committees in the community are usually good choices for a program champion. It can be helpful to find out who, from the hospital setting, works with cancer or lung societies or heart associations (e.g., American and Canadian cancer and lung associations/ societies, American Heart Association, Canadian and provincial Heart and Stroke Foundations, etc.). The hospital public relations department might be able to identify possible physician champions for the program by reviewing previous or current press releases on tobacco-related or disease prevention programs originating from the hospital and determining what physicians were involved. Hospital librarians, health educators, and substance abuse counselors might also know of physicians in the hospital involved with tobacco research, training, or treatment. These strategies should reveal at least one, if not a few physicians, who might be willing to be a program champion.

ADVISORY BOARDS

In addition to finding a physician champion in the hospital, it is helpful to have an advisory board. An advisory board may take various forms or have various mandates. They might be in place to ensure that the program meets institutional policies and regulations, serve as a resource for defining the standard of care for various patient groups, and/or help disseminate information about the program. They might be knowledgeable about resources in the community that could help support the program such as potential funding sources, potential partnership opportunities, public relations opportunities, and various resource sources for patient materials, post-discharge counseling services, quit lines, and even pharmacotherapy aid programs such as those offered through some public health departments.

The advisory board should include healthcare professionals whose expertise can be of use in the program design and function, whose patients will benefit from the program, and/or whose departments will be directly involved with the implementation and maintenance of the program. A broad representation of healthcare professionals is ideal in order to obtain as many perspectives as possible and to assist with the dissemination and buy-in across departments and disciplines—physicians, nurses, respiratory therapists, cardiac rehabilitation staff, pharmacists, psychologists, health educators, and social workers.

Non-health-related or non-hospital professionals can also contribute to the advisory committee. It might be helpful to consider top level administrators (to advise on hospital protocols and protect tobacco cessation agenda time in other hospital meetings), researchers (to advise on data collection and evaluation), admitting personnel (if the tobacco use question is added to the admitting records), information technology personnel (to advise on the technical aspects of patient identification and data collection), financial managers, attorneys, internal review board (IRB) members, and administrators familiar with reimbursement issues. Community representatives from local businesses, public health, and non-government organizations can also provide valuable input. They can serve as strong advocates who will lobby for programs and/or potentially contribute to funding for the program.

An advisory board might automatically be assigned to an inpatient tobacco program without any choice or input (e.g., the IRB for a research study), or a tobacco control or wellness committee might already exist and it might be a natural fit for the committee to take on the inpatient tobacco cessation initiative.

If a board or oversight committee has to be formed for the project, the methods suggested above for finding a physician champion might work to identify candidates for the board. A reasonable expectation for a board would be to meet approximately once per quarter (sometimes more in the start-up phase).

Case Example: An Advisory Board Makes Smoke-Free Grounds Happen

An example of how an advisory board can contribute to the approval and implementation process is provided by a Canadian hospital (Calgary Health Region, 2003; 2004). The hospital did extensive pre-program work and data collection to support a proposed 100% smoke-free grounds policy. The policy was complemented with coverage of tobacco cessation counseling and pharmacotherapy for patients and staff. The hospital used a number of advisory working committees to provide recommendations about specific patients groups such as mental health, long-term care, palliative care, and home care. Their reports included a literature review of best practices, challenges, and successes in the areas of smoking bans and cessation for their patient populations, outcomes from focus groups and interviews with staff and patients regarding the impending policy and program changes, and recommendations for their patient groups based on their literature reviews and interviews.

Another advisory board in the project helped to develop and facilitate the adoption of clear policies for tobacco company sponsorship of events related in any way to the regional health authority. Representatives from Human Resources and Protection Services served as an advisory committee and worked with the tobacco control committee to draft and implement more effective enforcement plans for the smoke-free grounds policy. The Executive Director and Vice President of each site involved in the region advanced the initiative by distributing memos providing information on policy changes and the types of tobacco cessation coverage that would come into effect for patients and staff.

All persons involved on the advisory working committees did so as part of their regular workload. The project had priority status which justified the amount the time and effort committee members put into it. This will not always be the case. It is probably more likely that time spent on an advisory board means time taken away from other work. When this is the case, few people like to serve on the board or committee so it is important to limit the amount of work asked of the members and keep the number and duration of meetings to a minimum.

STAKEHOLDERS

Stakeholders can be anyone and everyone involved directly or indirectly with the hospital or who will be affected in some way by the inpatient tobacco cessation program. Although stakeholders are often thought of only as those who will be providing the funding or those ultimately using the services, there are many others from whom support and buy-in will be either necessary or helpful in order for an inpatient tobacco cessation program to be approved and implemented, and without whose support the program might be an uphill struggle or might not happen at all. Stakeholders' wants and needs will be varied and might range from preventing or managing disease to keeping costs down or keeping moral up.

Garnering acceptance and support for the program will depend on the degree to which stakeholders and their needs can be identified and addressed. Acceptance can be as simple as not resisting the program, and support can take many forms, such as writing letters of support, providing funding, providing training, and offering incentives to staff to follow-through with the program.

How Are Stakeholders Identified?

The starting point for identifying stakeholders can be as simple as taking a blank sheet of paper and brainstorming about every possible person, committee, or board that might have a stake in the cessation program. Keep the list to the left side of the paper so that wants and needs can later be filled in on the right. Brainstorming can be organized around categories such as hospital executives, health education providers, committees, patient groups, hospital units, funding organizations, and patients' families. When it comes to committees or boards, it is helpful to identify individuals within these groups because some might be strong proponents of an inpatient tobacco cessation program and others might be strong opponents.

The more obvious stakeholders include hospital executives (CEO, CFO, COO, vice-presidents), department directors (e.g., nursing, patient education, human resources), chief of staff and physicians (specialists, family physicians, residents), non-physician front-line providers (nurses, respiratory therapists, pharmacists, health educators, social workers, kinesiologists), the hospital and partner IRBs (e.g., academic institutions), the hospital board of directors, patients (inpatients, outpatients, day surgery, emergency), and patients' relatives. Agencies, foundations, and philanthropists who might help fund the program are potential stakeholders, as are affiliated academic institutions that might appreciate the opportunity to collect and analyze data at all stages of implementation and delivery, and community partners (e.g., public health units, tobacco control coalitions, non-government agencies). Perhaps less obvious, but potential stakeholders, nonetheless, could include non-medical staff (administration, clergy, admitting, telecommunications, public relations, finance, laboratories), patient support and advocacy groups, hospital volunteers, and, media (e.g., local newspapers, cable television, radio).

This list will not necessarily be relevant to all programs nor is the list exhaustive because stakeholders will be institution-specific and the need to identify them will depend on the level of program support (in cases where support is high, identifying all stakeholders might not be necessary). The list does represent the broad range of stakeholders that could be considered to somehow play a part in the implementation and sustainability of the program. By taking the time to identify all possible stakeholders within the hospital, it becomes possible to look at potential positive and negative consequences or fallout prior to implementation using the list of stakeholders as the framework to guide thinking. The reason to consider stakeholders beyond hospital personnel, funding sources, and patients is that there might be ways to garner support from disparate sources that collectively will enhance the likelihood of implementation, overall success, and sustainability.

What Do Stakeholders Want and Need?

If stakeholder wants and needs can be identified, it becomes possible to collect and distribute information to them that they will appreciate and/or that might be necessary to get program buy-in. To determine what stakeholders want and need, it is helpful to start with information that is known about the stakeholders on the issue of tobacco use and interventions. Using the paper with the stakeholder names on the left, it is easiest to begin with a first line of questioning that addresses two key questions:

First Line of Questions:
> ➤ If anyone is speaking up, what do they say they want?
>> o For example, are staff physicians writing editorials and journal articles to support clinical practice guidelines for tobacco use and dependence?

> ➤ What do they know?
>> o For example, most hospital executives will be aware of the Joint Commission on Accreditation of Healthcare Organizations (JCAHO, 2005) requirements for tobacco cessation programs for specified patient groups.

For the second line of questioning, it is helpful to try to answer the questions about what stakeholders need to know and what they might want to know.

Second Line of Questions:
> ➤ What do stakeholders <u>need</u> to know to provide program buy-in?
>> o The needs might vary and include such concerns as what impact the program will have on patient care, how providers can get reimbursed for services, what resources providers will have to

contribute (e.g., clinic time), what a program will mean in terms of workload across all hospital staff, what data exist to build a business case, or what will be the return on investment.

> What do stakeholders <u>want</u> to know about the program in order to provide buy-in?
  o Some stakeholders might want to know a great deal because they want to ensure that it will not affect their resources or their own new initiatives.

> Is there a difference between want to know and need to know?
  o Some stakeholders might not want to know anything about the program because it is not in their area of accountability, but they will need to know about the program because they will have to approve in-service training in their departments.

> What is in it for the stakeholders (both positive and negative) if they support the program?
  o This will vary greatly. For example, for patients, consequences might include questions such as: "Will patients' healing time decrease?" For hospital administrators, consequences might be: "Will length of hospital stays decrease and free up waiting lists?" For hospital CEOs, consequences might be: "Will funds have to be diverted from another program to fund the inpatient program?" For clinicians, consequences might include: "Will anyone have to do more work?"

It is also helpful to determine what format would be the most efficient for dissemination of information to various stakeholders during the startup phase and beyond. For example, department managers who will not have hands-on responsibility for the inpatient program could be kept in the information loop through quarterly email or memo up-dates. A financial officer might want a monthly spreadsheet of costs and revenues. After the program is up and running, a clinical director might want a graph of cumulative enrollment by month. The director of nursing might want a comparison of cessation rates among different patient groups. And patients could be kept apprised of general access and cost information through patient newsletters or stories in the local media.

Stakeholder Data Collection

It might be helpful to administer surveys, hold focus groups, or interview stakeholders to find out what they know, want, and need, what their questions and concerns are, and what they perceive the barriers and facilitating factors are for implementation. This type of data collection might reveal the range of stakeholders' perceptions, needs, and wants. It can also elucidate the various agendas that might be operating within the hospital, how needs and expectations might vary across departments and disciplines, what the common problems or goals are with respect to tobacco use and cessation, and how to mobilize resources across departments. The data collected can be used to help define what the stakeholders will support in terms of the intervention and delivery options, who they believe should be ultimately responsible for the program, and who should provide it. Even if their desires cannot be met, the data can ensure that appropriate rationale are provided to support the decisions that are made.

Collecting information form the stakeholders might also reveal whether the overall support for a program is positive or negative. It might turn out that most staff are strongly in favor of a program and have been wanting something to happen for a long time, or it might be discovered that a program was tried years ago, it did not work because it put too much of a burden on staff nurses, and therefore the perception is that nothing has changed and it will not work this time either. The stakeholders might also be able to identify potential problems or suggest creative solutions or alternatives to barriers not initially considered.

After the information on stakeholders has been collected, the brainstorming sheet on stakeholders (suggested at the beginning of this section) can be completed by filling in the list with perceived needs and wants, the initial information stakeholders might require for buy-in, and the ongoing information they will require for continued support. It might also be helpful to create an overall summary to provide to the advisory committee or upper management. The summary could include:

> Who are the stakeholders?

> What do stakeholders know?

> What do stakeholders need to know to get buy-in in their department?

> What is in it for them?

> What is the level of support for the program?

> What form do the stakeholders want their information in?

This list will serve as the central organizing piece for ongoing reporting during implementation and the life of the program. When stakeholders are kept in the loop with the information they require or desire, or are simply thought of as being important enough to be kept in the loop, they are more likely to provide ongoing support for the program.

An added bonus to talking with stakeholders is that it might also be possible to identify the influential behavioral and environmental factors that will either facilitate or hinder the implementation of an inpatient tobacco cessation program quite apart from stakeholder needs and wants. For example, what clinicians already provide cessation services? Why do they do it? (Or why not?) Do clinicians believe they are individually responsible for providing cessation services to their patients? If not, who do they think should provide services? Do they systematically provide services or is it 'hit and miss'? What would increase their ability to provide cessation services? Other information could include factors that predispose clinicians to provide tobacco cessation services on a regular basis such as staff's knowledge, attitudes, beliefs, personal preferences, skills, and self-efficacy.

Environmental factors that can provide insight into implementation issues involving stakeholders can also be uncovered by talking with stakeholders. For example, the pharmacy can provide information on the availability and cost of medication cessation aids, and the patient education department can provide information on the availability of cessation resources. Those responsible for continuing professional education might be able to provide information on tobacco cessation counseling training programs for staff. Incentives and disincentives for staff to persist at providing cessation services such as social support for providing cessation services, supervisor or co-worker support, patients' responses, and acknowledgment or reactions from patients' families are also important pieces of information that can be collected from stakeholders.

COMMUNITY RESOURCES

It is helpful to find out what tobacco cessation services and resources exist in the community. Some of the major reasons to do this include potential partnering opportunities, finding supplemental help for patients, and clarifying the context for the inpatient program within the larger community. The Center for Tobacco Cessation (CTC) toolkit website might be helpful in providing tips and information about community tobacco cessation programs (CTC, 2005a).

Potential Partnering

It might be possible to pool efforts with others in the community. There are a number of ways partnering that could be beneficial. For example:

> ➤ If a tobacco cessation help line is provided in the community (local, regional, or state/provincial), counseling could be initiated in-hospital at the bedside through the inpatient tobacco cessation program and the help line could provide the follow-up telephone counseling.

Information on integrating quit line services with healthcare systems is available (Pacific Center On Health and Tobacco, 2003).

➢ Non-government agencies, such as cancer or lung societies, might be willing to provide printed materials for the program either free of charge or at a reduced rate. This could create a mutually beneficial relationship—the hospital receives easy access to established patient materials and the agencies receive distribution of their materials to a targeted audience of high risk tobacco users.

➢ Tobacco control coalitions or boards might be able to provide support for set-up and/or training.

➢ It might be possible to work with staff at other hospitals who run inpatient tobacco cessation programs in terms of joint training and information sharing, support, and possibly even coverage for vacation and sick leave.

➢ Local businesses might be willing to hire the services of the hospital cessation counselors to deliver cessation services to their employees. This might become either a stream of revenue for the hospital or serve as a cost recovery system to pay for the administrative structure of the program that is not reimbursable through insurance coverage.

Supplemental Help for Patients

Information about community resources can be collected and compiled to provide to patients. Resources can include support groups, private and group counseling services, print materials, free nicotine replacement therapy (sometimes provided or subsidized through public health units), web sites, and 1-800 help-lines. Patients will feel more secure knowing who or where they can turn to for help if needed after hospital discharge, and they will have an inventory of options, something they are unlikely to compile themselves.

Program Context Within the Community

Information about other tobacco cessation programs in the community can help developers of an inpatient tobacco cessation program gain a better conceptual understanding of what the service will look like and why, what need the inpatient program will be fulfilling, and what the demographic will look like compared to other programs that are offered. It will be easier to identify the unique advantages of the inpatient approach and explain them clearly when necessary if the program has a comparison context. If the inpatient program will be run on a cost-recovery basis, it will be easier to define, in business terms, the competitive position, market share distribution, barriers to entry, future opportunities and competition, the program's message, strategic partnerships, and viable marketing vehicles.

Competition. It is helpful to determine who the "competition" is in terms of tobacco cessation programs, what they are offering, and the range of rates for various types of services. It is especially important to know fair market value for tobacco services if there will be a charge for the inpatient tobacco cessation program, or if patients will have to pay or co-pay for the inpatient services.

Internal Program Conflicts. It will be important to determine possible tobacco cessation program conflicts within the institution. For example, if an outpatient tobacco cessation program is currently offered, both administration and the outpatient providers will likely want to know how the inpatient program will affect the outpatient program, especially if the outpatient program is a revenue-generating program. Likewise, the program administrator for the inpatient program will want to know how the inpatient program will be affected by the outpatient program.

For example, there was a fee-for-service outpatient cessation program at one of the hospitals we used in a randomized trial of Staying Free. Administration was concerned that our no-cost inpatient tobacco cessation program (funded through a research grant) would take potential enrollees away from the fee-for-service outpatient program. Likewise, we were concerned that patients randomized to receive the control treatment might enroll in the outpatient program and confound the results of the study. By talking with the program providers we discovered that the outpatient program was predominantly marketed to local businesses. Very few, if any, hospital patients had ever enrolled in the outpatient program. During the study, we found out why—the majority of the hospital patients (over 98%) were clear that they would not either seek out nor pay for a tobacco cessation program.

Possible Program Expansion. By finding out what programs exist in the community, possible ways to expand the inpatient program over time into the community might become apparent. For example, an inpatient program could have a five-year plan to expand into the community on a cost-recovery basis. Or the tobacco cessation counselors could expand the profile of the program by offering pro bono tobacco cessation talks at worksites as a service to employees. This would not only serve to promote the goodwill of the hospital, and possibly meet with the charity mandate of some hospitals to retain their non-profit status, but would also serve to heighten awareness of the inpatient program in the community so more patients would hopefully end up taking advantage of it if they were hospitalized.

Data Comparisons. It is also helpful to gain as much information as possible about community programs in terms of the target audience, reach, and efficacy, to serve as external local standards against which to measure the results of the inpatient tobacco cessation program. Since the cessation rates for inpatient tobacco cessation programs tend to be substantially higher than community-based programs for the general population, the comparatively high cessation rates for the inpatient program can be used to promote the success of the program to hospital administration, staff, patients, and patients' families. The inpatient program might also enroll a different population than those who seek out community programs. For example, the inpatient enrollees will likely represent a wider demographic than those who would enroll in a community program, and represent a more hard-to-reach population, especially in a universal healthcare system where patients range from financially independent to those on social assistance.

Triage. It might be possible to use the information from other programs to triage to appropriate care those patients who are not eligible for a given inpatient tobacco cessation program. For example, if short hospital stays for obstetric patients do not allow sufficient time to counsel women who have healthy deliveries, the nurses on the obstetric unit could potentially provide a brief bedside intervention and hand out information about community cessation programs offered to pregnant and postpartum women. This could fill one of the gaps in the inpatient service, which, in turn, could be measurable and reportable in monthly, quarterly, or annual reports.

Networking. By researching the programs and materials offered in the community, it is possible to make good contacts with people who are doing similar work and who have a similar passion for what they do. Others in the community might provide an ongoing support network, especially if a single individual will be running the inpatient program—it can get lonely and it is helpful and inspiring to connect with others doing similar work. In addition, by making these initial contacts, others in the community become aware of the inpatient program thereby increasing the word-of-mouth marketing.

SEEKING COMMUNITY RESOURCES

One place to start market research on tobacco cessation programs in the community is the city's yellow pages. Programs could be listed under tobacco cessation, psychologists, physicians, and personal change. Programs could also be offered through non-government health agencies such as lung associations, heart and stroke foundations, and cancer societies. Health units, hospitals, and clinics might provide counseling services. Universities and colleges might offer counseling services through their health services. Researchers might have ongoing tobacco cessation studies, which can be discovered by calling the office of research or checking the website at local universities or research companies. When contacting another program, it is helpful to ask what other programs the program personnel are aware of, and whether they have the contact information.

Websites and 1-800 help lines are also good resources to research. Due to the vast number of websites and help lines that exist, it is probably best to begin with government and non-government health agency 1-800 services and websites—in other words, the more common and trustworthy sites.

If the effort is made to find out about other programs in the community, it is best to find out as much information as possible about each program. It helps to create a worksheet with contact names and numbers (including email and web), program cost, and target audience (e.g., cardiac rehab patients, pregnant women) as shown in Figure 7. This can later be formatted into a useable form and passed onto patients as a resource list for extra support outside the hospital program.

Figure 7. Form for Community Resources General Information

Program	Contact Person	Contact Numbers	Cost	Target Audience

Additional information could be collected on a worksheet similar to Figure 8. This worksheet includes room to fill in the type and length of the program (e.g., 6 weekly clinic visits for a group program or 3 provider-initiated calls, etc.), components offered (e.g., face-to-face, pamphlet, workbook, video, group support, etc.), follow-up (e.g., mail-outs at 3 months post-quit, weekly email reminders, etc.), evaluation (reach, quit rates, change in confidence, nicotine replacement use, etc.), and actual outcomes (e.g., 3, 6, and 12-month quit rates).

Figure 8. Form for Community Resources Detailed Information

Type & Length	Components	Follow-up	Evaluation	Outcomes

In addition to passing this information onto patients for additional support, this type of information can be used to help solidify what the proposed inpatient program will look like relative to what is offered in the community, and the comparative information can be used in proposals, media interviews (the media will likely ask how the inpatient program differs from what already exists, as will patients and other providers), and as a point of comparison in regular reporting (e.g., as a comparison for reach and efficacy).

An environmental scan of community resources might take up to a week to complete including the documentation (as long as everyone called is available). It is helpful to store information using database software rather than a word processing or spreadsheet program—it is more easily searched and updated.

An unexpected but welcome advantage of doing a full search of programs in the community might be the discovery that someone else has already made a user-ready format of available cessation services that can be obtained and handed out to patients as an extra resource. For one of our studies, a local health unit had completed a pamphlet of tobacco cessation services available in the community, including national 1-800 numbers and web sites. It was ready for distribution just as we started our study. We received it at no cost to distribute to patients. However, even if a listing of cessation services already exists, it might still be helpful to research the details of each program for all the reasons listed above.

Once the initial work of identifying resources in the community is done, it is easy to up-date the service information once a year. Continued or regular contact with programs in the community can help open up new potential partnering opportunities. It is also helpful to keep apprised of other programs because there might be many questions from patients, clinicians, and the media about other cessation services and how the inpatient program is different or relatively advantageous. Signing up for the Center for Tobacco Cessation e-newsletter can also provide ongoing updates in the larger field of tobacco cessation (CTC, 2005b).

8

Financing and Budgeting

If inpatient tobacco cessation programs did not cost anything to deliver, every hospital in the U.S. and Canada would be providing them. In reality, even the most bare-bone programs incur costs. The costs fall into two categories: direct costs (e.g., administration, tobacco cessation counselor wages and benefits, patient materials, pharmacotherapy, etc.) and indirect costs (e.g., space, heating, lighting, etc.). The truth is that tobacco cessation programs, when all the items are considered, are expensive. Fortunately, many studies also find them to be cost effective (e.g., Goldman et al., 1996).

We begin this chapter with examples of how some hospitals have paid for their tobacco cessation programs, and then discuss options for paying for an inpatient tobacco cessation program. We finish this chapter by describing how to develop a budget based on the direct and indirect costs, and provide suggestions about what to consider for the most common expenses. The suggestions are made in a way that expenses can be adjusted to accommodate individual hospital budgets by adding or dropping program features that can or cannot be supported.

INSTITUTIONAL SUPPORT

All of the inpatient tobacco cessation programs we have helped develop, or are aware of, are supported at least in part by institutional operating budgets. Unfortunately, dependence on the institutional operating budget means that financial support for the program might compete with funds for other services or activities within the hospital. As such, administration often has to be lobbied in order to allocate resources to support an inpatient tobacco cessation program. The physician champion is usually instrumental in this process.

To prepare for the lobbying process, it might be necessary to make the business case for implementing an inpatient tobacco cessation program—that is, the cost-benefit or return on investment (ROI). A new website, developed by America's Health Insurance Plans (AHIP) and the Center for Health Research, Kaiser Permanente Northwest, is available to help advocates for tobacco cessation programs develop the business case for tobacco cessation by estimating the incremental ROI of evidence-based cessation interventions (Fellows et al., 2004). The calculator can also be used to estimate the actual costs of delivering a program tailored to the specific population being served (http://www.business caseroi.org).

Examples of Institutional Support

There is no "one size fits all" when it comes to institutional funding models for inpatient tobacco cessation programs. However, central to most programs is a financial commitment by the hospital for the basic operations of the program. Even if a dedicated tobacco cessation counselor is not hired and counseling is left to attending physicians and nurses, there is still a coordinating and administrative function that must receive financial support (see Chapter 4).

Following are examples of how five successful and long-standing programs in California, Wisconsin, and Ontario have found institutional support for their programs. The funding models presented cover only the direct costs involved with the program. Indirect costs are not explicit in these examples so they must be assumed to be covered by the hospital operating budget. Patient medication usually falls under insurance coverage and not the hospital operating budget but that is not always the case. For example, some hospitals in Canada that have implemented 100% smoke-free grounds policies provide counseling and nicotine replacement therapy (NRT) at no charge to patients and staff to complement and support the ban (e.g., Calgary Health Region, 2003; 2004).

Case A. A large community hospital in California offers the tobacco cessation program, Staying Free, at no cost to patients. It started with a small grant ($2,000) for a research project. The total annual cost is now $40,000/year and has since been absorbed into the cardiac rehabilitation budget, which has a budget of approximately $2 million/year. The budget for the tobacco cessation program covers approximately a 0.4 FTE (full-time equivalent) of a nurse's time to identify smokers, provide bedside counseling and follow-up, administrate the program, and maintain data on service delivery and outcomes. The hospital administration considers both the bedside counseling and the follow-up phone calls as part of its community service. Providing community-wide services is within the hospital's mission and one part of keeping its non-profit status. The money for the community-wide service comes from in-patient bed charges, cardiac rehabilitation and other charges, private donations, and other sources.

Case B. A large county hospital in California that services the uninsured offers the inpatient tobacco cessation program, Staying Free, at no cost to patients. As with Case A, this hospital also began the tobacco cessation program with a small research grant. It is now funded by the county Public Health Department's Tobacco Prevention Education Program, which receives yearly funds from the Tobacco Settlement Agreement (www.ncsl.org/statefed/tmsasumm.htm). The funding amount to the Staying Free program fluctuates from year to year depending on how much money the county is willing to give for the tobacco prevention and education program. For example, the inpatient tobacco cessation program received $71,000 in fiscal year (FY) 01-02, $72,000 in FY02-03, $80,000 in FY03-04, and $50,000 in FY04-05.

Case C. A large hospital in California offered the inpatient tobacco cessation program, Staying Free, at no cost to patients. The costs of the program were covered by the hospital's operating budget. The program had an annual budget of $80,000 that covered a 1.0 FTE (salary and benefits) of a nurse's time to identify smokers, provide bedside counseling and follow-up, collect data on service delivery and outcomes, and administrate the program. When nicotine replacement samples were available, they were distributed free of charge to the patients. Costs for start-up training and data analyses were covered by research grants obtained by researchers at the affiliated academic institution. The program expanded to include tobacco cessation services for hospital staff and staff of the affiliated academic institution, with costs covered through the employee health improvement plan. This program was initially championed by the chief executive officer of the hospital. However, when he left and the hospital underwent budget cuts, funding to the program was suspended The program has since been re-instituted, but this example highlights the challenges of program sustainability.

Case D. A large hospital in Ontario, Canada, specializing in treating heart disease, offers a tobacco cessation program at no cost to patients. Salary costs for a full-time nurse coordinator (1 FTE) and .5 FTE administrative support position are drawn from the global hospital budget received from the Ministry of Health and Long Term Care (MOHLTC). In addition, a family physician works in the outpatient clinic and bills for tobacco cessation counseling through the Ontario provincial health insurance plan. Research funds (peer-reviewed and industrial) are used to conduct specific projects, and staff are added or subtracted as required for these activities. of note, the decision to fund the cessation program was an internal resource-allocation decision made at the senior executive level with no special justification required for the MOHLTC. Hospitals in Canada do not yet have tobacco cessation services as a performance measure but accreditation committees have been impressed with the existence of the tobacco cessation program at this hospital during accreditation reviews.

Case E. A large hospital in Wisconsin offers tobacco cessation services at no cost to patients. The program is a combination of all clinicians responsible for counseling their own patients augmented by counseling by a tobacco cessation counselor. Financing was cobbled together and evolved over time. Determining who would pay for NRT, tobacco consults, and follow-up were initially issues that had to involve Human Resources because they were considered policy issues. The hospital worked with insurance companies to cover NRT. Over-the-counter NRT remains a challenge with some group plans. Reimbursement for counseling depends on the clinician. Respiratory therapists provide intensive counseling to patients and charge for a respiratory assessment because tobacco cessation remains a first line treatment recommendation for respiratory disorders. The cardiac rehabilitation department absorbs the costs as an in-kind service when the exercise physiologist provides tobacco consults to general hospital patients. Nursing staff provide tobacco consults as part of preventive care—considered part of patient education, there is no billing required for tobacco consults. Costs for program coordination were initially not covered—a health educator was allowed to coordinate the program as long as she continued to do everything she was already doing in her "real" job (i.e., she could basically do it on her own time). The physician champion for the program convinced the administrative board to cover program coordination (0.5 FTE) because the role fit into the health educator position. It has since evolved into a full-time position covered by health education. Initial training costs were covered by the Wisconsin Tobacco Control Board, which has since disbanded because funding dried up. The hospital was encouraged to use the state 1-800 quit line service as a resource for patient follow-up.

OTHER TYPES OF FUNDING SUPPORT

Grants and Gifts

Many hospitals find funding from private foundations, community organizations, and individuals with an interest in tobacco cessation. Such funds can be very useful to help defray start-up costs and can be very useful for sustaining a program. Targeted programs, such as reaching pregnant women or minorities who smoke might be attractive to some donors. In the U.S., the Tobacco Settlement provides funds for many programs through the Legacy Foundation (www.americanlegacy.org). In California, the anti-tobacco initiative (Prop 99) has also created revenues.

Local chapters of the American Heart Association, the American Cancer Society, and the American Lung Society, and comparable societies in Canada might be able to offer help. The program director/coordinator of inpatient tobacco cessation programs should regularly look for such sources of revenue. Many such grants and gifts are often one-time only and need to be considered in terms of how the services provided by the financial help can be continued.

Not to be overlooked are donations of medications from pharmaceutical companies, and more recently in both Canada and the U.S., NRT provided at no-cost to users by local public health units. Donations for patient materials might also be found through various government and non-government health agencies.

Research Funding

Research funding obtained by the hospital or affiliated academic institutions through national, state/provincial, or regional governments and agencies might be important sources of funding, as noted in the case examples above. Research funding can be especially important for start-up, program evaluation, determining and overseeing data collection, database design and management, data cleaning, analyses, and writing and publishing reports. Research funding can also be used to expand the program or used to test the efficacy and effectiveness with special needs groups, such as psychiatric patients, or with new target audiences, such as patients admitted to the emergency department or day surgery, patients' families, and parents of pediatric patients.

Fee-for-Service and Co-Payments

offering tobacco cessation programs on a fee-for-service, co-payment, or cost-recovery basis might be an option for some hospitals in an attempt to recover some of the operating costs. For example, one managed healthcare service charges participants $20 as a co-payment for tobacco cessation services (Krejci, 2000). The co-pay does not offset the delivery costs but is believed to enhance compliance by requiring a small investment by participants.

INSURANCE COVERAGE

One way to help fund an inpatient tobacco cessation program is to work with insurance plans to obtain coverage for tobacco counseling and pharmacotherapy. It is especially advisable to work with insurance plans to cover pharmaco-therapy because it is often the "carrot" that draws tobacco users to a cessation program (Krejci, 2000). As mentioned in Chapter 2, the Addressing Tobacco in Health Care National Technical Assistance office (NTAO) might be able to assist efforts to gain coverage of tobacco services (http://www.aahp.org/athc /ntaosum.htm). It is mandated to advance the integration of tobacco cessation into healthcare by increasing the number and quality of tobacco control initiatives within health insurance plans (Rosenthal, 2000). The NTAO is managed by America's Health Insurance Plans (AHIP), a national trade association representing nearly 1,300 member companies providing health benefits to more than 200 million Americans. And as mentioned previously in this chapter, AHIP has helped develop a calculator that can be used to provide ROI evidence to insurance companies for coverage of tobacco cessation services. The Center for Tobacco Control (2005a) also provides information about insurance benefits on their resource toolkit web page.

It is helpful to delineate the various types of coverage within a given hospital population because coverage does vary across insurance plans. For example, some, but not all, insurance plans require proof of behavioral counseling as a prerequisite for pharmacotherapy coverage. Table 8 provides an example of how pharmacotherapy in one large county hospital in California was reimbursed (see Chapter 2 for an overview of the new coverage by the U.S. Centers for Medicare and Medicaid, and billing options for physicians in the U.S. and Canada).

Table 8. Example the One Hospital's Experience with Pharmacotherapy Reimbursement

---

Classes for NRT/Zyban™ Coverage

1. For patients who have regular MediCal, they will receive Nicotro Patch™ 15 mg 16 hours for 6 weeks and Zyban™ 150 mg for a total of 8 weeks coverage if they can provide a certificate of completing a tobacco cessation class.

2. For those who have Blue Cross, they will be able to receive any patches for 12 weeks and Zyban™ for 3 months. Zyban™ restricted to failure of NRT for 6 weeks. If failed after 3 months, start over again. Patients need to provide certificate of completing a tobacco cessation program.

3. For Santa Clara Family Health Plan, they will be able to receive Nicoderm™ CQ for 12 weeks and Zyban™ 150 mg for 7 weeks in a year. Patients do not need certificate.

4. Those patients who have no known medical insurance nor ability to pay may be eligible to receive free Zyban™ for 8 weeks covered through the Medical Assistance Program. This is not a guarantee service because if patients have a history of seizure, liver or kidney diseases, currently receive psychotic medications, or are currently homeless or alcoholic, they cannot receive this medication.

DEVELOPING THE BASELINE BUDGET

Direct Costs

Direct costs are those that are directly associated with program delivery, and will depend on the type of program and delivery options chosen. Direct costs will comprise the majority of costs for the inpatient program. Examples of direct costs include the tobacco counselors' wages and benefits, patient print materials (if not donated), and long-distance telephone charges for post-discharge counseling. In some cases, patient-related costs such as pharmacotherapy also fall under direct costs. For example, in Canada when hospitals have made the decision to go 100% smoke-free grounds, some have added NRT to the hospital formulary and distribute it free of charge to patients and staff during a given transition period of going smoke-free (e.g., Calgary Health Region, 2003; 2004).

Indirect Costs

Indirect costs are those that support the existence of the program, such as office space, utilities, and "back office" help including technical support for hardware and software, purchasing, and accounts payable. Indirect costs are determined by institutional accounting practices, and are usually absorbed by the hospital operating budget. A section at the end of this chapter includes suggestions about what might be included for indirect costs. Since indirect costs are institution-specific, it is difficult to provide a general budget estimate that will apply to all programs. As such, the budget items below are based on direct costs.

Start-Up, Fixed, and Variable Expenses

Within the direct and indirect costs, there will be three types of expenses— initial one-time start-up expenses, fixed expenses, and variable expenses.

Start-Up Expenses. Initial one-time set-up expenses are costs that are incurred at the beginning of the program and are one-time charges that will not likely surface again, such as installation charges for a telephone line or high-speed internet, and equipment purchases. When possible, it is helpful to separate the initial start-up costs from the ongoing costs of running the program in an attempt to distinguish what the program will cost in the first year and what it will cost to maintain after it is set up.

Fixed Expenses. Fixed expenses are recurring expenses that are (relatively) constant over time. They are predictable, do not change from month to month, and come due whether or not any patients are enrolled in the program. For example, the monthly charge for a telephone line or high-speed internet service would be the same each month regardless of how many patients are enrolled in the program, as would wages and benefits for a salaried cessation counselor.

Variable Expenses. Variable expenses are costs that fluctuate with program demand, increasing when enrollment increases and decreasing when enrollment decreases. Whereas the monthly charges for telephone service are fixed and will remain the same regardless of how many patients are enrolled in the program, monthly long-distance charges for post-discharge counseling and follow-up will depend on how many patients who live outside the calling area are enrolled in the program at any given time. Similarly, the wages and benefits for a salaried cessation counselor will remain fixed month to month regardless of how many patients enroll in the program whereas the quantity of patient materials that need to be purchased will increase as enrollment increases. Having the variable expenses delineated from the fixed expenses is helpful for planning and for understanding why program costs might differ over time.

Getting Started with the Baseline Budget

The easiest starting point for estimating the preliminary budget is to begin with the direct program costs divided into three basic categories—wages and benefits, permanent equipment, and expendable supplies. These categories are often used by granting agencies in their applications, by governments for taxation categories, and by companies in their annual reports.

WAGES AND BENEFITS

Every program will have costs for wages and benefits. This holds whether a dedicated tobacco cessation counselor position is created to deliver the inpatient tobacco cessation program or whether cessation counseling becomes the responsibility of each individual clinician. If a dedicated position is created, a salary must usually be paid for the position, unless volunteers are assigned. If all clinicians are responsible for counseling their own patients or volunteers are assigned to a dedicated cessation position, a program director/coordinator will be required, a position that is usually salaried. If a dedicated tobacco cessation counselor position is created, this will be the greatest program expense. If a dedicated tobacco counselor position is not created or volunteers are "recruited" to provide counseling, a program director/coordinator will be the greatest expense.

Salaried Tobacco Cessation Counselor

The basic Staying Free model is to create a position for a tobacco cessation counselor. The position has traditionally been filled by a nurse who takes on the roles of both coordinator and cessation counselor. Compensation for the combined coordinator-counselor position has traditionally been a full time effort (1 FTE) nursing salary with benefits, calculated according to the hospital's wage scale for education and experience. However, the costs of hiring a full-time person might not be justified for all hospitals or programs—a caseload analysis should be performed using estimated enrollment (Chapter 6) and time and task analysis. In our Canadian study, one 0.5 FTE nurse per hospital was able to provide a brief in-hospital intervention with extensive data collection in hospitals with annual admissions ranging from 9,000 to 23,000 patients (approximately 20% tobacco use prevalence), and another 0.5 FTE nurse was hired to provide intensive bedside counseling, post-discharge telephone counseling, and extensive data collection.

An example budget entry for a full-time counselor is provided in Table 9. Also included in Table 9 are line items for coverage of counselor duties during scheduled vacation (2 weeks) and for the occasional missed day due to short-term illness (1 week). If financial consideration is not made for covering vacation and sick days, the program will come to a temporary halt while the tobacco cessation counselor is away. If the program comes to a halt, patients who are in the midst of receiving post-discharge counseling will miss their counseling and patients admitted to the hospital during this time will likely miss out on receiving cessation services. If data are being collected, there will be gaps in the data for these missed days. If coverage will be provided, it will mean that those who cover will either need training and/or require detailed job aids (see Chapters 12 and 17 regarding job aids).

Table 9. Example Budget for Full-Time Cessation Counselor-Coordinator

Position	Description	Begin	Hour	Weeks	Benefits	Amount
Cessation counselor	RN, 40 hr work wk	Jan 02/06	$31	52		$64,272
	18% benefits	Jan 02/06			18%	$11,569
Vacation coverage	RN for vacation	Jan 02/06	$31	2		$2,400
	18% benefits	Jan 02/06			18%	$432
Sick day coverage	RN for sick days	Jan 02/06	$31	1		$1,236
	18% benefits	Jan 02/06			18%	$222
Subtotal Yr 1						**$80,131**

Wages and benefits for a dedicated counselor/coordinator position would be considered a fixed expense because the expense remains constant regardless of how many patients are enrolled in the program. The example in Table 9 assumes that the counselor will be working from January 2, 2006 and the year-end is December 31, 2006, so the counselor is hired for 52 weeks in the first year. For year two, depending on hospital policies, a merit and/or cost of living increase to the hourly wage might be appropriate. The salary and benefits used in Table 9 are only examples and will vary by institution and by the qualifications of the person hired for the position. The easiest way to estimate what the salary and benefits will be is to decide what the education and background required for the position will be, and then contact the Human Resources department of the hospital to obtain the salary ranges and benefit options for the defined position, along with the annual cost-of-living and/or merit increases that are allowed for that position.

Release Time. Another salary and benefit consideration, not included in this example, would be covering release time for the cessation counselor. Covering release time might be desirable for ensuring quality programming and service through ongoing training such as continuing education or additional tobacco dependence training, or for program promotion, such as making presentations in the community and at professional conferences, or even to provide training to clinicians in other institutions (which could be done on a cost recovery basis).

Clerical Support. Clerical support for word processing, correspondence, photocopying, filing, and literature searches might also be a line item worth considering in a salaried tobacco cessation counselor model. In the case examples provided at the beginning of this chapter, Case D covered the salary and benefits of one 0.5 FTE administrative person to support the program. However, even one half-day per week or a full-day per month might suffice to keep up on paperwork and any extra administrative tasks, depending on the size of the hospital and the counselor's caseload.

Clinicians. In the Staying Free model, although a full-time tobacco cessation counselor is hired to provide intensive counseling and follow-up, all attending physicians and nurses are nonetheless responsible for providing cessation advise tailored to patients' medical conditions (i.e., the first and second of the "5 As" of the clinical practice guideline—*ask* and *advise*; Fiore et al., 2000). Because *ask* and *advise* take approximately one minute per patient, the attending physicians' and nurses' time are not charged to the program, patients, or insurance companies, but that might vary by institution.

Contract Wages

Some contract work might be involved in the start-up and ongoing operations of the program. Contract work can include any work that is out-sourced, either internally to another department or externally to a consultant or temporary contract worker. Contract work might include the design of a database for data collection, counselor training, project management consultations for start-up, data entry and/or cleaning (if not covered by administrative support), program evaluation, and technical assistance for computer services. It is difficult to put a dollar amount on these potential budget items because they will vary substantially depending on the needs of any given hospital and the state or province in which the work is being done. If using external contractors, accurate budget estimates will hinge on ensuring that the work to be done is clearly specified along with the timelines, deliverables, and taxes.

Many contract expenses will be start-up only (e.g., database design and training), some will be fixed (e.g., annual program evaluation), and some will be variable (e.g., data entry/cleaning and technical assistance for computer troubles). Computer servicing and data cleaning are variable expenses because that they are likely to fluctuate, and will not necessarily be constant in any given month or year. There could be years in which there is a minimal amount of cost with either contract position, but then something might happen and the amount of time required escalates (e.g., if a new computer software program with a number of bugs is installed it would affect both computer servicing and data cleaning). The amount of data cleaning will be dependent not only on the smooth running of the computer but also on the number of patients enrolled in the program (e.g., there might be peak times when more effort is required, and quiet times when relatively little effort is required). Weekly data cleaning ensures that data are being collected on all patients and accurately entered, can serve to dollar-cost average the services, and is far more cost-efficient than trying to retrospectively correct errors.

Cessation Delivery By All Attending Clinicians

When the responsibility for providing cessation services rests with all attending clinicians, estimating the budget for salaries is more complex than that of the dedicated cessation counselor approach. It will depend upon the institution, third party payers, patients' insurance coverage, and who the clinicians are. For example, if nurses provide the bedside consult, their time might not have to be charged to the tobacco cessation program—it might be covered under nursing education for patients as noted in the example of Case E at the beginning of this chapter. If physicians provide the bedside consult, they might be able to charge for it under the insurance plan for a tobacco consult—it will depend on the insurer and patients' coverage. Some hospital departments as noted in Cases A and E will absorb the costs of services provided to other departments as in-kind expenses. For these reasons, it is not possible for us to provide a generic estimate of the potential clinician costs of a model in which all attending clinicians are responsible for providing tobacco cessation services.

Program Director/Coordinator. A program director/coordinator is needed when the approach taken is to have all clinicians intervene with their own patients rather than having a dedicated tobacco cessation counselor. The process for making estimates for the program director/coordinator are identical to that of the dedicated tobacco counselor approach. That is, wages, benefits, and vacation pay would be obtained from Human Resources to match the education and experience of the coordinator. Funds might be considered for vacation and sick leave coverage, and the same basic contract work mentioned above for the dedicated tobacco cessation counselor approach would be applicable with one possible exception—program evaluation.

When the model used is to have all clinicians intervene and not have a dedicated counselor position, the costs for program evaluation will likely be substantially higher. Evaluation will tend to be more difficult and will also take substantially more time and effort. The reason is that data collection is not as systematic— there will be no one person to collect data so data collection will likely be relegated to retrospective chart review to identify patients who used tobacco and were counseled, and/or to gather basic demographic information. This translates into hiring someone to review the thousands of medical charts per year in any given hospital. Patient files then have to be set up in a database and information transferred from medical charts. Ensuring standardized charting itself poses a challenge and requires ongoing in-service training, which in turn, increases costs especially in terms of educators' and clinicians' time. If data collection is desirable, it is worth considering creating a tobacco cessation counselor position and include data collection as part of the job description.

Cessation Delivery by Volunteers

If tobacco cessation counseling will be delivered by volunteers, as it was in one of our studies (Taylor et al., 2005), the budget model will be similar to the approach in which all clinicians provide tobacco services to their patients. That is, the program will require a program director/coordinator, and all the other contract work (e.g., database design, computer technical assistance, program evaluation, etc.) mentioned above would be applicable.

EXPENDABLE SUPPLIES

The purchasing department will likely have purchasing policies and an approved supplier list from which all supplies must be purchased. Approved suppliers often have annual contracts negotiated with the institution so it is important to ensure that estimates made for a budget are still in effect at the time of purchase. It is also important to include any applicable taxes in the budget estimates, and to verify estimates with the purchasing and finance departments because some taxes are exempt for some institutions. For example, research projects run through academic institutions in Canada are exempt from provincial sales tax on all research purchases, but the federal goods and services tax (7% GST) is applicable to all purchases.

Patient Materials

The main expenditures for patient materials will be the purchase of take-home materials (e.g., workbooks, pamphlets, videos/DVDs, audiotapes, and/or cessation kits), paper and photocopying for information letters and informed consent in research studies, business cards for tobacco cessation counselors, and hard copy data collection forms. Even if patient data are entered directly into a computer at the bedside, hard copies of the data collection forms should be available to provide a backup if the computers go down.

Table 10 provides an example of the costs of patient materials and photocopying for data collection forms (costs are for example only, and will need to be estimated by each hospital). We have used 200 patients for the first year as the starting quantity for patient materials, based on our one-year enrollments across studies (see Chapter 6 for estimating enrollment). Staying Free includes a video, workbook, and relaxation audiotape, as well as two single sheet tri-fold pamphlets, one on how to quit smoking and one on cessation resources in the community. When patient information and informed consent must be collected, photocopying costs will have to be added as budget line items.

Table 10. Example of Patient Materials Budget Line Items

Patient Materials	Description	Cost/ Unit	Units	Total
Videotape	Preventing Relapse video	$5.00	200	$1,000
Audiotape	Preventing Relapse audiotape	$2.00	200	$400
Workbook	Preventing Relapse workbook	$3.00	200	$600
Pamphlet	How to Quit single page tri-fold	$0.10	200	$20
Pamphlet	Community resources 1 pg tri-fold	$0.10	200	$20
Business cards	Box of 250 cards	$65.00	1	$65
Photocopying	Inhospital forms (10 pg @ $0.10/pg)	$1.00	200	$200
	Telephone forms (10 pg @ $0.10/pg)	$1.00	200	$200
	Follow-up forms (6 pg @ $0.10/pg)	$0.60	200	$120
Subtotal Patient Materials				**$2,625**

Office Supplies

A number of basic items need to be purchased to set up an office at each hospital, and in the case of a multi-site study or hospital consortium, supplies will be needed for a coordinating center. Basic supplies include letterhead stationery, copier paper, envelops, binders, workbooks, clipboards, calendars, day-timers, and general office supplies (post-it notes, paper clips, staples, pens, pencils, tape, stapler, folders, labels, and files). Keeping the inventory of supplies stocked will be a variable expense.

Telecommunications

Initial one-time telecommunication costs might include the set-up and installation of a telephone line, a high-speed internet connection for email and internet access, and/or the initial registration/activation for a cell phone or pager. These one-time expenses will depend on the program options and the situation. For example, if a health educator takes over the tobacco cessation counselor position and continues to use his/her own office in the health education department, there might not be any initial set-up expenses.

Fixed telecommunication expenses can include monthly rental of telephone lines, internet access, paging service, and/or cell phone service. Variable expenses might include long-distance, roaming charges for cell phones, and fax charges. To estimate long-distance charges, the geographic catchment of the hospital should be assessed and an estimate can be made as to what the monthly long-distance charges will be using caseload estimates (see Chapter 6 for estimating enrollment). It might be worthwhile checking into 1-800 line options. If a flat fee is charged for a 1-800 number and all long-distance calls can be made via the 1-800 service, long-distance costs will move to the fixed expense category. Some 1-800 lines operate like a regular long-distance service and each call is charged, meaning it becomes a variable expense that depends on usage.

Computer Supplies

Computer supplies include software for the computers, laptop or handheld computer batteries and battery chargers, ink cartridges, ethernet cards, and CDs and/or memory sticks for back-up. "Must-have" software includes an operating system, virus protection, word processing, presentation program (e.g., Microsoft Powerpoint ™), and a spreadsheet program (e.g., Microsoft Excel ™). "Nice to have" software includes a database program (e.g., FileMakerPro™ or Microsoft Access™), statistics package (e.g., SPSS™ or SAS™), email package (e.g., Eudora™), and a bibliography package (e.g., EndNote™). Many of these programs might be available through institutional licenses for an annual fee rather than having to purchase them.

Cotinine Collection and Analyses

If saliva samples will be taken for biochemical confirmation of tobacco status, there will be a number of expenses incurred. Supplies will include vials, cotton swabs, hard candies including special candies for diabetics (to help patients increase saliva), hand protection, soap, paper towels, freezer gel packs, insulated bags for short-term storage until samples can be safely stored in a freezer, and freezer bags for storage and/or transporting samples to the laboratory. There might also be freezer storage 'rent' for saliva samples, transportation of these samples to a laboratory for analyses (e.g., courier or staff mileage and parking), mileage and parking for personnel who make home-visits for saliva collection, and parking for patients who return to the hospital or clinic to provide saliva samples. The cost for cotinine analyses will vary from lab to lab.

Miscellaneous

Cessation counselors will require nametags and possibly white lab coats. We have used white lab coats because they serve as an easy visual cue, identifying cessation counselors as part of the clinical staff to both patients and staff. If a multi-site program is being launched, parking might be considered for monthly meetings at a central site (possibly even mileage) as well as a parking allowance for the project manager to visit multiple sites. In-service training might incur costs such as handouts (paper and photocopying), overheads, and refreshments. Promotion might factor into expenses including posters, announcement postcards or letters (and postage), brochures, advertising (including the initial advertising for the counselor and/or coordinator positions), give-aways (e.g., motivation buttons), and even the occasional treat (e.g., basket of fruit) for the nursing units to provide ongoing reminders of appreciation for support and cooperation with the program.

PERMANENT EQUIPMENT

Before ordering any permanent equipment, it is important to check with the purchasing department to find out the protocol for obtaining quotes and ordering equipment. In fact, the purchasing department is usually responsible for obtaining quotes for equipment and will likely be under contract with a limited number of suppliers from whom equipment can be purchased. As with expendable supplies, it is important to include any applicable taxes in the budget estimates and to check with the purchasing and finance departments regarding possible tax exemptions.

Office Furniture

Regardless of the office space provided, at the very minimum, the office for the cessation counselor and/or coordinator will require basic office furniture—a desk, chair, and filing cabinet. This will most often be provided by the hospital and will not have to be purchased.

Computer Equipment

A computer will be required for viewing electronic medical records for patient screening, as well as required for preparation of reports and preparation of training materials. It might also be required for data input, data analyses, email, and internet-access, depending on the scope of the program. All staff clinicians will likely have pre-established access to a computer either through their own offices or through computers in the nursing stations on each unit so computers might not have to be purchased. For dedicated counselor approach, it is almost essential that the tobacco counselor/coordinator has his/her own computer so a computer might have to be purchased. Although it is possible to borrow the use of computers on the different hospital units, we have found that computers on the units are often tied up for long periods of time and the cessation counselor must yield to the regular attending staff.

Optional, but useful if funds are available, is either a laptop or handheld computer to enable entry of patient data at the bedside. This will substantially reduce the requirement for clerical personnel and data entry. It is helpful to compare the costs of purchasing these items and their docking stations against the ongoing costs to input data (either by the tobacco cessation counselor or clerical staff). If a multi-site program is being implemented, it might be desirable to have a central 'master' computer that will house a main database that receives data from the satellite sites; in this case, each site will have either a desktop or a handheld/laptop computer for screening and data input. Multi-site programs might also opt for web-based data entry, which might incur a monthly rental fee for space on the server (line item for expendable supplies) and consulting charges for reports, report templates, web-master services, and/or technical services for data storage (line item for wages and benefits).

Printer

For a dedicated counselor approach, access to a printer is helpful in order to receive a hard copy of the daily hospital census. Although the daily census can be searched electronically without a hard copy, a hard copy is easier to work from and can serve as a good system to keep track of patients who need to be seen for a consult. A printer might be necessary for sending letters to physicians to keep them apprised of their patients' tobacco consults in-hospital. A printer is also helpful for producing reports (e.g., weekly, monthly, quarterly, and annual reports), printing pamphlets, and for preparing other documents such as manuscripts for publication.

Television, VCR/DVD, and Audiovisual Cart

If a video/DVD will be shown at the bedside as part of counseling, which is what we do with Staying Free, it might be necessary to purchase a television, VCR/DVD player, and audiovisual (AV) cart. Some hospitals will have access to in-room television/VCRs/DVDs in every patient room whereas others will have limited or no access. It is important to check hospital-wide access before purchasing equipment. If the program will be provided in more than one building, it might be desirable to set up some form of a share system for AV equipment with other departments, especially those housed in other buildings—it can be an onerous task to push a television on an AV cart from unit to unit or building to building (especially in the wintry northern climes).

Telephone Equipment

Telephones might have to be purchased or rented. It is helpful to get a model that has the ability to accept a jack for a headset. If post-discharge telephone counseling or tobacco status data are collected, it is important to provide a headset to avoid arm, shoulder, neck, and back strain. A headset also facilitates direct entry of data during the call into a computer because both hands are free. Cell phones and pagers might also have to be purchased depending on the program.

INDIRECT COSTS

In traditional accounting, indirect costs are called overhead costs, referring only to costs related to the "roof over one's head" such as rent, utilities, and insurance. Many people use the term overhead costs as an umbrella term for all expenses including wages, supplies, and equipment. We will use it in the more traditional sense, referring to costs that are indirectly related to providing the program. These costs include rent, utilities, cleaning, maintenance, property taxes, insurance, depreciation, and some types of administration such as accounting, human resources, internal review board, and public relations.

Determining what costs will be charged to an inpatient tobacco cessation program will have to be verified by management. Some hospitals will charge a square footage fee for the office, some will not charge floor space but will charge a utility fee, and others might charge a percentage of estimated program revenues. If the inpatient program will be housed in a building independent from the main hospital and is separately metered, the rent on the building would normally be considered fixed overhead because the rate would not change over the year and the utilities would be considered variable overhead costs because the monthly costs will vary month to month (e.g., heating costs in the winter, air conditioning in the summer).

Some hospitals might require transfer payments to each department that becomes involved with implementation of the program. For example, the hospital finance department might charge a fee to the inpatient tobacco cessation program for managing the financial account as part of the hospital's operating budget, so a budget line for financial management would have to be added to the inpatient tobacco cessation budget. Or if cessation consults are charged to insurance companies, part of an accounts receivable staff's salary and benefits might be charged to the inpatient account for collecting from insurance companies. The information technology department might require a transfer payment for services such as adding the tobacco status question to the admitting records. The only way to verify what costs will be involved is to ask the finance department what the usual cost structures are, and then verify the estimated budget with management in the departmental home of the inpatient tobacco cessation program.

Part II Program Development

9

Tobacco Cessation Providers

Who will provide inpatient tobacco cessation services is a decision that must be made. There are three basic approaches to guide decisions about who will provide the inpatient tobacco cessation program. We refer to the three approaches as the decentralized clinician approach, the centralized counselor approach, and the hybrid approach. The decentralized clinician approach is one in which all clinicians are responsible for identifying among their patients those who use tobacco, and then intervening by providing tobacco cessation services. The centralized counselor approach is the approach in which a dedicated position is created for a tobacco cessation counselor who has the responsibility for identifying all hospitalized patients who use tobacco and intervening with tobacco cessation services. The hybrid approach is a combination of the decentralized clinician and centralized counselor approaches—all clinicians are responsible for at least minimally intervening with their own patients who use tobacco and a tobacco cessation counselor is available to provide more in-depth education and counseling.

From a systems-level strategy, the minimal recommendation of the USDHHS clinical practice guideline is that of the decentralized clinician approach—all clinicians in all healthcare settings should be encouraged to provide their patients with simple counseling advice, support, and appropriate pharmacotherapy (Fiore et al., 2000). The guideline further suggests that in order to facilitate all clinicians intervening with all patients on every encounter, tobacco dependence interventions should be included in the job descriptions and performance evaluations of salaried clinicians and included as a reimbursable inpatient consultation activity for fee-for-service providers.

The clinical practice guideline also suggests that a clinician (or clinicians) should be identified in every hospital to deliver tobacco dependence inpatient consultation services (Fiore et al., 2000). This recommendation aligns with the hybrid approach, putting the emphasis on the decentralized clinician approach— all clinicians intervening with all patients and clinicians' intervention efforts supplemented by a tobacco specialist. Staying Free represents another model of the hybrid approach with an emphasis on the centralized counselor approach— the tobacco cessation counselor is central to providing tobacco cessation services to all patients, and the tobacco counselor's efforts are supplemented by all clinicians intervening with all patients on every encounter with a brief intervention consisting of at least ask and advise from the "5 As".

We begin this chapter with the relative advantages and challenges of the decentralized clinician approach to providing inpatient tobacco cessation interventions, and include a special section on physicians and nurses with respect to the decentralized clinician approach. We then provide the relative advantages and challenges of the centralized counselor approach, and include a section on providers in the centralized counselor approach. We end the chapter with a brief discussion of the hybrid approach models, and include the relative advantages and challenges of each.

DECENTRALIZED CLINICIAN APPROACH TO INPATIENT TOBACCO CESSATION

The decentralized clinician approach is one in which all clinicians are responsible for providing tobacco cessation services to all patients on every encounter. Although the guidelines suggest that all clinicians should intervene with tobacco dependence treatments, the focus has been primarily on physicians, and to a lesser extent nurses. However, clinicians can be physicians, both specialists (e.g., oncologists) and generalists (family physicians), nurses, or any other healthcare provider in the hospital (e.g., respiratory therapists, physiotherapists, dentists, pharmacists, etc.).

Advantages of the Decentralized Clinician Approach

If all clinicians are responsible for intervening with all patients on every encounter, tobacco interventions are technically available 24 hr a day, 7 days a week during hospitalization, especially if one considers the around-the-clock coverage provided by nursing shifts. Also, if all clinicians intervene with all patients on every encounter—inpatient, outpatient, and physician's office, wide coverage of tobacco interventions is possible, and the repeated consistent messaging across clinicians can help shift the paradigm from tobacco as a lifestyle issue to that of a medical concern.

The repeated contact within and between clinicians should also have a positive effect on cessation according to the meta-analyses used to develop the clinical practice guideline (Fiore et al., 2000). In addition, if all clinicians intervene even minimally, the amount of time spent by each individual clinician can remain at 3 minutes or less per encounter, yet the cumulative time due to the repeated contact at multiple encounters across medical care settings will add up and should enhance the likelihood of cessation and long-term abstinence as indicated in the meta-analyses in the guideline (Fiore et al., 2000).

The Role of Physicians in the Decentralized Clinician Approach

Physicians have high credibility with smokers, smokers cite physician advice to quit as an important motivator for attempting to quit smoking, and smokers quit more frequently when a physician provides advice and/or help (Cromwell et al., 1997; Ockene, et al., 1994; Pederson et al., 1982). Although tobacco cessation intervention is becoming more accepted in the culture of medicine, such as evidenced by residency programs providing training in tobacco interventions (e.g., Hartmann et al., 2004; Ockene et al., 1988); data suggest that only slightly more than half of all physicians intervene with their patients (Marbella et al., 2003). However, the culture is shifting in the positive direction. As the culture continues to shift, tobacco cessation advice and counseling on the part of physicians is expected to increase.

The Role of Nurses in the Decentralized Clinician Approach

Nurses are also an important clinician group to intervene with patients on tobacco use. They comprise the single largest health professional group in the hospital, they spend the most time with patients, and the support and caring attitudes of nurses are often cited as therapeutic processes in patients' recovery (Dennis & Prescott, 1985). "If only half of all nurses helped one patient per month quit smoking, more than 12 million smokers would overcome their addictions every year" (Bialous & Sarna, 2005).

By having staff nurses trained to provide tobacco interventions, they can decrease the burden on physicians to counsel, make counseling more likely to happen, and cessation can be increased compared to physician advice alone (Hollis et al., 1993; Rice, 1999; Rice & Stead, 2000). In terms of convenience, staff nurses can be available to the patient on an ongoing basis, can mention tobacco every time they come in and out of patients' rooms, and due to how nurses' shifts are scheduled, there is always someone available to follow-up on patients' questions about tobacco use and quitting regardless of the time of day or night. Nurses can also chart the encounters so physicians can be kept apprised of tobacco interventions, thereby allowing a seamless and synergistic effect between or among clinicians attending to any given patient. For example, a physician could respond to the nursing notes in a patient's chart by saying:

> *I see that* <<name of nurse>> *talked to you about the importance of quitting smoking in order to decrease your chance of having another heart attack. That's good. You really must quit. She mentioned in your chart that you are ready to quit and that you have developed a plan with her to prevent going back to cigarettes when you leave the hospital. If you would like to talk about medications that might help, or if you*

have other questions, please let me know. In the meantime, congratulations on quitting. Please continue to work with <<name of nurse>> and she will help you to remain a nonsmoker.

Just as physician groups and medical schools are beginning to support tobacco interventions, nursing associations, such as the American Nurses Association (ANA), are becoming strong advocates of tobacco interventions, and position and policy papers are being written (American Nurses Association, 1995; ANA Nursing World, 2005; Cataldo, 2001; Tobacco Free Nurses, 2004a). The Nursing Leadership Task Force on Tobacco Control met in March 2004 as part of the Tobacco Free Nurses Initiative funded by the Robert Wood Johnson Foundation—more than 481,000 nurses from 21 organizations participated (Tobacco Free Nurses, 2004b). Each organization was mandated with developing an action plan for their organization to support cessation for nurses, implement cessation services for patients, and/or increase the involvement of nurses in tobacco control policy issues. Included in the action plan were two and five year target goals for the percentage of nurses projected to conduct the "5 As" with their patients. A website for nurses has also been designed, both to help nurses quit smoking as well as provide resources for nurses to help others quit (Tobacco Free Nurses, 2004c).

Challenges with the Decentralized Clinician Approach to Inpatient Tobacco Cessation

Despite the positive movement toward, and the positive outcomes of, all clinicians intervening with all patients who use tobacco on every encounter, there are a number of challenges with the decentralized clinician approach. The main challenges are a disinclination for physicians and nurses to intervene with tobacco cessation services, the work involved in coordinating and institutionalizing the approach, and data collection.

Disinclination Among Physicians to Intervene with Tobacco Cessation. When physicians do intervene with tobacco cessation, they tend to engage only in the first two steps of the "5 As"—*ask* if patients use tobacco and *advise* them to quit, if they intervene at all (Humair & Ward, 1998; McBride et al., 1997). Few physicians comply with the full recommendations to also *assess* willingness to quit, *assist* with quitting (or enhance motivation if not willing to quit), and *arrange* follow-up contacts to prevent relapse. In our studies of Staying Free, we have found that appropriately only 50% of physicians provide cessation advice to patients during hospitalization, even when prompted with a scripted cessation message for patients placed in patients' charts (Houston Miller et al., 1997). This lack of intervention occurs even though physicians are only asked to provide advice alone—they are not being asked to counsel or follow-up, and patients are sufficiently motivated to quit based on their willingness to enroll in our intensive intervention programs. These findings are consistent with findings from primary care settings such as physicians' offices and clinics (Marbella et al., 2003; Thorndike et al., 1998).

There are a number of reasons that physicians do not intervene, many of which can be challenging to overcome. Reasons for not intervening, collected from a number of published articles (Cabana et al., 1999; Fiore et al., 2000; Kottke et al., 1994; McBride et al., 1997; Thorndike et al., 1999), include:

> ➢ lack of patient interest in quitting along with the perception that patients do not seem to listen

> ➢ lack of self-efficacy to counsel—physicians see some success with their efforts (approximately 7% of patients quit), but the numbers are small

> ➢ lack of time due to the pace of everyday practice

> ➢ lack of follow-up and feedback systems—abstinence data are usually not collected on the number or percentage of patients who quit due to the physician's efforts, so feedback on physicians' efforts, which could potentially encourage physicians to counsel, is lacking

> ➢ lack of financial reward—counseling is often not compensated

> ➢ lack of emotional reward to the physician—immediate rewards are rare because abstinence takes time

> ➢ lack of peer support—colleagues do not value it

> ➢ lack of staff support (many staff smoke)

> ➢ lack of interest on the part of the physician, preferring to provide acute care treatments for acute problems and seeing positive outcomes from acute care efforts

> ➢ lack of knowledge about how to identify smokers quickly and easily

> ➢ not knowing what tobacco treatments are efficacious

> ➢ not knowing the relative efficacies of different treatments

> ➢ not knowing how efficacious treatments can be delivered

> ➢ inadequate clinic or institutional support for routine assessment and treatment of tobacco use

> ➢ resistance to training because many physicians still view tobacco use as a lifestyle choice rather than equivalent to a chronic disease that requires attention and continuous follow-up

When physicians do provide tobacco cessation interventions, there is a tendency for them to intervene more with patients who are suffering tobacco-related diseases or for whom tobacco use exacerbates the presenting problem, such as those with cardiovascular disease, and less of a tendency to intervene with other patients, such as those admitted for gynecological reasons (Houston Miller et al., 1997; Thorndike et al., 1998).

Providing hospital meetings, such as grand rounds, seminars, and in-service trainings, and adding diagnostic and billing code check boxes to coding sheets might help encourage physicians to provide tobacco cessation counseling to their patients (Fiore et al., 2000). Other mechanisms encouraging a shift toward tobacco intervention on the part of physicians include position papers and guidelines encouraging tobacco cessation intervention within medical specialties (e.g., Ahuja et al., 2003; Canadian Thoracic Society Workshop Group, 1992).

Disinclination Among Nurses to Intervene. Just as there is a disinclination for physicians to intervene with tobacco cessation services, the majority of nurses do not provide tobacco interventions to their patients despite many feeling a responsibility to do so (Faulkner et al., 1983; Goldstein et al., 1987; Katz et al., 2004; Solberg et al., 2001). One of the biggest barriers to counseling on the part of nurses is the tobacco use status of the nurses themselves—across studies, nurses who smoke are significantly less likely than non-smokers to counsel patients to quit (Goldstein et al., 1987; Sarna et al., 2001). In addition to being a current tobacco user, one study found that nurses least likely to provide tobacco counseling tended to be young, less likely to have an advanced degree, had administrative responsibilities, or was a nurse practitioner (Sarna et al., 2001).

Other barriers to counseling summarized in a series of articles (Faulkner et al., 1983; Goldstein et al., 1987; Katz et al., 2004; Solberg et al., 2001) include:

> ➢ not knowing how to counsel

> ➢ not finding it rewarding

> ➢ feeling it takes too much time

➤ not having the training

➤ not believing all patients should be counseled

➤ not being asked by physicians to counsel

➤ fear that they will antagonize patients

Coordination Challenges of the Decentralized Clinician Approach. The work involved in coordinating and institutionalizing the decentralized clinician approach is substantial. There needs to be at least one part-time tobacco program director/coordinator who will do the developmental work from a systems-level perspective to implement and institutionalize the program. The program director coordinates or performs start-up tasks, such as those indicated for the program director in Chapter 4, and then continues to coordinate the program to ensure that it stays on track. For example, one hospital in Wisconsin required the half time effort (0.5 FTE) of a health educator to launch the inpatient tobacco cessation program and train clinicians to provide cessation services. After two years, the program was only 60% implemented (Sakis, 2004, personal communication). The position later became full-time due to the workload. Training was the biggest time-taker. Arranging trainings within every department and scheduling clinicians' time for training can be a challenge. Training itself will take 1-2 hours per session, depending on what clinicians will allow. Training often entails going back to each department multiple times to ensure all clinicians receive training. And training should never be a one-time event. It must be ongoing due to staff turnover and the need to keep the program on track and clinicians updated.

Resistance to Training. There is often resistance to training, from both management and clinicians. The resistance can include any number of the reasons listed for the disinclination of physicians and nurses to intervene with tobacco cessation, but time often seems to be the main resistance. Some medical care systems are chronically understaffed with clinicians strained to provide even the acute care they are "hired" and "paid" to do. And, anecdotally, stronger resistance might come from managers and clinicians who use tobacco. If department managers are tobacco users, there might be greater difficulty getting the department onboard with the program, getting the department to schedule training, and getting the department to comply consistently with tobacco interventions. Individual clinicians who use tobacco might simply refuse to attend trainings and/or intervene with patients unless mandated to do so.

Data Collection and Evaluation Challenges with the Decentralized Clinician Approach. Systematic data collection to evaluate clinicians' and patients' participation and program outcomes is difficult to do with the decentralized clinician approach. Data collection with this approach will likely be minimal, comprised of what is traditionally available in patients' charts (e.g., age, gender, medical condition) unless standardized measures, such as those developed by JCAHO (2005), are adopted and implemented. To collect more elaborate assessment data, such as smoking histories and psychosocial data, would involve a relatively substantial amount of work and time for clinicians, with the amount of work depending on how much and what type of data are collected (most data collection will take at least 10 to 20 minutes/patient not including counseling time). Although clinicians can be expected to chart tobacco interventions in patients' charts according to hospital protocol, they cannot be expected to collect extensive data—it is too time consuming. As a result, basic demographic and smoking history variables, beyond those traditionally collected as part of a patients' history, will likely not be recorded. Even if basic demographic data are available in the charts, a mechanism must be devised to systematically extract the data for analyses. This usually involves manual chart review, a labor-intensive process.

Missing and/or unreliable data might also pose problems with the decentralized clinician approach due to the resistance by some clinicians to chart tobacco consults. And what gets documented might not be standardized and might vary among clinicians, thereby making data collection and evaluation difficult. For hard copy charts, reading handwriting might pose an additional challenge.

Systematic collection of post-discharge short-term and long-term abstinence might also pose many challenges. One consideration is whether a mechanism can be put in place to ensure that patients are informed during hospitalization that they will be called at some time after hospital discharge to find out their tobacco use status. This could be done during tobacco consults by the attending clinicians or with a written note. Another consideration with collecting post-discharge abstinence data is the ability to identify what patients used tobacco at the time of hospitalization and/or received tobacco cessation services. Unless some sort of data collection system is set up to automatically pull off tobacco intervention data from patients' charts, some degree of ongoing retrospective chart review and data recording will be necessary.

The actual timing for post-discharge follow-up and the ability to create consistent equivalent post-discharge follow-up periods for tobacco use status across patients can also be challenging. Since abstinence is a measure relative to a specific time frame, data collection requires some sort of scheduling mechanism to trigger tobacco status calls to patients at specified intervals (e.g., 3 or 12 months post-discharge). Without a prompting system, charts must be continually screened, searching for patients who self-reported using tobacco and/or who received counseling, which as mentioned, is labor-intensive.

Depending on how regularly charts are screened, some patients might be called at 12-months post-discharge, others at 16-months, etc. Therefore, abstinence outcomes might have to lean more to broad brush-strokes of abstinence over wider time frames (e.g., abstinence collected between 12 and 18 months post-discharge).

CENTRALIZED COUNSELOR APPROACH TO INPATIENT TOBACCO CESSATION

The centralized counselor approach is one in which a dedicated position is created for a tobacco cessation counselor who becomes the central person responsible for providing cessation services to all patients hospital-wide. Having all tobacco dependence intervention activity organized and orchestrated by a central position is the defining, unique relative advantage of the centralized counselor approach from which all relative advantages flow.

Advantages of the Centralized Counselor Approach

The centralized counselor approach is easier to set up than the decentralized clinician approach, especially in terms of training because only one person—the person hired as the tobacco cessation counselor, needs to be fully trained, with perhaps a few others trained to cover vacation, sick days, etc. Since only one person needs to be trained, the program can be up and fully functioning, from inception to complete in-hospital delivery, post-discharge follow-up, and data collection, within a few weeks, rather than potentially years as indicated in the example in the decentralized clinician approach section.

Regardless of the background of the person hired for the position of tobacco cessation counselor in the centralized counselor approach, none of the challenges associated with the disinclination of clinicians to intervene evidenced in the decentralized clinician approach apply, even if a nurse or physician takes over the position. This is because only one individual is hired and/or trained for the position of tobacco counselor (albeit more than one person could be hired depending on the size of the hospital and job-sharing arrangements), so the responsibility is not diffused over hundreds of clinicians. The counselor who is hired is usually someone who applies or volunteers for the position, rather than someone who is assigned unwillingly to take over. As such, the counselor will likely be enthusiastic about assuming the role and responsibility, likely be compensated for it, have the time to deliver the services, believe all patients should be counseled (not only those with tobacco-related diseases), and will likely find the work rewarding. It would be quite unusual for a smoker to apply for the position, which eliminates one of the main barriers identified among staff nurses providing tobacco treatment.

Due to the focused responsibility of the cessation counselor, delivery of tobacco interventions will be more consistent, all patients who are appropriate for intervention according to the hospital's criteria will receive an intervention if they are interested (i.e., not only those with smoking-related diseases), and patients will not be excluded from receiving tobacco cessation services as they might be in a decentralized clinician approach if a clinician does not want to risk upsetting patients with repeatedly counseling them to quit. Patients will also be more likely to receive a more intensive intervention in the centralized counselor approach and will be more likely to receive post-discharge follow-up counseling, both of which enhance cessation.

Data collection also becomes seamless with the centralized counselor approach by becoming part of the job description of the counselor, and carried out during the counseling sessions, with the cessation provider having the time and tools to systematically record data in real time. This makes data collection easier, more efficient, more complete, and more systematic. In turn, it allows more accurate and timely program evaluation, goal setting, and dissemination of results.

Tobacco Cessation Counselors in the Centralized Counselor Approach

According to the USDHHS guideline recommendations, a tobacco cessation counselor can be any clinician or non-clinician who is trained in tobacco dependence and treatment. This can include nurses, health educators, physiotherapists, respiratory therapists, clergy, pharmacists, dentists, exercise physiologists, oncologists, etc. (Fiore et al., 2000).

Most of our work with Staying Free has involved training nurses to assume the role of the tobacco cessation counselor as their full-time job. Our initial choice for nurses was based on the points mentioned earlier in this chapter—nurses comprise the single largest health professional group in the hospital, they spend the most time with patients, and the support and caring attitudes of nurses are often cited as therapeutic processes in patients' recovery. In our studies there was also the need for the cessation provider to be able to tailor the risks of tobacco and the benefits of cessation to patients' medical conditions, the ability to read medical charts to determine eligibility for tobacco interventions, the binding ethics of the nursing profession in the care, treatment, and confidentiality of patients, and the ability to professionally address difficult issues that other allied medical professionals or lay counselors might not be able to, such as depression, substance abuse, and/or contraindications of cessation medications. Nurses can also provide continuity of care between hospital and home—during follow-up, they might be able to identify medical problems and/or contraindications to medications that patients might be experiencing post-discharge, and be able to triage patients to the appropriate health services.

Despite our initial reasons for hiring nurses to deliver Staying Free, we have since found that many providers from various disciplines are willing and able to provide cessation services, and we have trained a variety of other providers when we have put the program into standard practice outside of the tight controls of a research project. These providers have included physicians, lay volunteers, and clergy (Taylor et al., 2005). All types of providers can be efficacious in helping patients with tobacco dependence. However, we have found that those paid to deliver the services as part of their job description are more consistent than those who do so on a volunteer basis (Taylor et al., 2005).

Full or Part-Time Counselors? Many factors will determine whether a tobacco cessation counselor needs to be hired full-time or whether part-time will suffice. Some of these factors include the intensity of the program that will be provided in terms of the amount of time the in-hospital portion of the intervention takes, the amount and mode of post-discharge contact, and the amount of data collection required.

Also important to consider is whether the role will be dedicated to patient counseling only or whether it will also involve program administration, training, and promotional aspects as discussed in Chapter 4 (factors that must also be considered in the decentralized clinician approach in the form of a program director/coordinator/administrator). For example, program administration can include basic administration to keep the program going, such as ordering supplies and patient materials, basic program organization and management, program evaluation and reporting, and ensuring quality assurance and fidelity of intervention delivery. Training and promotional activities can include in-services, special training in tobacco dependence, brochure/pamphlet/poster design and distribution, updates to stakeholders, publication in the hospital newsletter or nursing journals, publication in scientific journals, media interviews, community presentations, and answering inquiries or requests for information from patients, community, and staff.

In one of our studies we found that one cessation provider working 50% time per hospital (20 hr/wk) was sufficient for screening, recruiting, providing brief in-hospital tobacco intervention, and collecting and inputting extensive data, including recording basic information on all patients admitted to the hospital in order to provide the population parameters for calculating tobacco prevalence and program reach. This held across three different hospitals with very different annual patient flow and make-up of the hospital units and specialties. When an intensive intervention with post-discharge telephone counseling was added, a full-time position was required. If a full-time position is not in the budget, options can be explored for every component over and above direct inpatient contact, such as using an existing 1-800 help-line service for the post-discharge counseling, having hospital volunteers do the 3, 6, and 12 month follow-up, having the research department responsible for data input, evaluation, analysis, and reporting, having the patient education department responsible for in-servicing and community presentations, and having the public relations department responsible for promotion, media interviews, and article preparation for the hospital newsletter.

Challenges with the Centralized Counselor Approach to Inpatient Tobacco Cessation

There are fewer challenges to the centralized counselor approach compared to the decentralized clinician approach. The main challenges of the centralized counselor approach are cost and timing-related. Cost can be a challenge if a new position for a tobacco cessation counselor must be funded from the hospital operating budget and funds are tight. As mentioned in Chapter 1, evidence suggests that healthcare savings can be seen immediately with cessation during hospitalization due to shorter hospital stays, decreased recovery time, decreased intra-operative and post-operative complications, and decreased utilization (DiFranza & Lew, 1996; Egan & Wong, 1992; Leung et al., 2003; Lightwood et al., 1999; Moller et al., 2002; Simon et al., 1997; Sorensen et al., 2002; Wagner et al., 1995), so it might be advantageous for a hospital to fund such a position. Building a business case based on return on investment (ROI) might be necessary to justify funding. As mentioned previously, an ROI calculator is available free of charge on the web (http://www.businesscaeroi.org).

From a timing perspective, the tobacco cessation counselor might not be available when the patient is ready for a consult, or the patient might not be available for a consult when the tobacco cessation counselor is available. Repeated bedside visits to check on patient availability does not guarantee that the patient will ever be available and these repeated visits can not only be time-consuming, but due to the trend for shorter hospital stays, patients might be discharged before the tobacco cessation counselor has a chance to intervene. So unless other attending clinicians are trained to provide at least brief interventions or even just advice at the bedside, patients will not necessarily receive support from the whole hospital staff. And finally, unlike primary care physicians who have the opportunity to intervene with tobacco services continuously over a number of years with any given patient, the only opportunities tobacco cessation counselors have to intervene with patients are during hospitalization and scheduled post-discharge sessions following a hospitalization. However, the time that a counselor can spend with a patient can be supplemented by the patient's other clinicians.

HYBRID APPROACH TO INPATIENT TOBACCO CESSATION

The hybrid approach is a combination of the decentralized clinician approach and the centralized counselor approach, with all clinicians responsible for at least minimally intervening with their patients, and a tobacco cessation counselor, either in-house or affiliated with an organization that offers tobacco cessation services, providing either a more intensive intervention to complement the brief clinician-delivered intervention, and/or providing follow-up post-discharge. There are two main hybrid models. One is to approach inpatient tobacco services from the decentralized clinician perspective, and the other is to approach tobacco services from the centralized counselor perspective.

Hybrid Model the the Decentralized Clinician Approach

The starting point for the hybrid approach from the decentralized clinician perspective is to have all clinicians responsible for providing some level of brief intervention on every encounter with their patients who use tobacco, and then be responsible for calling in the tobacco cessation counselor to provide more in-depth education, counseling, and/or to provide or arrange post-discharge follow-up. In this model, the tobacco cessation counselor plays a supplementary role. This approach would, fortunately, entail all the advantages of the decentralized clinician approach—wide coverage, availability 24/7, reinforcement by multiple providers, and hopefully a change in medical culture and a paradigm shift to tobacco being a medical concern not a lifestyle issue.

Despite the advantages, the hybrid approach from the decentralized clinician perspective would also, unfortunately, entail all the challenges of the decentralized clinician approach. The primary responsibility for tobacco cessation intervention and for triggering additional intervention would rest on hundreds of individual clinicians, all of whom would need to be trained and sufficiently motivated to intervene consistently (i.e., the disinclination to intervene challenge). It would also involve the program coordination and training challenges of the decentralized clinician approach. Although data collection would be more easily accomplished with the tobacco cessation counselor working with patients, due to the time lag between clinicians and counselors seeing patients, patients could easily be discharged before being seen by the counselor, and therefore there would be a tendency to have missing data for evaluation purposes.

Hybrid Model the Centralized Counselor Approach

The hybrid approach from the centralized counselor perspective would involve having the tobacco cessation counselor as the central organizing person responsible for identifying all patients who use tobacco and delivering the in-hospital interventions and post-discharge follow-up. The counselor would prompt attending clinicians to intervene. In this model, patients' attending clinicians would play a supplementary role, which would usually be comprised of at least providing advice to quit, if not a brief intervention that played to the strengths of the clinician, such as tailoring cessation messages to patients' medical conditions (see Chapter 11 for ideas).

The hybrid approach from the centralized counselor perspective entails all the advantages of the centralized counselor approach—easier to set up, especially in terms of coordination and training, only one person needs to be trained, the program can be up and fully functioning within a few weeks, delivery is more likely to be consistent, patients are more likely to receive a more intense intervention and post-discharge follow-up counseling (both of which enhance cessation), and data collection is seamless, thereby facilitating program evaluation, goal setting, and dissemination. It also entails all the advantages of the decentralized clinician approach—by having all attending clinicians intervene with all patients on every encounter, there is wide coverage, repeated contact, interventions are available 24/7 by attending hospital staff, and the culture around tobacco use and intervention changes from viewing tobacco as a lifestyle issue to a medical concern.

Moreover, with the hybrid approach from the centralized counselor perspective, the advantages of both the centralized counselor approach and decentralized clinician approach combine synergistically by having a dedicated counselor who can ensure the consistency of interventions across all patients, provide more intense interventions, and ensure that post-discharge follow-up is provided as long as patients are willing. The counselor can also serve as a resource to attending clinicians who are not tobacco treatment specialists but who provide services to their patients as part of general healthcare delivery. The type of help they can provide includes training in counseling, providing consultation on difficult cases, and providing specialized assessment services (Fiore et al., 2000). From an institutionalization perspective, tobacco cessation counselors can help develop office and clinic procedures to increase the rates of tobacco use identification and treatment by clinicians, as well as provide evaluation services for treatment activities and procedures.

A unique advantage of the hybrid approach from the centralized counselor perspective is that attending physicians and nurses tend to become more willing and likely to provide advice to patients to quit because their role in tobacco cessation is minimized and it becomes perceptibly more doable and within their acute care mandate. There is not as much resistance to training with the hybrid approach once clinicians realize that they do not have to do it all—that they can ask, advise, and say *"I'm sending in the tobacco specialist"* or *"I see that the tobacco specialist has been in to see you. That's good. Quitting tobacco is the single most important thing you can do for your health.*" Because they do not have to do it all, training can be as simple as a 5-10 minute in-service during regular staff meetings, so scheduling and training of staff ceases to be an issue.

There are no unique challenges to the hybrid approach from the centralized counselor approach, although some of the challenges with the centralized counselor approach itself might prevail, depending on the institution, the degree to which the hybrid approach is implemented, and the willingness of clinicians to provide at least a brief intervention. The hybrid approach from the centralized counselor approach was actually designed to address the challenges of the decentralized and the centralized counselor approaches.

10

Systems for Tobacco Use Identification and Documentation

Institutionalization of the identification and documentation of tobacco use are key recommendations of the USDHHS clinical practice guideline for treating tobacco use and dependence (Fiore et al., 2000). Institutionalization requires systems-level changes. Systems-level changes, in turn, can enhance the likelihood that clinicians will intervene with patients who use tobacco.

When designing systems-level changes, it is important to focus first on areas that are most amenable to improvement, on changes that are simple to do, and on changes that will have the highest impact (Institute of Medicine, 2001; Revell & Schroeder, 2005). It is also important to consider the burden of adjustment being placed on clinicians when designing systems-level changes. Changes that require minimal adjustment in clinicians' behavior will tend to have the most impact—this is especially true with respect to physicians (Cabana et al., 1999; Eisenberg, 2002). Even when systems-level changes are simple to do, will have high impact, and require minimal adjustment in clinicians' behavior, there will usually still be some of level of resistance to change. The resistance can include concerns about compromised productivity, perceived threats to autonomy, and lack of time to adjust to or be actively involved in redesigning systems (Berwick, 2003; Grumbach et al., 2002).

This chapter focuses on systems-level changes to institutionalize the consistent identification and documentation of tobacco use of patients admitted to the hospital. Identification and documentation of tobacco use are systems-level changes that are amenable to improvement at low to no cost, are relatively simple to do, will have high impact, and yet do not require major behavior change from clinicians. The chapter begins with the definition of tobacco use and the relationship of tobacco use definitions to interventions. It then discusses centralized and decentralized approaches to the identification and documentation of tobacco use, and the challenges involved with identifying tobacco use.

DEFINITION OF TOBACCO USE

In order to document tobacco use, an agreed upon definition of tobacco use must be made within each institution. Although the definition of tobacco use seems simple at first glance, there are actually various definitions of tobacco use, and various definitions of tobacco use relative to what it means for intervention. With Staying Free, we have defined tobacco use as any use, even a puff or chew, in the month prior to hospitalization. It is documented as a dichotomous outcome (yes/no) on patients' admitting forms. The reasons for considering tobacco use in the previous month are: 1) to ensure that occasional, non-daily tobacco users are identified; 2) to encourage and support patients who quit smoking for a planned hospitalization; since these patients have already quit, an intervention might help them decide to remain tobacco-free; and, 3) recent quitters might be able to benefit from additional help and support, especially within the first month of quitting, which tends to be the most important time for remaining tobacco-free after a quit attempt.

Tobacco use has also been defined as currently using tobacco at time of hospitalization without any reference to a time frame (i.e., Do you use tobacco products?). This definition, however, might miss occasional users and recent quitters. Other definitions of tobacco use include a time-frame that is shorter or longer than one month prior to assessment. For example, the Joint Commission on Accreditation of Healthcare Organizations (JCAHO, n.d.^{c}) defines tobacco use as any use over the previous year. The National Heart, Lung, and Blood Institute definition of tobacco use can be inferred from its definition of abstinence—no tobacco use for the previous seven days (Ossip-Klein et al., 1986)—this is the most common definition of abstinence in research trials.

Other definitions of tobacco use include a minimum requirement that the person has smoked at least 100 cigarettes in his/her lifetime in addition to current use defined by some timeframe. This definition is usually reserved for adolescent populations to screen out those who have experimented or are currently experimenting with tobacco but who have never moved past the experimentation stage. If the inpatient tobacco cessation program will be offered to adolescents, including a quantity of cigarettes in the definition of tobacco use might or might not be an important consideration depending on the outcome goals of the program. If the program goals are simply to provide tobacco cessation services to all patients, quantity will not be an issue; however, if cessation rates will be reported as an indicator of program success, including "experimenters" and regular users together for outcome analyses might serve to artificially inflate the cessation outcomes. Adding quantity might add a level of complexity for recording, requiring data recording beyond a yes/no response, and might require a memo field for clarification of the response.

Another option for the definition of tobacco use is to ask a two-tiered question. One version would be to begin by asking patients if they have ever used tobacco (yes/no [or never]), and if they have, ask whether they are current or former users. Another version of a two-tiered question would be to begin by asking if patients currently use tobacco (yes/no). Those currently using would be coded current. Those not currently using, could be asked if they have ever used tobacco and coded as former or never. This latter approach is the approach recommended by the clinical practice guideline (Fiore et al., 2000). A two-tiered tobacco use definition does add a level of complexity and might require a memo field for clarification of the response (e.g., quit 20 years ago).

Relationship of Tobacco Use Definitions to Interventions

In the simplest form, current use of tobacco warrants an intervention that focuses on quitting and relapse prevention. Use of tobacco within a defined period of time, such as the month previous to hospitalization might require an intervention that focuses on quitting (if patients have not yet quit) and relapse prevention, or only on relapse prevention if they have been tobacco-free for at least some defined period of time, such as one week.

The USDHHS clinical practice guideline (Fiore et al., 2000) provides an algorithm definition of tobacco use that guides clinicians to the appropriate level of intervention (Figure 9). At the first level of the algorithm, patients are asked about current use of tobacco (yes/no). The algorithm branches for current users versus those who do not currently use tobacco. For current users, the algorithm moves to asking patients about their willingness to quit. For those who are willing to quit the guidelines recommend providing a tobacco cessation intervention. For those not willing to quit, the guidelines recommend providing an intervention to enhance motivation to quit. On the other side of the algorithm, patients who do not use tobacco should be asked if they have ever used tobacco. For never users, the guidelines recommend encouraging them to remain tobacco-free. For previous users, the guidelines recommend providing a relapse prevention intervention. In practice, this latter recommendation might seem a bit strange for patients who quit using tobacco in the distant past.

Figure 9. Definition of Tobacco Use Algorithm (Fiore et al., 2000)

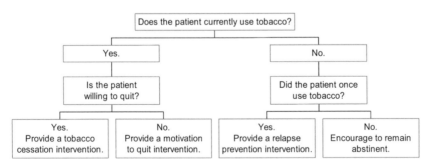

After the definition of tobacco use and how to phrase and answer the question of tobacco use have been clarified, a system needs to be developed in order institutionalize the consistent identification and documentation of tobacco use. If possible, it is best to identify and document the tobacco use of all patients, not only the target population. This allows calculation of tobacco use prevalence within the target group population and the hospital as a whole, as well as allows tobacco use prevalence to be compared to other subgroups of patients not currently considered part of the target group.

INSTITUTIONALIZATION OF TOBACCO USE IDENTIFICATION AND DOCUMENTATION

Centralized Approach to the Identification and Documentation of Tobacco Use

The seemingly simplest and most efficient means of systematically identifying hospitalized patients who use tobacco is to centralize the process by having a tobacco use question added to the admitting forms and asked by admitting staff. This system immediately institutionalizes the process—every patient, if conscious and coherent at the time of admission, should be asked about tobacco use on every visit as part of the routine of admission to the hospital. From a documentation perspective, having the tobacco use question on the admitting form ensures a standardized location for tobacco use on patients' records. It also ensures a standardized coding system for status even though tobacco use might also appear in other parts of patients' medical charts, such as in the history and physical or physician and nursing notes. Once in the system with a standardized location and documentation code, tobacco use data can be used to satisfy many different types of reports involving tobacco use, such as those required by JCAHO (2005).

Ironically, many hospitals in the past had a tobacco use question on the admitting forms—it was when smoking rooms were available and admitting staff needed to determine what type of room patients preferred (smoking or non-smoking). When hospitals became smoke-free and it was no longer necessary to admit patients to a smoking or non-smoking room, many hospitals removed the tobacco question from the admitting form. We have had to convince many hospitals of the need to put the question back on the admitting form, this time for a very different reason, and then train or retrain admitting staff to ask the question.

No-bypass Field. If electronic or computerized admitting records are used, it is helpful to have the tobacco use question as a "no-by-pass" field to enhance the likelihood that the question does get asked of and answered by every patient. "No-by-pass" field means that admitting staff cannot pass the question and get to the next question on the admitting form without providing an answer to the tobacco use question. A no-by pass field does not guarantee accuracy, however. We have found admitting staff might insert "no" for the tobacco use item in an attempt to get past the item because it is new or they do not believe it is important, to save time, or to avoid asking about tobacco use due to their own discomfort around the subject. As such, the program director will need to monitor the accuracy of this information.

Daily Hospital Census as a Complement. If the tobacco use question is added to the electronic admitting forms, a good complement for identifying patients who use tobacco is a printout of the daily hospital census that shows all new admissions along with a column added for tobacco use. This allows quick and efficient identification of all patients who use tobacco by the tobacco cessation counselor. The daily census might look something like that shown in Figure 10, with a "Y" for yes, the patient uses tobacco, "N" for no, the patient does not use tobacco, and "U" for tobacco use is unknown.

Figure 10. Example of Adding Tobacco Use to the Daily Census

Hospital Daily Admissions, January 21, 2006

Name	Unit	Gender	Age	Admit Reason	Tobacco
Jones	Medical	M	60	chest pain	Y
Latta	Medical	M	72	SOB	N
Pellini	Pediatric	M	16	overdose	U

Unknown Tobacco Use Status. It is important to include an option for tobacco use "unknown". It is not possible to collect tobacco use on all patients at admission. Some patients are admitted emergently or directly to a unit and by-pass central admissions; other patients might not be able to provide personal information due to being unconscious, medically unstable, confused, in too much pain, incoherent, aphasiac, suffering from dementia, or simply because they refuse to answer the question. In some medical systems, transfer from one hospital unit to another within the same hospital requires that the patient be discharged on paper from the original unit and then re-admitted on paper to the new unit. In such a case, information about tobacco use might not transfer with the rest of the records. However, unknown status can often be quickly verified by checking other sections in patients' charts such as the history and physical, nursing notes, or physician notes, by asking the attending staff nurse, or by approaching patients at the bedside.

In-service Training. If a centralized approach using the admitting department is taken, admitting staff should receive an in-service training that clarifies what they are expected to do (e.g., ask the question for every patient for every admission) and how the information will be used (e.g., identify patients who use tobacco so they can be offered a service free of charge). The important role played by admitting staff in the bigger picture should be stressed. Staff should be informed that without the identification of tobacco use during admission, many patients who use tobacco will not be identified so they will not receive tobacco cessation services, and/or comprehensive hospital data such as that required by quality assurance indicators will be incomplete. It is helpful to let admitting staff know that patients who use tobacco are offered a special service to help them quit, a service that most patients appreciate (especially if it is free of charge). It is also helpful to ensure that the role played by the admitting staff is recognized and appreciation for their contribution is shown, especially in the early learning phase.

Paper Versus Computerized Admitting Forms. If the admitting forms are paper rather than electronic, the tobacco use question can either be added to the paper form or separate cards with the tobacco use question and room for identifying patient information can be provided. Our earliest system for using the admitting department, prior to electronic admitting becoming the norm in many hospitals, was to provide admitting staff with a stack of recipe-size cards that had a tobacco use question on them along with space for patient identifying information. Admitting staff were requested to ask the questions on the cards of every patient admitted to the hospital. The recipe card system involved extra work that was separate from the admitting staff's regular admitting duties, but there was hospital support for this system and so the work was done.

With most hospitals now on some sort of electronic admitting system, the cards, at least for our purposes, have fallen by the wayside. Cards might still be useful, however, for hospitals that will not add the tobacco use question to electronic admitting, to bridge time lags in adding the question to electronic admitting records, or for hospitals that are still on a paper system. Even with cards, it is advisable to have a printout of the daily hospital census in order to have a full record of all admissions in order to calculate smoking prevalence. The card method, however, requires the added step of entering tobacco use by hand onto the printout of the daily census if a printout is available.

A centralized approach to identifying and documenting tobacco use does not mean that healthcare providers should not continue to be responsible for asking each patient about tobacco use. Even if tobacco use is recorded in the admitting records by admitting staff, it is still important for every provider to ask every patient on every encounter about tobacco use—that is, the first **A** "*ask* about tobacco use" of the recommended "5 A" approach for clinicians (Fiore et al., 2000). The more times a patient is asked about tobacco use, the better, because it brings the issue to the forefront and increases the saliency and importance of tobacco use.

Decentralized Options for the Identification and Documentation of Tobacco Use

In the previous section, we referred to the strategy of adding the tobacco use question to the admitting records to be asked by admitting staff during the admission process as a centralized approach. We called it centralized because there was one centralized process in place to ensure that the question was asked by a few identifiable staff rather than leaving it to the many hundreds of clinicians to ask of their own patients. In this next section, we provide two options that are more decentralized in nature—adding the question to the vital signs and going bed-to-bed to ask patients whether they use tobacco. Although both options could have a central place on patients' charts to record tobacco use, the actual process of asking is decentralized, either because many individuals, possibly hundreds, are involved and/or because it could happen at any point in time rather than in a specified order as part of a standardized process.

Add to Vital Signs. If the tobacco use question cannot be centralized by adding it to the admitting records, other options for systematic identification and documentation must be identified. The most commonly used option is to add the question to the vital signs section of patient charts. In fact, the clinical practice guideline recommends expanding the vital signs section of medical charts to include tobacco use (Fiore et al., 2000). The question can be asked by nurses or others responsible for measuring the vital signs. Adding tobacco use to the vital signs means that tobacco use usually appears on the history and physical (H & P) section of the medical chart; however, it might also end up in the nursing history, physician or transcription notes, or on the problems list.

The challenge with using the vital signs method of recording tobacco use is that tobacco use might not be asked as consistently as it is when admitting staff are responsible for the question. One of the reasons is the sheer number of medical staff who could be responsible for collecting this information. The more people that are involved, the more diffused the responsibility for asking about tobacco status will be, the more individual differences there will be, and the more difficult it will be to provide adequate in-service training and to track problems or inconsistencies simply due to the large numbers of clinicians involved. In contrast, the more centralized the process, the more consistently the question will be asked, and the easier it will be to control the fidelity of documentation.

Having each provider responsible for asking about tobacco use might also add a time-delay to screening of patients who use tobacco by the tobacco cessation counselor relative to the immediacy of recording when admitting staff ask the question. When the question is on the vital signs section of the chart, adding tobacco use by hand to the printout of the daily census or other documents used to organize and track tobacco cessation consults will be required. This was the case in one of our study hospitals that added tobacco use to the H & P to be asked by nursing staff versus admitting staff. Because tobacco use was not on the admitting form in a standardized field, it could not be printed with the daily census. As a result, it was more work for the cessation counselors on a daily basis to identify patients who used tobacco—it involved printing a hardcopy of the daily hospital census and transferring tobacco status from each newly admitted patient's medical chart to the census.

However, in another hospital having a decentralized system worked well. The nursing staff added tobacco use to their nursing history and assessed the patients' interest in quitting. If patients were using tobacco and interested in quitting they received a card which was handed to the ward clerk for the tobacco cessation counselor to pick up. This system provided a high yield of interested patients and helped bring the nursing staff into the program delivery.

Bed-to-Bed. The last option for identifying tobacco use is to go bed to bed and ask patients if they use tobacco. The bed-to-bed method can provide more accurate information than other methods, but it is a tremendously labor-intensive and costly way to collect information and should only be used as a last resort (or as a fidelity check of other methods).

Moreover, the bed-to-bed approach cannot result in complete data because there will always be patients who are discharged before they are seen, patients who are medically complicated or incoherent and cannot provide their status, and patients who are simply never available (they might be away from their room, sleeping, in too much pain, undergoing procedures, etc.). In addition, depending on the hospital and whether data will be collected for external reporting, informed consent might have to be obtained from each patient who is approached and asked about tobacco use at the bedside.

The bed-to-bed approach also requires a lot of needless work because it necessitates a visit to every bed in order to find the 10%-30% of patients who use tobacco. That is, most likely, more than three-quarters of the patients in the hospital will be non-smokers.

The bed-to-bed method also requires manually adding tobacco use to the daily census or other tracking instrument if tobacco use prevalence data are being collected. Although this sounds like an impossible situation, it unfortunately happened in one of our studies; we made it work for the study, but it would not be sustainable over time as a program in standard practice.

CHALLENGES IDENTIFYING TOBACCO USE

Discomfort Asking About Tobacco Use

Some admitting staff and clinicians might be uncomfortable asking patients about tobacco use for fear of upsetting them. In one of our studies we found that admitting staff who did not ask tobacco use did not ask it in an attempt to protect patients—they were concerned that patients who used tobacco were going to somehow be harassed by medical staff. When we clarified that patients would be receiving a special patient service that most patients appreciated, admitting staff became very willing and consistent in recording tobacco use.

Another reason for discomfort asking patients about tobacco use is the personal tobacco use status of the admitting staff and clinicians. Those who use tobacco tend to be reluctant to ask others about tobacco use (Heath et al., 2004). The solution is to provide regular in-service training. For clinicians, it helps to frame asking about tobacco use as equivalent to asking about other health-related issues, such as blood pressure and diabetes that are central to the patients' healing. It is also helpful to reinforce to staff and clinicians who smoke that patients who use tobacco want to be encouraged to quit by health professionals, and that patients are more satisfied with their care when they are offered a tobacco cessation intervention (Solberg et al., 2001).

Back Lash of a No-By-Pass Field

If the centralized approach to identifying and documenting tobacco use is implemented (i.e., having the tobacco use question on the admitting form and asked by the admitting department), putting the tobacco use question as a no-by-pass field on admitting records can result in some staff answering 'unknown tobacco use status' or 'no' for every, or almost every patient, just to get past the question. Although a certain number of patients who are admitted to hospital are unconscious, incoherent, unable to answer questions, or are otherwise in an emergency situation, such that admitting information is abbreviated, most patients are able to answer the question.

When tobacco use is not being asked by admitting staff of those patients who can answer, it is often a relatively easy problem to correct (unlike in a decentralized approach in which hundreds of clinicians are involved). With the support of the admitting department, it is possible to track admitting entries to determine whether this is a universal problem with all admitting staff or whether it is person-specific. In one hospital we found that one admitting staff person on the midnight shift answered 'unknown' tobacco use for all patients. As it turns out, she always worked the midnight shift and did not attend the day shift in-service training about asking the tobacco use question. It was simply a lack of awareness. When she was properly informed by the admitting supervisor about asking the question, the 'unknowns' ceased.

The 'unknown status' problem will tend to surface either when the question is first added to admitting records, when new staff are hired, or when staff miss the in-service. The in-service training needs to clarify that tobacco use status is important, that it is information being tracked by hospital administration or research staff and complete data are necessary (e.g., to meet performance requirements), and that if the question is not asked, patients will miss out on a program that most patients appreciate being offered.

The Tobacco Use Question Is 'Extra Work' or Not Part of the Routine

If the tobacco use question is not programmed as a no-by-pass field on admitting records, but rather appears as a field that can be by-passed, is added as an additional question at the bottom of the old form, or requires a sticker or stamp to a hard copy record, it might go unanswered or be answered inconsistently. Some staff might perceive it as extra work over and above their regular jobs. Others will miss it because it is not part of their habitual routine. Both problems can usually be corrected with regular in-service trainings that stress the importance of asking the question, as well as providing some type of cueing and/or reminder system. In one of our hospitals, admitting staff (on their own accord) posted yellow sticky notes on their computers to remind themselves to ask the tobacco use question that was an extra question tacked onto the bottom of the admitting form. If the tobacco use question is to be asked by clinical staff rather than admitting, frequent in-services across all or most units might be required, especially in large hospitals with large numbers of staff and/or turnover. When the question is asked by admitting staff, the in-services are simple and can be reinforced regularly.

Wording of the Question

An odd challenge we came up against in one of our hospitals was that admitting personnel preferred to ask patients whether they "smoked" rather than if they used "tobacco". It was easier and more natural for them to say "smoked" because that is what they called tobacco use in their everyday life. They tended to trip over the word "tobacco", and "tobacco" for some reason confused some patients—they were not clear what they were being asked, which in turn meant the conversation around tobacco was extended, thereby adding an element of discomfort on the part of the staff. To remedy their discomfort and the confusion of the patients, they changed the question to "Do you smoke?"—it was easier for them to say and it was understood immediately by all patients. In this hospital, it was not a huge problem because 99.9% of all patients "smoked"—smokeless tobacco use was not at all prevalent. An alternate question could be "Have you smoked or used other tobacco products in the last month?".

Fidelity of Tobacco Use Data

A change in pattern of documented tobacco use, such as substantially more non-smokers or unknown status, might signal a lack of fidelity in asking the tobacco use question. In one of our studies that relied on admitting staff to ask the tobacco question, we noticed a substantial increase in non-smokers at one hospital over a short period of time. It turned out that smoking prevalence had not actually decreased; rather, admitting staff were filling in the tobacco use question as 'non-smoker' without ever asking patients whether they used tobacco products.

In another hospital, we noticed a drop-off in the number of tobacco users for a very different reason. Tobacco use identification in this hospital relied on physician referrals and the tobacco cessation counselor informally asking patients if they used tobacco. Over time, the counselor and the physicians began to approach only the patients they felt most comfortable in asking about tobacco use. This is a good example of how an expert-based rather than systems-based approach can lead to inconsistent identification and documentation.

If tobacco use is not being correctly identified, it helps to determine whether there are any patterns to the discrepancies (unit, time of admitting, medical condition, etc.). A relatively easy way to look at discrepancies is to work backwards from an estimate of what the tobacco use prevalence is in the targeted population. For instance, if tobacco use prevalence is approximately 20% on the units where the program is delivered, then 20 of the 100 patients seen on those units should be tobacco users. If only 10 patients are identified over the course of 100 admissions, then the system needs to be evaluated.

Occasional fidelity checks can provide ongoing evidence for quality assurance. If the admitting and medical charts are fully electronic, the tobacco use recorded by admitting staff can be assessed for fidelity by comparing it with tobacco use recorded in other parts of patients' chart such as in the history and physical, nursing notes, or physician notes. However, this comparison relies on clinicians consistently asking patients about tobacco use. An alternate, and arguably the most effective fidelity check, is to visit patients bed-to-bed and ask them whether they use tobacco. Their answers can then be compared to the tobacco use recorded in their admitting or medical record.

Fidelity checks can be done over a 1 to 2 week period to verify tobacco use recorded by admitting staff or providers. In large hospitals, specific units can be targeted for fidelity checks, rotating the units that are checked over the year.

These checks allow identification of discrepancies in tobacco use. For the most part, patients coded as non-smokers or unknown tobacco use status are the target for checks because the tobacco use of patients coded as smokers will automatically be verified when they are screened for eligibility for the cessation program. Fidelity checks might be especially important when the question is first added to the admitting forms to ensure that the systems are working smoothly.

Cost

Some hospitals have balked at the cost of adding a tobacco use question to the admitting forms. The costs can involve changing computer programs, re-doing forms, and training admission personnel. These costs, in practice, have proved minor. We have generally recommended that hospitals make the changes at times they are making other changes in forms and programs.

11

Intervention Delivery Options

The USDHHS clinical practice guideline for treating tobacco use and dependence recommends that all clinicians intervene with all patients who use tobacco on every encounter (Fiore et al., 2000). Intervention should include providing advice to quit, assessing patients' willingness to quit, and at a minimum, providing brief counseling using a treatment recommended as effective in the guidelines, and intensive interventions should be offered whenever possible.

The USDHHS guideline makes recommendations for both effective brief and intensive intervention strategies. All of the recommended strategies are evidence-based, with conclusions based on meta-analyses performed as part of the development of the guideline (Fiore et al., 2000). The strategies represent general concepts in tobacco education and counseling. The specific education and counseling content for any given patient will be dictated to some degree by the patient and the patient's circumstances. The guideline does, however, provide content examples of what to include.

In this chapter we use the USDHHS clinical practice guideline (Fiore et al., 2000) as the framework for making choices about what intervention components to include in an inpatient tobacco cessation program and how to "intensify" interventions to make them more effective. We have used the USDHHS guideline as the basis for making choices because it is relevant to all clinicians—it is not discipline or patient population-specific whereas many of the other clinical practice guidelines are, such as those for the British, Canadian, and American Thoracic Societies and the American Psychiatric Association (American Psychiatric Association, 1996; British Thoracic Society, 1998; Celli et al., 1995; O'Donnell et al., 2003). The recommended strategies in the USDHHS guideline are also consistent with those recommended by other clinical guidelines.

The focus of this chapter is to stimulate thinking about the structure of intensive interventions. It does not focus on counseling content or content sequencing, nor have we provided suggestions for what a complete intervention would look like, aside from providing examples from Staying Free (the full content and sequencing of Staying Free are provided in Chapter 3). Doing so would be an impossible task given all the possible iterations of what makes an effective intensive intervention, including the number of providers involved, the number of sessions, the length of each session, and the various formats and adjunctive therapies that might be included.

EFFECTIVE INTERVENTION STRATEGIES

In terms of a broad perspective of "effective" intervention strategies, the USDHHS guideline (Fiore et al., 2000) provides recommendations to use the "5 A" approach to guide sequencing of interventions for patients willing to make a quit attempt, and a combination of the "5 A" and "5 R" approaches to guide interventions for patients not willing to make a quit attempt. The guideline also includes general recommended counseling strategies considered effective within the "5 A" and "5 R" approaches (e.g., skills counseling and motivational counseling; see Figure 11).

The overarching "5 A" and "5 R" approaches and the recommended counseling strategies within each apply to both brief and intensive interventions. The intensity of each counseling strategy can be adjusted as a function of practical factors—patient preference, time available, training of clinicians, and resources available.

What the guideline does not provide are recommendations for specific content within each of the recommended counseling strategies, although it does provide suggestions. The most appropriate content will be determined by circumstances such as patients' needs, wants, and life situations, and providers' time constraints and training. The guideline also does not recommend or single out specific intervention programs that have been tested or that are currently in practice. Nor does the guideline rank-order interventions in terms of efficacy or compare among different types of interventions (e.g., pharmacotherapy versus social support training).

Effective Brief Interventions

Brief interventions can be completed within three minutes of a clinician's time (Fiore et al., 2000). The identification of effective brief intervention strategies for any given patient begins with following through with the first three "As" of the "5 A" strategy—*ask* whether the patient uses tobacco, *advise* patients who use tobacco to quit, and *assess* the willingness to quit among those who use tobacco. It is the assessment of patients' tobacco use status (current, former, and never) and their willingness to make a quit attempt that elucidates the most effective type of intervention strategy for the last two "As" of the "5 A" strategy—*assist* patients in their quit attempt using effective counseling strategies, and *arrange* follow-up. A graphic representation of the effective brief treatment strategies for current users and former users are provided in an algorithm in Figure 11. Never users are (not included in the algorithm) should be congratulated and encouraged not to start using tobacco (Fiore et al., 2000).

Figure 11. Clinical Practice Guideline Effective Intervention Strategies

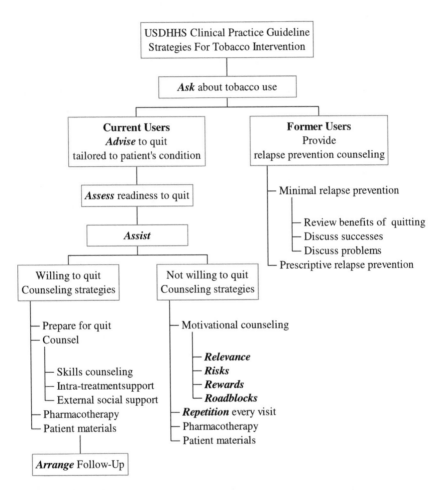

Current Tobacco Users Willing to Make a Quit Attempt. Among current tobacco users who are willing to make a quit attempt, assistance should include helping them prepare for their quit attempt, providing cessation counseling using recommended strategies (skills counseling, intra-treatment support, and external social support), providing education and counseling for pharmacotherapy (and when appropriate, prescriptions), and providing take-home materials (Figure 11). Arranging follow-up could include arranging repeat counseling visits with the provider or referral to another service (e.g., a 1-800 cessation service).

Current Tobacco Users Unwilling to Make a Quit Attempt. Among current tobacco users who are not willing to make a quit attempt, assistance should include counseling to help motivate them to quit guided by the "5 Rs"—the *relevance* of using tobacco to the patient, the *risks* of continuing to use tobacco, the *rewards* of quitting, and the *roadblocks* to quitting that patients might be facing. Motivational counseling should be *repeated* on every visit.

Ideally, all recommended steps for each brief strategy should be followed on every encounter with every patient. However, brief interventions will be bound by time constraints and other factors, so recommendations are to include as many steps as possible in the time allowed during encounters with patients. Although many clinicians who do intervene tend to only *ask* and *advise*, they should also be able at a minimum to *arrange* other cessation services, such as a referral to a tobacco cessation counselor or quitline (Revell & Schroeder, 2005), even though they, themselves, might not have the time, inclination, or training to provide the assist and arrange components of the "5 A" approach. The Pacific Center On Health and Tobacco (2003) provides an instructional document on integrating quitlines with healthcare systems that may be helpful.

Effective Intensive Interventions

Intensive interventions should be provided when possible because they significantly increase cessation rates (Fiore et al., 2000). Intensive interventions can be provided by healthcare providers, tobacco cessation specialists, or by both. Effective intensive interventions follow the same algorithm for brief interventions strategies (Figure 11). Brief strategies become intensive interventions by "intensifying" the counseling strategies for patients willing to make a quit attempt. The next section provides insight into ways to intensify interventions to make them more effective.

INTENSIFYING INTERVENTIONS

The USDHHS guideline provides insight into intensifying interventions based on conclusions made from meta-analyses of published research studies on tobacco cessation interventions (Fiore et al., 2000). Interventions can be intensified by: 1) involving more than one type of clinician; 2) increasing the amount of time per session to at least 10 minutes; 3) increasing the total number of sessions to four or more person-to-person sessions, each lasting more than 10 minutes; 4) increasing total counseling time to a minimum of 30 minutes; and, 5) including more than one type of format (e.g., individual and group counseling as well as proactive telephone counseling). Aversive therapies are also recommended as an intensive strategy. Intensifying interventions involves adding as many of the "intensive" components deemed effective as possible (Table 11).

of note, the guideline does not compare among the various types of intensive intervention strategies, such as comparing interventions with two or more formats with interventions that have 30 minutes or more of total counseling time. These types of comparisons are not possible due to the lack of studies for any given isolated intervention component, in addition to the fact that most studies on which the meta-analyses were based were not designed to isolate and comparatively test the individual components within an intervention.

In this section, we have taken the guideline evidence for effective intensive interventions and used them to make suggestions and provide decision-making tools to strategically intensify interventions while staying within the budgetary and time constraints faced by hospitals and clinicians. The "intensifying" intervention components covered include involving more than one type of provider, the length of time spent with a patient in each session, the number of sessions, the total time spent with a patient summing across the number of sessions, and the type and number of delivery formats (Table 11).

Table 11. Intervention Intensity Factors: USDHHS Guideline Recommendations (Fiore et al., 2000)

Intensity Factor	Minimum	Recommended Intensity
Number of clinicians	1clinician	2 or more clinicians
Time per session	3 minutes or less	10 minutes or more
Cumulative time	1 to 3 minutes	31 to 90
Number of sessions	1 session	8 sessions or more
Format	self-help	individual phone counseling individual face-to-face counseling group counseling
Number of formats	1 format	3 or 4 formats

Involving More Than One Type of Provider

Involving more than one type of provider increases the intensity of interventions and increases cessation (Fiore et al., 2000). When considering what clinicians to involve with tobacco interventions, some consideration must be given to time. Although the minimum recommended is only three minutes per session for brief interventions, the ideal is to aim for a more intensive intervention, defined as up to eight or more sessions of at least 10 minutes each, for a total of 31-90 minutes

(Fiore et al., 2000). Some providers (e.g., tobacco cessation counselors) might be able to provide 10 minutes or more per encounter whereas others might not. The following are a few suggestions for what different types of providers could bring to the collective mix. Involving more than one provider also inherently increases the number of sessions, cumulative time spent with patients, and potentially the number of formats.

Physicians. Given the time constraints of most physicians, a decision might be made to have physicians assist patients using a single three minute session at the bedside following a recommended strategy from the guideline that speaks to physicians' strengths in medical science and clinical skills. For example, they could provide advice to quit tailored to patients' medical conditions. Or they could focus on pharmacotherapy, such as providing education/information on withdrawal symptoms, how medication can help with withdrawal symptoms, when to seek help for withdrawal symptoms, and/or provide a prescription for cessation medications when required. They could also educate patients regarding specific withdrawal symptoms that sometimes occur and could cause concern, such as depression, constipation, and mouth sores, and when and if to seek medical treatment for these conditions.

Staff Nurses. Staff nurses could provide three minutes of counseling using the brief intervention strategies recommended in the USDHHS guideline that speak to nurses' strengths in medical sciences and patient care. For example, they could provide advice to quit tailored to the patients' medical conditions and offer to speak with family members about social support post-discharge (e.g., making houses and cars smoke-free). They could also offer in-hospital support, such as arranging for and/or providing nicotine replacement therapy for withdrawal symptoms, providing information on cessation services available during and after hospitalization, distributing patient materials such as pamphlets and videos/DVDs, and/or arranging appointments with an in-house tobacco cessation counselor.

Pharmacists. Depending on time restraints, the hospital pharmacist could provide three minutes or more of education around pharmacotherapy (Vitale, 2000). Pharmacotherapy is one of the recommended strategies in the USDHHS guideline (Fiore et al., 2000). Pharmacists could provide written materials as well engage in face-to-face counseling around nicotine replacement therapy and/or bupropion, including when, why, and how to use each medication, combining two or more cessation medications, what to expect from the medications, the course of medication use and titration protocols, contraindications (with other medications, medical conditions, and substances such as alcohol), possible side-effects, and side-effects that require medical attention.

Other Providers. There are a host of other clinicians and healthcare providers in the hospital, such as respiratory therapists, exercise physiologists, occupational therapists, physiotherapists, psychologists, social workers, health educators, and even massage therapists, that could offer at least a three minute brief intervention to patients who use tobacco. All providers could provide healthcare occupation-specific advice to quit tobacco tailored to patients' medical conditions. For example, respiratory therapists could speak to lung function, exercise physiologists could speak to the effect of nicotine and carbon monoxide on the cardiovascular system, and massage therapists could speak to blood flow and oxygen delivery to various parts of the body. All providers could also offer various types of support during hospitalization and take responsibility for distributing patient learning materials. In addition, they could arrange additional assistance for cessation services both during hospitalization (e.g., with a pharmacist and tobacco cessation counselor), as well as arrange post-discharge follow-up (e.g., through patient rehabilitation services, social workers, community services, 1-800 cessation services, etc.).

Tobacco Cessation Counselors/Specialists. Tobacco cessation counselors/ specialists can include someone hired specifically to provide tobacco cessation services or they could be any number of other health professionals in the hospital specially trained to offer tobacco cessation services as part of the other health services they provide (e.g., respiratory therapists, health educators, or exercise physiologists). Tobacco cessation counselors/specialists can provide a foundational 30 to 60 minutes of bedside education and counseling based on the strategies recommended in the guideline, or supplement other providers' efforts with a 10-30 minute intervention. Because of the extended amount of time that might be available to tobacco cessation counselors/specialists to spend with patients, they could provide more depth and breadth of education and counseling for each of the recommended strategies than other providers might be able to do.

Tobacco cessation counselors/specialists could also arrange follow-up and might be in the position to provide the recommended minimum of one to five months of post-discharge counseling (France et al., 2001; Rigotti et al., 2003). Time permitting, the tobacco cessation counselor/specialist could also perform detailed patient assessments to allow more personalized counseling, and collect data for program evaluation.

For example, tobacco cessation counselors/specialists with the Staying Free program provide patients with in-depth education and counseling around preparing to quit including the importance of creating smoke-free environments, avoiding high risk triggers (e.g., alcohol), weight gain, withdrawal, and cravings, and they formalize a quit contract with the patient. Skills counseling includes how to make choices when cravings hit, how to make low fat food choices, exercise, how to identify high risk situations for relapse and develop strategies to remain tobacco-free, how to deal with slips, urges, and social pressure, and how to use past quit experiences to develop strategies to remain tobacco-free. Intra-treatment support includes focusing on special issues that might be relevant to a given patient, such as withdrawal during hospitalization or lack of spousal support. Counselors also provide up to 3 months of post-discharge counseling and collect data for program evaluation.

Length of Time Per Session

In the USDHHS guideline (Fiore et al., 2000), program intensity defined as length of contact time in one session, is broken down into categories of no contact time (i.e., self-help), 3 minutes or less, more than 3 minutes but less than or equal to 10 minutes, and more than 10 minutes. Although the evidence used to develop the guideline showed that even 3 minutes or less of counseling is better than no counseling at all, cessation increases with the amount of time spent in a counseling session, and the recommended time per session for an intensive intervention is more than 10 minutes (Table 12).

As covered in the previous section, it might not be feasible for all clinicians to deliver 10 minutes of tobacco cessation counseling on every encounter with every patient. It might be feasible, however, for some clinicians, such as physicians, to provide a minimum of three minutes of brief intervention, and for others, such as tobacco counselors, pharmacists, respiratory therapists, and exercise physiologists, to provide more, closer to, or exceeding, the recommended 10 minutes. Again, this satisfies the intensifying characteristics of more than one provider, increased number of sessions, increased total time, and increased number of formats.

Table 12. Recommendations for Session Length in Minutes

	Not Recommended	Minimum		Recommend
Time	0 min	≤ 3 min	3 to 10 min	> 10 min

Total Time Spent

Evidence from meta-analyses presented in the guideline suggests a dose-response for cessation and the total amount of time spent counseling, with treatments offering a total of 31-90 minutes of counseling showing significantly higher cessation than those with one to three minutes of counseling (Fiore et al.,

2000). The total time does not have to occur in one session, but can be spread out over a number of sessions. There is no evidence, however, that increasing the total time to more than 91 minutes increases cessation further (Table 13).

Table 13. Guideline Recommendations for Total Time Spent with Patients

	Minimum		Highly Recommended	Inconclusive	
Minutes	1 to 3	4 to 30	31 to 90	91 to 300	> 300

As mentioned previously, there are creative ways to make up the total duration by involving a mix of providers that could each strategically provide the minimum three minute brief intervention and their combined efforts could make up the equivalent of 31 to 90 minutes of total counseling time. Moreover, the combination of having more than one provider also increases cessation. For example, if physicians and staff nurses each provided three minutes of brief intervention at the bedside and the pharmacist provided five to 10 minutes, the total amount of time would add up to 11 to 16 minutes with only minimal effort on everyone's part. Even 15 minutes of additional counseling with a tobacco cessation counselor during hospitalization would bring the total counseling time up to the minimum ideal floor of 31 minutes. If 45 minutes of counseling by a tobacco cessation counselor was provided during hospitalization (instead of only 15 minutes), along with at least three 10-minute post-discharge counseling calls over the first five months post-discharge, the total counseling time would reach the ideal recommended ceiling for intensity of 91 minutes.

Staying Free offers a total of 85 to 100 minutes—45 to 60 minutes for the intensive education and counseling session during hospitalization, and four post-discharge counseling calls of approximately 10-minutes each, all provided by a tobacco cessation counselor. In the most recent randomized trial of Staying Free with general hospital patients, we added three additional post-discharge calls, bringing the total time spent to 130 minutes, but the additional sessions did not increase cessation beyond previous studies that provided a total of 85-100 minutes of total counseling (Smith et al., submitted).

Number of Sessions

Meta-analyses used to develop the USDHHS guideline (Fiore et al., 2000) show a dose-response with cessation and number of tobacco cessation sessions, with cessation increasing with increasing number of sessions. Interventions that offer more than eight sessions show significantly higher cessation than treatments offering three or fewer sessions (Table 14).

Table 14. Guideline Recommendations for Number of Sessions

	Minimum		Highly Recommend
Sessions	0 to 1	2 to 3	4 to 8	> 8

As with total time spent counseling patients, if physicians, staff nurses, and the hospital pharmacist all provide a brief three minute intervention, the number of sessions is already at three. Adding additional counseling with a tobacco cessation counselor—one visit during hospitalization and five sessions post-discharge, brings the total number of sessions up to the ideal of more than eight. Referral to a quit-line is another way to increase the number of contacts—these additional contacts are more likely to happen, however, if the telephone calls are proactive, initiated by a provider, rather than left for the patient to self-initiate.

In its original form, Staying Free offers six sessions—brief advice from a physician, an intensive bedside session during hospitalization with a tobacco cessation counselor, and four provider-initiated post-discharge counseling calls. Although the Staying Free protocol offers only six contacts, as mentioned in the previous section, the total counseling time achieves the recommended total time of 91 minutes of counseling, thereby achieving the benchmark of a highly intensive intervention. In the most recent randomized trial of Staying Free with general hospital patients, we did add three additional post-discharge calls, bringing the total number of sessions to nine, but the additional sessions did not increase cessation over what we have found in other studies with a total of six contacts (Smith et al., submitted).

Post-Discharge Follow-up and Call Attempts. Post-discharge telephone counseling for the first one to five months after hospitalization is an important way to increase the number of counseling sessions and significantly increase long-term cessation (France et al., 2001; Rigotti et al., 2003). However, contacting patients by telephone post-discharge can be a challenge, especially if multiple calls are scheduled over a short period of time, such as weekly or biweekly calls. Difficulty contacting patients means decisions will need to be made regarding the number of attempts that will be made to reach patients for each scheduled call, and thought must be given to what clinicians will be able to provide the time for post-discharge counseling sessions considering that calls might require multiple call attempts for any scheduled session.

Our recommendation is to keep call attempts to a minimum. They can be costly and administratively complex. For example, if seven attempts were allotted for each of four scheduled post-discharge counseling contacts, up to 2.5 weeks of call attempts alone (not including counseling time) could result over a one-year period. This estimate assumes one minute per call attempt (7 attempts x 4 scheduled calls as per the Staying Free protocol), a utilization rate of 200 patients/year, and a workweek of 37.5 hours. Although not all call attempts take one minute, and not all patients require more than one call attempt, many attempts take a substantial amount of time (e.g., speaking with participants' friends and family, and attempts to find those lost-to-follow-up often involving a search of '411' services or participants' contacts). To maximize contact availability for post-discharge counseling calls, it would be optimum to schedule specific telephone appointments at specific times as one would schedule a face-to-face appointment rather than leaving it open-ended for a given day.

Type and Number of Delivery Formats

Tobacco cessation interventions can consist of self-help materials alone, some form of person-to-person contact (telephone, group, face-to-face), or some combination of the two. The meta-analyses used to develop the USDHHS guideline suggests that any intervention format (i.e., self-help materials alone or person-to-person contact) is better than no intervention at all, although the results are less stable for self-help materials alone (Fiore et al., 2000).

Providing two or more types of formats (e.g., self-help materials and telephone counseling) results in higher cessation than providing a single format (Table 15; Fiore et al., 2000). Increasing the number of delivery formats for tobacco services during hospitalization does not have to be onerous. If physicians, staff nurses, and/or pharmacists provided a brief intervention during hospital, each encounter would represent one face-to-face counseling (i.e., one format, multiple sessions). Each provider could also offer pamphlets during their brief intervention, thereby increasing the number of delivery formats to two (with multiple sessions). Referral to group or individual counseling or quit-line services for post-discharge continuity of care each provide another type of counseling contact, thereby reaching the recommended number of formats and offering multiple sessions.

Adding counseling by a tobacco cessation counselor during hospitalization could potentially cover at least 3 or 4 formats. For example, Staying Free incorporates a number of different delivery formats by including physician advice at the bedside, individual face-to-face counseling at the bedside provided by a tobacco cessation counselor, self-help take-home materials (relapse prevention video and workbook, how to quit pamphlet, community resource pamphlet, and relaxation audiotape), and post-discharge telephone counseling follow-up.

Table 15. Guideline Recommendations for Type of Delivery Format

	Minimum	Recommended
Format	Self-help	Multiple choices of self-help, phone, group, and face-to-face counseling
# formats	1 format	3 or 4 formats

12

Training Providers

Training should supply clinicians with sufficient knowledge about effective intervention strategies as well as enhance their skills to assist patients with the motivation and skills to make a quit attempt. Training should also foster an attitude toward tobacco dependence as a standard of good practice (Kottke et al., 1992). The USDHHS clinical practice guideline for treating tobacco use and dependence recommends that healthcare systems offer clinicians regular credit-based training in tobacco dependence treatment through lectures, seminars, and in-services (Fiore et al., 2000).

The focus of this chapter is on the issues related to training providers to deliver tobacco cessation interventions. Key factors to keep in mind are that the type and extent of training will be determined by the background of the individuals who are selected to provide the intervention. We have trained many physicians, nurses, respiratory therapists, psychologists, social workers, and non-healthcare professional volunteers. The passion, professionalism, interpersonal sensitivity and effectiveness of the individual seem more important than what type of healthcare training they received. And while our data suggest that paid healthcare professionals are more adherent to the intervention than are volunteers, we have had many volunteers from many disciplines who are very successful in recruiting patients and providing the interventions.

GOALS OF TRAINING

Despite what is known about training, research is still needed to clarify what constitutes the most effective elements of successful training (Fiore et al., 2000). For example, some training programs have focused on teaching general counseling skills, such as reflective listening, thought likely to enhance the effectiveness of the intervention. However, these skills are more difficult to teach than specific techniques for intervening directly with tobacco dependence, and it is probably better to select individuals to provide the intervention who already exhibit them. At a minimum, the goals of training in tobacco cessation should be:

1. To increase **knowledge** about issues related to tobacco dependence and treatment.

2. To increase provider confidence (**efficacy**) to deliver an effective intervention.
3. To teach the necessary **skills** specific to delivering the intervention.
4. To help clinicians recognize and interpret relapse as a reflection of the chronic nature of dependence rather than as a reflection of their personal failure to intervene adequately or their patients' failure to remain abstinent (**attitudes**).

Knowledge

Healthcare professionals interested in delivering tobacco cessation interventions should have adequate knowledge about the risks of tobacco use and the benefits of quitting. Training programs often include standardized knowledge assessments. Those providing an intervention to a specific population (such as pregnant women or individuals with lung disease) might need more knowledge about the effects of tobacco use on those specific conditions and the benefits of quitting. Providers need to know about the pharmacology of nicotine use and cessation, including what happens physiologically and psychologically when individuals stop using tobacco. It is also important for providers to understand the theoretical models guiding the intervention and the rationale for the intervention model. For our intervention, Staying Free, this would include a basic knowledge of stages of change theory (Prochaska & DiClementi, 1983), self-efficacy theory (Bandura, 1986), relapse prevention (Marlatt & Gordon, 1985), nicotine addiction, social support, motivational interviewing, and medication aids such as bupropion and nicotine replacement therapy.

Self-efficacy

Self-efficacy is a term used to refer to a person's situation-specific confidence to engage in a particular task (Bandura, 1986). In general, self-efficacy levels are strongly related to actual behaviors. Individuals with higher levels of efficacy to provide tobacco cessation counseling have been shown to be more likely to provide the intervention.

The training program developed for Staying Free uses counselors' pre- and post-training counseling self-efficacy to determine the effectiveness of training. The self-efficacy questionnaire consists of nine items that the counselor is asked to rate on a scale from 0 (not at all confident) to 100 (extremely confident). The items are related to the specific skills required to provide the intervention, such as confidence to take an adequate tobacco use history, determine situations in which a patient is most likely to relapse, and how to effectively use nicotine replacement therapies. In general, self-efficacy items have high test-retest reliability, construct validity, and predictive validity (Etter et al., 2000). Self-efficacy items can be specifically written for or tailored to any training program.

Counselor self-efficacy to deliver training and patient self-efficacy to remain abstinent from tobacco are two different types of efficacy. In contrast to the self-efficacy items mentioned above for training, counselors who deliver the Staying Free program must learn to interpret and use patients' self-efficacy to remain abstinent in various situations in order to prioritize and individualize the intervention. Patients complete a 14–item self-efficacy instrument (Baer et al., 1986). The counselor then identifies areas where the patient reports less than 70% confidence to cope with an urge to use tobacco and then helps provide skills to increase the patients confidence if the area is important.

Skills

Training in intervention skills is the most complicated aspect of training. Reviews of studies on how to train individuals in tobacco cessation skills consistently find that practice and feedback, such as use of standardized patient instructors role playing with other providers and actors, are more effective for teaching tobacco interventionists than are traditional didactic methods alone (Spangler et al., 2002). Another way to provide immediate feedback involves shadowing providers using a standardized counseling aid during real-time intervention. An example of a performance aid for the first fours steps involved in the daily preparation for identifying patients who use tobacco is provided in Figure 12. Practice and feedback are key.

Figure 12. Training Performance Checklist

Learner: _____ **Date:** _____

Y = acceptable N = needs work

Steps for Daily Preparation	1st Practice	2nd Practice	Notes
1.1 Print daily census.	Y	Y	
1.2 Highlight patients $\geq$ 18 yr old in eligible units who have a "yes" in the tobacco use column.	Y	Y	
1.3 If tobacco use is missing, check patient chart under nursing & physician notes, problem list, history & physical, and emergency records.	N	Y	
1.4 If tobacco use missing from chart, visit patient during daily rounds or check status with nursing staff.	Y	Y	

To use this aid, the learner would proceed through the steps involved with the daily preparation, and the instructor would shadow and evaluate the learner's performance. Tools such as these allow specific pinpointing of components that require improvement and components that are being done well—both positive and negative performance can benefit from immediate feedback. Aids such as this can be created for all aspects of program delivery, from daily preparation to identification of tobacco users, screening charts, approaching patients at the bedside, delivering the intervention, providing post-discharge follow-up, and various aspects of record keeping, data collection, and administration.

STANDARDIZED TRAINING

In determining how to train counselors and maintain counselor skills, a number of factors need to be considered, including the type of intervention offered and the counselors' previous experience with the intervention. Programs also need to consider how much time can be spent in training, how many people need to be trained and to what depth, and how training can be reimbursed. It is probably more cost-effective for most hospitals to send counselors to be trained in some of the existing programs than to develop the hospitals' own training program.

Nationally accepted standards do not currently exist for training, although there are many initiatives currently underway in the United States and Canada to develop training and accreditation standards. A training program based on the USDHHS clinical practice guideline is offered online free of charge and provides continuing medical education credits (Treating Tobacco Use and Dependence: Online Continuing Medical Education Course, 2003). A number of training resources are also listed on the Center for Tobacco Cessation toolkit website (2005a).

Many models have been developed to train counselors in tobacco cessation. In general, training has focused either on brief training or intensive training. Brief training models have been designed to help physicians, nurses, or other healthcare workers provide brief interventions, such as following the "5 As" and "5 Rs" recommended by the USDHHS guideline (Fiore, 2000). Intensive trainings have been designed by tobacco treatment specialists to help counselors deliver more intensive interventions.

Brief Training

Brief training programs for tobacco dependence counseling include at least one seminar, in-service, or workshop. The sessions are brief, usually lasting 1-4 hours, sometimes lasting a full day. They are designed to accommodate healthcare professionals' busy schedules and limited time for training.

Table 16. Outline for *Staying Free* Onsite Smoking Cessation Training Program

---

(1) Introductions, evaluations (30 minutes)

(2) Overview of Smoking Cessation and *Staying Free* Intervention (30 minutes)
       Smoking as an addiction and habit
       Overview of tobacco statistics
       Medical consequences of smoking and quitting
       Randomized controlled trials of smoking interventions
       Relapse prevention model related to smoking
       Pharmacological interventions

(3) Skills Training for the *Staying Free* Intervention (90 minutes)
       Determining a patient's willingness to quit
       Delivery of a strong message to quit tailored to patients' conditions
       Use of self-help materials
       Undertaking a smoking history and self-efficacy scale
       Formalizing commitment through contracting
       Review of tobacco use history and efficacy items
       Addressing withdrawal symptoms
       Addressing family and social support
       Addressing weight gain
       Addressing the benefits of relaxation and exercise
       Addressing loss and deprivation
       Addressing other patient-specific areas—alcohol, depression
       Focusing on the need for pharmacological therapy
       Focusing on high-risk situations—developing cognitive, behavioral, and social skills
       Highlighting issues about relapse prevention

(4) Telephone follow-up (30 minutes)
       How to effectively implement telephone follow-up for smoking cessation
       Conducting a telephone interview
       Maximizing reach through telephone follow-up

(5) Videotape of a bedside counseling session (30 minutes)

(6) Role-playing in dyads (90 minutes)

(7) Questions and answers (30-45 minutes)

We have developed a six-hour brief training workshop for Staying Free that we offer quarter-annually and on a request basis (btaylor@stanford.edu). The training focuses on increasing knowledge, skills, confidence, and attitudes, and goes beyond the "5 A" and "5 R" brief intervention approaches (see Table 16).

Intensive Training

Most intensive training programs provide some sort of certification for completion. Some programs also provide continuing education credits, which can be an incentive for providers to attend. We have provided examples of three different programs below.

Mayo Clinic Nicotine Dependence Seminar. The Mayo Clinic Nicotine Dependence Seminar is a four-day, 30-hour intensive program for counselor training (http://www.mayoclinic.org/ndc-rst/conference.html). The program covers a broad array of topics in nicotine dependence counselor training and program development. In addition, the program includes small group networking sessions that focus on special topics of interest including counseling applications and advanced counseling skills workshops.

California Smoker's Helpline. Zhu and his colleagues (1996) developed a training for counselors operating the California Smoker's Helpline, that might also be helpful to those providing any type of tobacco intervention. Counselors complete a 60-hour training that includes extensive general counseling skills training and a variety of tobacco cessation skills: nicotine replacement therapy, self-efficacy, and situational analysis of relapse. Trainees engage in role-playing sessions with veteran phone counselors in addition to observing these veterans at work. Trainees are not certified until they pass a written exam and they successfully demonstrate their skills in a role-play with the director.

Massachusetts Tobacco Control Program. The Massachusetts Tobacco Control Program (MTCP) has developed a comprehensive statewide tobacco training and certification program (Pbert et al., 2000). To become certified, participants need to complete a basic and advanced course and accrue 2000 hours of experience. The basic course is two days of training, designed for clinicians who encounter tobacco users in their practice. The six-day core certification training provides intensive instruction in the biology and pharmacology of nicotine dependence, counseling, and cessation-related issues.

MAINTENANCE OF SKILLS

How to monitor, refresh, enhance, and in other ways, provide for the maintenance of skills is an important training consideration. Surprisingly, there is little information on strategies to maintain skills post-training yet there is evidence suggesting that the use of tobacco use interventions by healthcare professionals tends to decrease post-training (Cameron et al., submitted; Lancaster et al., 2000).

As part of ongoing training, it is critical to identify options for providing continuing training and act on them. There are substantial data from social learning theory about issues related to maintenance of skills. In practice, success with the application of the skills (and related to the expectations of the individual) affects maintenance, as do feedback and monitoring (Bandura, 1986). It is likely that the educational strategies developed for training in other behaviors and skills, such as prompts and feedback, are applicable to counselors sustaining intervention skills.

Skills are also more likely to be maintained in organizations that implement system-wide tobacco cessation guidelines, policies, and procedures (Taylor & Curry, 2004). Other options include booster sessions with the original training program, scheduling routine seminars, case-conferences, doing literature reviews, bringing in consultants, or encouraging attendance at national meetings that include issues related to tobacco cessation (e.g., Society of Behavioral Medicine, and Society for Nicotine and Tobacco Research).

TRAINING FORMATS AND PARAMETERS

Web-Based Training

Although training has traditionally involved face-to-face sessions, web-based training will play an increasingly important role in healthcare education (e.g., Leong et al., 2003). Thousands of on-line continuing medical education (CME) programs are available and some medical school curricula are provided almost entirely on-line (e.g., Harden & Hart, 2002). Such trainings should theoretically be as effective as computer-based instruction and have the advantage of added features like real-time videoconferencing, support groups, follow-up mailings/information, etc.

Nevertheless, very few studies have evaluated this methodology. Those that have, found web-based instruction is effective for increasing knowledge and self-reported competency (e.g. Curran et al., 2000; Francis et al., 2000). Healthcare practitioners, who have used web-based CME programs, like the convenience and would choose well-designed on-line courses again to meet their continuing education units (Francis et al., 2000). Self-study programs (including web-based ones) are probably effective in providing knowledge but not skills, and, as mentioned, didactic programs without experiential learning are limited in their effectiveness.

Support Materials and Handouts

Regardless of the training format, handouts should be available to cover the required material and help with the intervention. At a minimum, handouts should include reference material and source information for the topics covered in the training. Job aids, such as a standardized delivery protocol (e.g., Figure 12) and laminated algorithms for intervention as suggested in the USDHHS guideline (Fiore et al., 2000), are also helpful.

Quality Assurance and Ongoing Skills Development

Quality assurance involves adherence to providing the intervention in the designated way. In the Staying Free training system, counselors submit an actual audio-taped patient interview that is then scored based on the number of the specific skills delivered. Counselors are given feedback about areas of the intervention that they omit. Using this system in one of our studies, we found that healthcare professionals covered most of the steps whereas non-professional volunteers were much less likely to (Cameron et al., submitted). This finding speaks to the need for careful selection of who should provide the intervention.

Quality assurance based on outcomes (e.g. six month tobacco cessation rate) is a more complicated issue. We believe that the responsibility of the interventionist is to deliver the intervention, and the responsibility of the program designer is to provide an effective intervention. In the best case, with a highly select population (e.g. post MI patients)—25%-40% of patients will relapse within the first year; in a more general population, the relapse rate is 70%-85%. Feedback of these rates can be discouraging and might reflect the limitations of the intervention rather than the skills of the interventionist. However, failure to meet outcome targets should prompt review of how the intervention is being delivered and can serve as a opportunity to encourage further training.

Provider Morale and Burnout

Because many patients relapse, idealistic providers, faced with high workloads are subject to burnout and poor morale. Those in charge of tobacco cessation programs need to routinely assess the morale of the individuals providing the intervention. In preventing burnout and poor morale, it is important that providers put their success (or perceived lack of success) in context. For instance, for those following up on patients involved in our intervention programs, about 75% of patients might be back to tobacco use at the six-month follow-up. This means that an idealistic counselor might face "failure" with 3 out of 4 clients, depending on the population addressed. To counter what can be a demoralizing feeling, it is important for counselors to remember such things as: tobacco use is as addictive as heroin, that a 25% success rate has a huge public health impact, that their responsibility is to deliver the intervention as designed, and that the lack of success in terms of cessation is related to our still imperfect knowledge of tobacco cessation. Other ideas to consider are to balance the job so that directly rewarding tasks are part of one's everyday activity, to create a support system, to create networks with other professionals involved in this work to learn new techniques, and generally to be aware of looking after oneself.

13

Program Evaluation

Every inpatient tobacco cessation program should have some level of evaluation for accounting and program administration purposes. At its core, evaluation involves systematic collection of data that are then analyzed to provide evidence or insight about what is happening with some or all aspects of a program. The data can be used to provide feedback on goals and quality assurance; to determine if the program is working, how well it is working, and how it might be improved; to provide information to stakeholders; to inform decision-making; or, to justify the program's existence by providing quantifiable and qualitative information.

This chapter provides an overview of evaluation, combining both research and program-in-practice perspectives. It is not meant as a definitive guide to evaluation; rather it is designed to provide broad brushstrokes of ideas for evaluation planning. The chapter begins with clarifying the purpose behind doing an evaluation and the importance of stakeholders in evaluation planning. The chapter includes a discussion of pre-program evaluation and how to use models such as the Precede-Proceed Planning Model (Green & Kreuter, 1991) to guide planning given sufficient time and funding. The chapter also provides information on process, impact, and outcome evaluations, and ends with a brief discussion on time-line considerations. For readers new to program evaluation, the National Center For Chronic Disease Prevention and Health Promotion (CDC; 2005) provides a comprehensive introduction to program evaluation.

CLARIFYING THE EVALUATION PURPOSE

The purpose of program evaluation can and will vary from institution to institution. Hospitals implement cessation programs for many reasons, some because a top level executive believes in the value of a tobacco cessation program, others because of a need to adhere to quality assurance indicators such as those required for adult smoking cessation by the Joint Commission on Accreditation of Healthcare Organizations (JCAHO, 2005), and still others for financial reasons such return on investment. It is important to be clear about why the evaluation will be done because the purpose will clarify what needs to be measured, how it needs to be measured, when it needs to be measured, who needs to receive the evaluation, and in what form. Ultimately, the purpose of the evaluation will be clarified by clarifying the primary aims, scope, and objectives of the program (see Chapter 5).

Once the program's primary aims, scope, and objectives are clearly documented, questions that can stimulate clarity around the purpose of the evaluation and data to be collected for an inpatient tobacco cessation program include:

> What are the key questions that require answers?

> Who requires the information, by when, in what form, and how will the information be used?

> Is there urgency for any specific type of information?

> If the ultimate outcomes will take months or even years to be demonstrated, what are the short-term outcomes that can provide ongoing feedback that will aid in sustainability of the program over time?

To facilitate the process of evaluation, a plan should be developed at the outset that includes a clear definition of the purpose of the evaluation and the objectives. The plan should include a summary of the stakeholders and the type of information they require and at what intervals, as well as an identification of existing information and data sources that might be available to assist with the evaluation. Program evaluation planning models, such as the Precede-Proceed Planning Model (Green & Kreuter, 1991) and the RE-AIM model (Glasgow et al., 2004), can be very helpful in the planning process. They not only provide a map or framework for evaluation planning, but can serve to highlight issues and possible areas for evaluation that might not be intuitively apparent at the outset. Following a planning model can also lead to a much more rigorous evaluation than might otherwise be performed.

STAKEHOLDERS AND EVALUATION

Stakeholders are central to program evaluation. Ultimately, they dictate what must be measured and evaluated, and what will be reported and in what form. The most useful way to look at the relationship of stakeholders to evaluation is to think in terms of what data do the various stakeholders want and need in order to continue to support the program and in what format do they want their information (see Chapter 7 for determining what stakeholders might want and need). For example, the JCAHO (n.d.[c-e]) measure sets for acute myocardial infarction, heart failure, and pneumonia require specific measures for adult smoking cessation advice/counseling performance data. The data include the number of patients with a history of smoking cigarettes anytime during the year prior to hospital arrival, the number of patients who receive smoking cessation advice or counseling during the hospital stay, admission date, adult smoking history, birth date, discharge status, and ICD-9-CM principal diagnosis code. The data collection approach for JCAHO requires retrospective data collection from administrative data and medical records, and data are to be reported as a proportion using aggregate data generated from frequency counts.

Similarly, the Health Plan Employer Data and Information Set (HEDIS) medical assistance with smoking cessation measures require the percentage of smokers or recent quitters who received advice to quit smoking from their practitioner; the percentage of smokers or recent quitters whose practitioner discussed smoking cessation medications; and, the percentage of smokers or recent quitters whose practitioner discussed smoking cessation strategies with them (National Committee for Quality Assurance [NCQA], 2004). To provide the denominator for these percentages, a frequency count of all smokers must be tabulated, which in turn requires that tobacco use data be collected on all patients. In order to calculate the numerator of these percentages, physicians must chart when they provide advice, when they discuss cessation medications with their patients, and when they discuss cessation strategies. These data must then be extracted from patient records and summarized for evaluation and reporting.

Internal reporting requirements might be similar or quite different from those of external quality assurance bodies such as JCAHO and HEDIS. For example, department managers might request quarterly up-dates via email on enrollment and one-year cessation numbers by department—this would require daily data collection on enrollment and one-year post-discharge tobacco use status. In contrast, the chief financial officer of the hospital might want detailed hard-copy monthly budget reports—budget reports require up-to-date tracking and reporting of all expenses and revenues, possibly evaluating the actual versus projected budgets. Even public relations could play into evaluation. For example, keeping the local media updated by providing them with semi-annual faxed testimonials about patient satisfaction and cessation success might be important for creating a presence for the program—this type of evaluation would require on-going interviews or surveys with patients regarding their experiences and outcomes.

For research studies, evaluation is often more straight forward, and often better funded, thereby allowing more in-depth data collection. Research evaluations are planned to provide funding agencies, other researchers, and healthcare providers with objective evidence of the implementation process, impact on knowledge, skills, attitudes, and behavior, and outcomes such as cost-effectiveness and cost-benefit. Studies are designed to collect data that will provide answers to specific questions such as *"Does it work?"*, *"For whom does it work?"*, *"Under what conditions does it work?"*, *"How much does it cost?"*, *"Is it more cost-effective than the current gold standard?"*, *"How does it work?"*, *"What is the reach?"*, *"Was it implemented as intended?"*, etc.

Similarly in practice, process, impact, and outcome evaluation are desirable, but rather than simply providing an objective evidence base, evaluation in practice is usually used to make decisions. It is often necessary to satisfy accountability requirements throughout the organization, demonstrate program feasibility to management to assist in decision-making (such as whether to keep or eliminate a program), provide financial outcomes (such as return on investment) to department heads and the chief financial officer, determine employee morale relative to the new program, and/or provide feedback that will inform goal-setting, delivery, training, and maintenance that will ultimately improve patient care.

PRE-PROGRAM EVALUATION

Evaluation can begin before the inpatient tobacco cessation program is actually implemented. Pre-program evaluation can be performed any time prior to a program launch, and can include creating a baseline on various aspects of the organization, policies, patients, providers, social climate, culture, and any other factor that will in any way affect, be affected by, facilitate, or inhibit implementation, delivery, and/or sustainability of the program. Pre-program evaluation can include performing a needs analysis to determine the number of patients who will benefit from an inpatient program and what they want and need from a program. A needs analysis can also be performed to determine staff's perceptions for an inpatient program, who they believe should be responsible for it, what it should entail, and what they believe their involvement should be. Needs-analyses at various ecological levels can help build the business case for the program. The various components of a pre-program evaluation are well-captured in the Precede-Proceed Planning Model (Green & Kreuter, 1991).

Precede-Proceed Planning Model

The Precede-Proceed Planning Model (Green & Kreuter, 1991) provides a framework for pre-program evaluation that is conceptualized as performing a series of "diagnoses" across all ecological levels of the proposed intervention—individuals, interpersonal relationships, organization, and even community. The five phases of diagnoses include social, epidemiological, behavioral and environmental, educational and organizational, and administrative and policy. Whatever is measured prior to the program as a diagnosis can be used as a baseline, and then the same factors can be measured for comparison during implementation, delivery, and program maintenance to determine the effect the program has on the factors of interest.

Social Diagnosis. A social diagnosis, considered Phase 1 in the Precede-Proceed Planning Model, can be done to determine what the implementation process and the program will mean to the various people who will be affected by it, especially in terms of quality of life (Gielen & McDonald, 1997). For example, some staff might have strong opinions about what an inpatient tobacco cessation program will mean to their work life, who should have access to it, and who should provide it. There might be stronger support if they believe a program will impact positively on quality of care and resistance if they perceive a program as a burden placed on them to do more work. For patients, quality of life concerns could include an improvement in health status or a decrease in hospitalizations.

Epidemiological Diagnosis. An epidemiological diagnosis, considered Phase 2 in the Precede-Proceed Planning Model (Gielen & McDonald, 1997), can help clarify the importance of tobacco and health for the institution in terms of the prevalence of tobacco-related diseases and the costs related to treating tobacco-related diseases. Epidemiological data can come from existing published data and papers, and from hospital records. An epidemiological diagnosis can also help identify target groups for intervention and the size of these groups within a given hospital (e.g., post-MI patients, pregnant women, psychiatric patients, etc.).

Behavioral and Environmental Diagnosis. A behavioral and environmental diagnosis, considered Phase 3 in the Precede-Proceed Planning Model, can be performed to identify influential behavioral and environmental factors that will either facilitate or hinder the implementation of the program (Gielen & McDonald, 1997). It can include data collection to determine whether staff already provide cessation services and why or why not, what would increase their ability to provide services, and whether there is currently support from supervisors to counsel patients about tobacco. Behavioral factors for both staff and patients can be tracked over time to determine whether the trends are in the right direction for variables of interest.

Other environmental factors that could influence tobacco counseling include insurance coverage for cessation counseling and cessation aids (bupropion and nicotine replacement), the ability of clinicians to charge for tobacco consults, and environmental perceptions such as social/cultural factors that would increase staff's ability to provide cessation services. Environmental factors involving patients could include the availability of the cessation provider, privacy of counseling during hospitalization, and the availability of print materials and electronic equipment in patients rooms to allow viewing or listening to cessation videos/DVDs, audiotapes, and/or CDs.

Educational and Organizational Diagnosis. An educational and organizational diagnosis, considered Phase 4 in the Precede-Proceed Planning Model, can be performed to identify the predisposing, reinforcing, and enabling factors that encourage and/or sustain the change processes (Gielen & McDonald, 1997). Table 17 provides examples of predisposing, reinforcing, and enabling factors that could be measured based on staff and patient input.

Table 17. Examples of Predisposing, Reinforcing, and Enabling Factors for Educational and Organizational Evaluation

Staff	Patients
Predisposing Factors	
➤ motivation to counsel patients	➤ motivation to quit
➤ tobacco counseling knowledge	➤ risk and benefit knowledge
➤ attitudes towards counseling	➤ attitudes towards quitting
➤ beliefs about tobacco counseling	➤ beliefs about quitting
➤ personal preferences about counseling	➤ personal preferences about quitting
➤ skills to counsel	➤ self-adjustment skills to quit
➤ self-efficacy to counsel	➤ self-efficacy to quit
Reinforcing Factors	
➤ incentives to counsel	➤ incentives to quit
➤ disincentives to counsel	➤ disincentives to quit
➤ supervisors' support to counsel	➤ support from friends and family
➤ co-workers' support to counsel	➤ social support at work
➤ unions' support to counsel	➤ smoke-free workplace
➤ patients' responses to counseling	➤ smoke-free home & car
➤ reactions from patients' families	➤ existence of triggers to smoke
➤ satisfaction with the program	➤ satisfaction with the program
➤ enhanced self-efficacy to counsel	➤ enhanced self-efficacy to quit
Enabling Factors	
➤ training	➤ program availability
➤ required charting	➤ insurance coverage
➤ availability of referral services	➤ program cost
➤ availability of patient materials	➤ social support

Most of the factors in Table 17 could be measured before the program is implemented and then again after the program is implemented to determine where changes might lie. For example, pre-post measures of predisposing factors could include staff's knowledge, attitudes, beliefs, and self-efficacy about providing cessation services. Pre-post measures of reinforcing factors could include social support for providing counseling and/or patients' responses (positive or negative) to being provided tobacco cessation services. Pre-post measures for enabling factors could include availability of cessation resources such as patient materials or training programs for staff. A few of the factors shown in Table 17, such as satisfaction with the program, can only be measured after the program is implemented.

Administrative and Policy Diagnosis. An administrative and policy diagnosis, considered Phase 5 in the Precede-Proceed Planning Model (Gielen & McDonald, 1997), can be performed to identify the policies, resources, and circumstances in the organization that will facilitate and hinder the implementation and sustainability of the program, and/or create boundaries of operation. For example, there might be policies regarding program delivery, data collection and storage, pharmacotherapy, privacy of patient information, charting, cost recovery, and in-service training.

PROCESS EVALUATION

Process evaluation, corresponding to Phases 6 and 7 in the Precede-Proceed Planning Model, begins in the implementation and program launch phases and can continue over the life of the program (Gielen & McDonald, 1997). Process evaluation typically involves determining the extent to which the program was implemented according to protocol (fidelity of implementation). This type of evaluation can also provide insight into exactly what took place during implementation, what went well and what did not, the barriers and facilitating factors encountered, the barriers that were successfully overcome, and the barriers that remain challenging and why. After the initial program launch, process evaluation can include an ongoing evaluation of the program activities (e.g., the number of trainings per month) and fidelity of program delivery, where the program is successful and where it is breaking down, and what might be needed in order to enhance program delivery.

As previously mentioned, if a pre-program evaluation is performed, process evaluation can be designed to measure progress on all of the factors measured in the pre-program diagnosis. In addition to what might have been measured pre-program, the following are some specific suggestions for process evaluation of factors that could only happen during or after implementation. Evaluation of these factors can be helpful for providing updates at regular monthly meetings.

Process Evaluation of Training

Process evaluation can provide immediate and informative feedback relative to training. Evaluation could include any or all of the following aspects of training:

> ➤ degree of training across departments (e.g., 45% of departments have received at least one training)

> ➤ frequency counts of training by department (e.g., ICU has received 3 trainings, ER has received 2 trainings, etc.)

> ➤ frequency counts of how many staff are trained (total, by department, by profession, etc.)

> ➤ number of trainings required to train all staff in each department (e.g., surgery required 7 trainings to reach all clinicians, medicine has received 5 trainings thus far but only 70% have been trained, etc.)

> ➤ identification of departments that are easy and difficult to schedule for trainings and why

> ➤ extent of training (e.g., ICU has thus far only received training on withdrawal and nicotine replacement therapy)

> ➤ duration of training (e.g., nurses are able to attend 1 hour trainings, physicians have been able to attend only 15 minute sessions, etc.)

> ➤ skill-building activities (e.g., role playing, practice patients, etc.)

For example, a 2-month process evaluation report might show that the cessation counselor has provided at least three in-service trainings per week over the first three months of operation, 40% of departments have had at least one in-service, and Unit A has been difficult to schedule due to flu outbreaks and floor closures.

Process Evaluation of the Identification of Tobacco Use

Assessing the fidelity of tobacco use identification will likely be a key component of process evaluation. Fidelity of tobacco use identification systems can be determined by comparing a bed-to-bed check of tobacco use with tobacco use recorded in patients' charts. It is also helpful to identify patterns in missing or incorrectly recorded tobacco use data. For example, if tobacco use is on the admitting forms and asked by admitting staff, a fidelity check for tobacco use recording across staffing shifts might reveal patterns.

Process Evaluation of Program Delivery

Fidelity of program delivery can be determined by recording how much of the program is being delivered to each patient. Data can be collected by shadowing cessation providers with a detailed checklist of program components, by tape-recording counseling cessations, and/or by creating self-report program delivery sheets with an inventory of components that the cessation counselor completes.

Process Evaluation of Post-Discharge Counseling and Status Follow-Up

If post-discharge counseling and follow-up of tobacco use status are performed by telephone, the completeness of each call according to protocol can be measured using self-report checklists, shadowing, and tape-recording calls (with patients' permission). Evaluation can also be designed to determine the total number of call attempts performed for each scheduled call, the number of call attempts it takes to reach patients, the number of scheduled calls that are abandoned because patients cannot be reached, the reasons for missed calls, and the number of patients who receive each scheduled call. If post-discharge counseling is face-to-face, appointments can be audio or video-recorded (with patients' permission), supervised, or counselors can self-report on what was covered using a standardized checklist.

Process Evaluation of Data Collection

The accuracy and completeness of data collection and entry can be evaluated by performing data checks. This could be considered a quality assurance check as much as process evaluation. Fidelity checks for data collection could include reviewing the hardcopy and electronic data collection forms for missing data, completeness of answers, and patterns of missing data. For example, we have found that data questions that are frequently missed are those that have to do with retrospective recall about events that might have taken place in the distant past, such as the number and duration of quit attempts, reasons for relapsing, dates, and number and reasons for previous hospitalizations. Other data collection errors include ranges where only a single number should be (e.g., 17-20 cigarettes/day versus 20), text where numbers should be (e.g., patient usually smokes 1 or 2 before getting out of bed versus "2"), and date reversals (e.g., using today's date for a birth date).

If data collection is computerized, it can also be easily checked for aggregated data error patterns, out-of-range values, outliers, and incorrect responses such as date reversals. Data accuracy can be reported as a frequency or proportion. Fidelity checks of data collection and data entry serve to identify and correct problems with data collection early on in the implementation and delivery process as well as on an ongoing basis.

Process Evaluation of Marketing and Promotion

Promotion efforts can be evaluated and should not be overlooked as part of the process evaluation. Evaluation can include the time and cost spent on promotion (e.g., design, printing, distribution), and the degree to which the program was promoted and where. For example, the number of notices sent to physicians, the number of in-service trainings, the number of stories appearing in the local media, the percentage of patient rooms and staff lounges in which a poster promoting the tobacco cessation services was posted, and the number of staff adhering to promotional requests, such as wearing badges that advertise the program, could all provide sources for process evaluation.

IMPACT EVALUATION

Impact evaluation, corresponding to Phase 8 in the Precede-Proceed Planning Model (Green & Kreuter, 1991), involves examination of the direct results of the program relative to changes in behavioral and environmental factors and to changes in the predisposing, reinforcing, and enabling factors. If a pre-program evaluation was performed as a baseline, an impact evaluation can be designed to measure changes in the factors that were measured pre-program.

For example, changes in behavioral factors could include an increase in the number of clinicians recording tobacco consults in patients' charts. Environmental impact could include an increase in the number of posters advertising the inpatient tobacco cessation program displayed in patients' rooms and staff lounges. A change in predisposing factors could include changes in clinicians' knowledge, skills, attitudes, self-efficacy, and motivation following training (in a positive or negative direction). A change in reinforcing factors could include an increase in the percentage of supervisors that encourage staff to counsel patients on tobacco cessation. A change in enabling factors could include an increase in resources such as pamphlets or workbooks provided to each unit. Some of these variables are captured in the pre-program evaluation section (see also Table 17).

Impact evaluation can also include various aspects of the reach of a program. Reach can be operationalized as the percentage of all new admissions identified as tobacco users, the percentage of all identified tobacco users who were offered an intervention, the percentage of all tobacco users who accepted tobacco services, and/or the percentage of all tobacco users who received at least one post-discharge follow-up call. Impact evaluations can also include program awareness in terms of how many people have heard about the program (both patients and staff), what they know about the program, and satisfaction among staff and patients regarding the program and delivery.

Other impact factors could include a description of who is participating in the program (i.e., who is impacted by the program and who is not) described by demographics, smoking history, and/or medical condition, repeat participation rates, cessation rates at various time points (e.g., in-hospital, and 3, 6, 12 months post-discharge), and behavioral changes in tobacco use, such as cutting back cigarettes on the number of cigarettes smoked per day. Evaluation of the impact of the program on environmental changes could include increases in insurance coverage for tobacco counseling and medication to assist in cessation. RE-AIM (Glasgow et al., 2004) is an excellent model to guide impact evaluation.

OUTCOME EVALUATION

Outcome evaluation, corresponding to the final phase (Phase 9) of the Precede-Proceed Planning Model (Green & Kreuter, 1991), involves evaluation of the ultimate goals of the program, such as the effect of the program on health, quality of life, cost indicators, or the degree of compliance with external regulatory bodies such as JCAHO (2005). As with process and impact evaluations, an outcome evaluation can be designed to mirror the pre-program evaluation.

Outcomes are often long-term in nature, taking many years to actualize, such as decreased healthcare utilization with cessation (Wagner et al., 1995). Therefore it is important to collect as many short-term indicators of outcome as possible. Short-term indicators among patients can include perceived health related to quitting status (as a proxy to actual improved health), and perceived quality of healthcare as a result of receiving the cessation program. Other short-term patient outcomes could include changes in post-surgical complications, length of hospital stay, and well being, although these outcomes are multi-determined so it might be difficult to attribute positive changes in these variables to cessation alone or negative outcomes to continued tobacco use. Among providers, short-term outcomes can include comparisons between pre-program and post-launch perceptions or satisfaction with quality of patient care, quality of work life, and morale. Institutional short-term outcomes can include various cost indicators such as cost per quitter, cost per enrolled patient, cost per extra quitter over 'usual care' (such as an outpatient cessation program), and cost per year of life saved compared to 'usual care'.

EVALUATION TIMELINES

Program evaluation can be thought of in phases or stages according to the status of program implementation. The objectives written at each phase—pre-program, launch, delivery, and maintenance, serve as milestones against which data are evaluated. The most useful way to look at the phases is to think in terms of what data can or should be collected at each phase of implementation and why, based on the objectives for each phase. The key is to think in terms of who needs to know what and when.

In terms of scheduling evaluations, it is helpful to think in measurement cycles. What makes sense for a cycle? Are there different cycles for different aspects of the program? For example, do monthly cycles make sense for financial evaluations, quarterly cycles make sense for evaluating recruitment into the program, and annual cycles make sense for measuring the satisfaction of clinicians and cessation counselors with the program? Cycles can be determined from a feasibility perspective, such as the effort required, as well as from a practical perspective, such as making cycles short enough to catch problems or errors that benefit from quick solutions and that would over time pose serious challenges if not corrected (e.g., errors in data collection). It is also helpful to determine organizationally what data are being collected for other purposes and when, and try to cross-reference, map onto their timelines, and share, if the data will be helpful for supporting the inpatient program (e.g., patient flow statistics).

14

Data and Measurement

Data choice will be determined by the primary aims and objectives of the inpatient tobacco cessation program and by the proposed evaluations. In this chapter, we review common measurement considerations to take into account and highlight a few basics of database software and design. We finish the chapter with suggestions for the type data to consider collecting using our studies of Staying Free as the reference point. Although the ideal scenario would be to have sufficient funding to collect data for ongoing process, impact, and outcome evaluations, the reality is that funding and the time available for evaluation are usually limited, with data collection typically involving at most, program context, participant demographic and psychosocial variables, and cessation.

MEASUREMENT CONSIDERATIONS

Data Sources

Data will likely come from four basic sources—direct contact (e.g., face-to-face interviews or counseling), patients' medical records, distributed surveys (e.g., mailed or emailed to patients and staff), and from data that are collected by others (e.g., published population health or state/provincial hospital data, individual hospital data, such as annual live admissions, etc). Each data source will have unique challenges. For example, using data collected by others, including data included in patients' charts and published population data, means that choice might not be available in terms of what and how data are measured. There might be interpretation difficulties for some data collected by others, and challenges might arise with reading hand-writing from patients' hardcopy medical charts. There might also be challenges extracting data collected by others, especially from electronic records, and formatting it into a useable form for evaluation of the tobacco cessation program.

Collecting data directly from patients and staff can also have challenges, such as communication difficulties, missing data due patients not being available or discharged, and patients unable or unwilling to provide information. Data collected via surveys can meet challenges of distribution, cost, readability, interpretation, and low response rates.

Close-Ended Items

It is advisable to use close-ended items that can be easily quantified, summed, averaged, or categorized, rather than using open-ended questions. Responses to close-ended items can be recorded with a simple checkbox whereas open-ended questions require writing text, which takes more time. Open-ended responses are not easily summarized, and terminology and handwriting can pose challenges for those who must read or input the data into a computer from the hard copy.

Closed-ended items are also ready to analyze as soon as the data are inputted, and can be analyzed by anyone proficient at data analyses. Open-ended items require interpretation and categorization, which is more time-consuming and might require someone with special training to do the work. For example, in one of our studies, patients' primary reason for hospitalization was recorded as an open-ended memo field. When it came time to analyze the data, we required someone with a medical background to code the data into categories so that frequencies could be calculated. We now use closed-ended forced choice items that the tobacco cessation counselor codes during the initial counseling session with the patient. This speeds up the process for data collection and analyses.

Continuous and Categorical Data

Closed-ended questions data will be either continuous (e.g., age, number of cigarettes smoked per day) or categorical (e.g., marital status—married, widowed, etc.). It is advisable to keep continuous data continuous (e.g., 26 yr. old) rather than creating artificial categories (e.g., 26 to 35 yr. old)—continuous variables can always be categorized during analyses. When categories are used, they should be standardized whenever possible to allow comparison with other programs and published studies. Standardized categories can be obtained by checking the published literature and by checking with the hospital research department and ethics committee; the latter might have measures considered standard for a given hospital (e.g., the categories used to code ethnicity).

Response Burden

The burden put on participants to answer questions in terms of time and effort is called the response burden. It is important to keep the response burden to a minimum by ensuring that the data being collected are necessary and yet sufficient. One-item screens can minimize the response burden. For example, we use a one-item screen for depressed mood rather than a longer multiple item depression questionnaire. The one-item screen correlates significantly with the short form of the Beck Depression Inventory and has been found to differentiate between non-depressed and depressed patients (King et al., 1989). There is now a two-item for depression that might be preferable to our one-item screen

(Kroenke et al., 2003). When using one-item screens, consideration needs to be given to reliability and validity, and the reason the data are being collected (i.e., for counseling or for predicting outcomes).

Another response burden issue involves data required to test theoretical models of behavior change. Theoretical testing often requires repeat measurement, pre- and post-intervention, to determine whether the intervention resulted in changes to the theoretical variables (e.g., attitudes toward quitting) and if, in turn, these changes resulted in behavior change (e.g., more positive attitudes were related to long-term abstinence). Although many funding agencies require an underlying theory or framework for data collection, data required to test *causal* models of behavior change can push up the patient response burden and substantially increase the time it takes to collect the data, so careful thought must be given to how important it is to include causal testing and what purpose it will serve.

For example, Fishbein and Ajzen's theory of reasoned action (1975), one of the most popular and successfully-tested causal models of behavior change, requires up to 35 to 40 questionnaire items to test the basic constructs in the theory (e.g., attitudes, expectancy-value behavioral beliefs, etc.). These data would be in addition to whatever other data are being collected such as socio-demographics and tobacco history. When theoretical variables are being measured, it is important that the measures have high reliability and validity. Therefore it is usually desirable to use published scales—developing new measures with adequate psychometric properties is a long process.

Reliability of Patient Recall

Patient recall might be poor, unreliable, or biased for some types of data such as dates (e.g., quit dates), frequencies (e.g., previous use of medication or number of quit attempts), duration (e.g., the length quit attempts), amounts (e.g., dosage of bupropion or nicotine replacement), and reasons for doing what they did (e.g., relapsing after a quit attempt). One reason for poor recall is simply the passage of time—many of the questions, such as those related to quit attempts, refer to the distant past, often 10-20 years in the past. If patients did not purposefully track their behavior at the time of the quit attempt, or the quit attempt was not associated with a life event (e.g., turning 40 years old), poor recall should be expected and data choices should be made with recall considerations in mind.

Descriptive and Counseling Data Versus Predictive Data

It is important to differentiate among data that will be used to describe the population and data that will be used to predict outcomes. For example, most tobacco histories inquire about the age patients were when they started to use tobacco on a regular basis. The majority of patients will have started using tobacco before turning 20 years of age. That means there will be little variability in the measure of age of uptake, which is not a problem if it is being used to simply describe the population, but renders it questionable for predicting specific outcomes, such as cessation, due to the lack of variance.

Similarly, it is equally important to differentiate between data that are helpful for counseling and data that will be used to predict specific outcomes. Data that will be used to predict outcomes should be collected using standardized measures with published psychometric properties, if possible. This will ensure some level of validity and reliability. In contrast, information collected during counseling sessions to gain a better understanding of patients' experiences and perceptions about such things as previous quit attempts, might be useful from a counseling perspective to help the patient with the current quit attempt, but might tend to be idiosyncratic and/or suffer from recall bias (especially as noted above) so it might not be helpful from a data analysis perspective. For example, information about previous quit attempts can be helpful during a counseling session in terms of having patients reflect on previous successes and potentially high risk situations for relapse. This type of information, however, might not be helpful at an aggregate level for statistical analyses to predict or explain cessation outcomes because most patients will have had experiences unique to their own environments, emotions, and physiology.

DATABASE SOFTWARE AND DESIGN CONSIDERATIONS

In order to facilitate easy access and analyses of the data, it is essential to have some sort of computerized storage of the data. The best option is database software rather than spreadsheet or word processing software because it is more malleable for creating reports and substantially easier to search and update. The rule of thumb with software solutions is to keep it as simple as possible to get the job done.

The sophistication of the database will depend on how it will be used and by whom. If the database will only be used by one person in one hospital at any given time, it can programmed as a regular database program on a single computer. This may allow an off-the-shelf database program that can be easily designed to meet evaluation needs to be used, such as Microsoft Access^{TM} or FileMaker Pro^{TM}. Most people with a general comfort level with computers can learn to tailor basic off-the-shelf database programs to meet their needs. If more than one person at a time will require access to the database files through multiple computers or if multiple sites will be using the database, a file format that can be accessed through the web simultaneously by many people would be the better choice. Although many database programs, such as FileMaker Pro[TM], have the capacity to connect many users to the same program, designing the database for multiple users might require more complex programming by a computer programmer.

Before the information technology (IT) department in the hospital (or a computer programming consultant) is approached for help or suggestions, it is important and cost-efficient to clarify exactly what data will be collected, how the questions will be formatted (e.g., closed-ended with four options numbered 1-4), when the data will be collected, and by whom. The data collection forms, along with "data codes" fore each item (e.g., the 8 digit maximum required by SPSS, such as "educ" for "education") should be typed so that the items, response choices, and data codes are clear.

The following are a few suggestions to ease the process and minimize the cost of database design:

➢ Decide whether to add a "do not know" or "not answered" category for each item. Doing this in the preparation stage is less complicated than revising the computer program.

➢ Add sufficient notes/memo/text fields for explanations. For example, some items, such as the longest time a patient has been off cigarettes, might seem straight forward, but some patients might have been unintentionally off cigarettes for a month due to a severe illness and hospitalization and this will need to be noted—it might be important to capture this type of information for descriptive and statistical purposes.

➢ Include scripts on the data collection forms that guide counselors through the form. For example, if a patient has never had a quit attempt, it is helpful for the counselor to follow a script on the data collection form that directs the counselor to the first item following the quit attempt questions because the quit attempt questions will be not applicable to patients who have never had a quit attempt. Also determine how these skipped items will be coded (e.g., not applicable [n/a]), so that they will not appear as "missing" data.

➢ Clarify the sequential order of the data collection forms beginning with tobacco use identification and screening and progressing to in-hospital data collection and post-discharge follow-up. The order is a necessary part of the programming.

➢ Determine whether the database needs to "talk" to any other computer programs such as the electronic medical records or a daily planner. For example, it might be possible to extract information directly from medical records, such as admission or discharge dates, and it might be possible to program post-discharge follow-up calls in a daily planner based on discharge dates.

> If multiple sites will be involved and each will be using their own desktop programs rather than a web-based software program, clarify how and when the data will be integrated into a single master database, and how updates and changes to patient files will be integrated into the master database. Even in individual desktop applications, it is important to determine how frequently data will be updated and how it will be done. Most, but not all, database programs have the capacity to update information—make sure this feature exists when choosing an application.

After having used a number of databases, and often being held hostage to the intricacies of them, we highly recommend taking a course in working with the database that will be used and to get as familiar with it as possible, including expanding skills to make small changes to the program, such as adding a data collection item or adding an item option to a question already in the database.

Data Entry

A computerized system for storing prevalence data is highly recommended. Data can be entered directly into a computer at the time of collection, or recorded first on paper and then entered into a computer later for storage and easy tabulation and analyses. Our preference is to enter data directly into a computer during data collection—it is less time-consuming and more cost-efficient. Direct data entry into a computer at the bedside requires either a laptop or handheld computer, both of which can be programmed to download easily to a desktop computer for data analyses and reports. Bedside entry highlights the need to have as many of the questions as possible formatted with closed-ended options that allow a single click on an answer box.

If data are recorded first on paper, it is advisable to enter the data daily into the computer to avoid backlogs that can become considerably time-consuming for data entry. Daily entry of data also enables almost effortless updates or reports of program status to be prepared at any time.

Creating Reports Effortlessly Using a Database Program

If a database program is designed and data are entered daily and cleaned frequently (daily or weekly), creating reports should be relatively effortless. Effortless reports require determining what information the various stakeholders need, when they need it, how often they need it, and in what form. Template reports can be designed by the IT department (or computer programmer) that focus specifically on the information required by the various stakeholders.

When templates are developed as part of implementation planning, creating a report becomes as simple as pulling up a given report template and executing the command. For example, a department head might want to know the number of tobacco users admitted to the hospital over the previous month, the percentage of patients who accept and refuse tobacco cessation services, and year-to-date cessation rates. If this template has been designed and the data have been cleaned as part of the daily or weekly work routine, it will take literally seconds to generate the report.

Although reports are easy to produce and can be scheduled as part of the regular work routine, their importance should not be underestimated. Regular reports can showcase a program and the providers, and potentially provide the ongoing information necessary to keep the program alive and well (and in the budget).

WHAT TO MEASURE

Although the actual data that will be collected by each institution will be determined by the primary aims of the program and will vary by the various types of evaluation that are planned, the following section provides suggestions for the types of patient data that can be helpful for counseling purposes as well as impact evaluation (we included more detailed information about big picture process data in the previous chapter on evaluation). The suggestions are based on our work with Staying Free. In general, what to measure should ideally include contextual information and program description, screening, reach, participant data (demographics, psychosocial and socio-environmental, tobacco history, and medical conditions), and tobacco cessation.

Context and Program Description

It is helpful to document basic information about the program, providers, facilities, and program procedures/methods at the outset. This type of information will provide the basic context into which the program is implemented. Once documented, it can be used for internal reports such as in an inventory of programs offered by the hospital or for various hospital promotions, and will provide basic information for new providers taking over the position of tobacco counselor. Externally the information might be used in publications submitted to scientific or medical journals or newsletters, or to provide an overview for the contemporary media.

Context information can include:

> a description of the types of counselors involved with the program, including educational background (e.g., BScN-trained nurses)

> the length and type of training for the cessation program (e.g., one week of theory, role-playing, and shadowing by a cessation specialist)

> the facility (e.g., type of hospital, number of beds, location)

> the patient materials used along with their source information and costs (e.g., workbooks from a non-profit agency at $2/each)

> the process of informed consent if applicable, and documented clearance/approval by the review boards involved

> the recruitment methods and timing (e.g., approach patients at the bedside after they are sufficiently medically stabilized)

> where and how the intervention take places (e.g., in-hospital, post-discharge by telephone, etc.)

> the components of the program (e.g., face-to-face and telephone counseling, take-home materials, group sessions, etc.)

> the timing of delivery (one hour during hospitalization, four 10-minute post-discharge telephone counseling contacts)

> quality assurance and/or goals of the program

Tobacco Use Prevalence

The tobacco use prevalence of all hospitalized patients over a given period of time can be calculated (or estimated) using a ratio—all new daily admissions to the hospital, regardless of tobacco-use status, serves as the denominator, and the number of identified tobacco users serves as the numerator. A frequency count of all daily admissions along with tobacco use status can help determine the change in tobacco use prevalence over time, which might become an important factor as tobacco use prevalence in the general population decreases.

Reach

In our work, we have operationalized reach as the percentage of identified tobacco users that accept tobacco cessation counseling. In order to calculate the percentage who accept, the number who are ineligible by program criteria and the number who refuse also have to be calculated. The daily hospital census can be used to identify the total number of patients who report using tobacco—this serves as the denominator. Table 18 provides an example of the daily admissions data collection system we developed for one of our recent studies to calculate the number of patients who accept the program—this serves as the numerator in the ratio to calculate reach.

Table 18. Example Data Collection Form for Program Reach

Week: Jan 2-8, 2006	S	M	T	W	...
Ineligible to screen	6				
OB	1				
Newborns	2				
Pediatrics	1				
Psych/Substance	2				
Eligible to screen	9				
Total new admits	15				
Among Eligible to Screen					
< 45 yr old smokers	2				
≥ 45 yr old smokers	1				
Total smokers (30%)	3				
Enrollment					
Accept program	1				
Excluded	1				
Med. complicated	*(1)*				
Confused					
< 36 hours					
Communication					
Refuse program	1				
Do not want to quit					
Quit on own	*(1)*				
Other					

Data collection for ineligibility/eligibility can be done relatively expediently with access to patient charts and using a yes-no closed-ended item format for each exclusion criterion (e.g., pediatric—yes/no). Even with the tight eligibility criteria for randomized trials, we have found that 98.5% of ineligible patients can be identified from a chart review. Acceptance and refusal data, however, require a trip to the bedside. Keeping accurate data on the number of patients who do not meet inclusion criteria (e.g., patients with a psychiatric disorder) helps to objectively determine whether the numbers are large enough for any exclusion category to warrant designing new program delivery formats that are more inclusive.

Screening Data

Screening data should include frequencies of reasons for program ineligibility, program acceptance, program refusal (see Table 18), and at least minimal demographic data such as age, gender, and primary reason for hospitalization. If it is possible to collect them, demographic data allow a basic description of who is enrolling in a program and who is not.

Table 19 provides data from one of our dissemination studies (Smith et al., 2002). of note, is that broad categories for primary reason for hospitalization are used. As previously mentioned, we recommend presenting the categories as closed-ended options for data collection with a back-up memo field to describe specifics. Memo-only data make data entry difficult by someone who does not understand medical terminology. However, having a memo backup for specifics is helpful because it allows reliability checks for primary reason categorization.

In one of our recent studies we also included closed-ended specifics for each of the subcategories of reasons for hospitalization (e.g., gastro-intestinal under the general category of other internal medicine) but found that there were few patients for any specific reason so analyses by specific reason were not meaningful. The one exception is with cardiovascular disease—it is useful to identify patients who have had a myocardial infarction (MI). Post-MI patients tend to be the most likely to enroll in a tobacco cessation program. They also tend to have the highest cessation rates of all patients so the overall cessation rates for any given program will be affected by the number of post-MI patients enrolled, such that overall cessation rates will increase as the number of post-MI patients enrolled increases.

Participant Data

If data for the program will be published, it will be necessary to collect basic participant data such as demographics (e.g., age, gender, employment, marital status, education, ethnicity, etc.), tobacco history, in-hospital tobacco use, and psychosocial, socio-environmental and medical/hospitalization-related data. These data are usually collected prior to delivering the cessation intervention, and provide a baseline description of participants. Some of the variables might also be collected during the intervention and follow-up to show change over time. It is most efficient to enter baseline data into a database program at the time it is collected, using a laptop or handheld computer. If patients will be followed up after hospital discharge, it will be necessary to collect basic contact information including the addresses, phone numbers, email, and the names and phone numbers of three of the patient's friends, family, or co-workers who would be able to contact the patient or provide change of address/number information if the patient moves.

Table 19. Example Presentation of Screening Data: Ineligibility, Acceptance, and Refusal By Demographic Characteristics

	Ineligible	Participated	Quit on own	Don't want to quit
Age	54 ± 17	52 ± 14	56 ± 16	52 ± 16
Males	12%	53%	18%	17%
Ethnicity				
Caucasian	9%	61%	20%	10%
African-American	25%	46%	21%	19%
Hispanic	11%	63%	16%	9%
Asian	0%	51%	17%	29%
Other	15%	42%	15%	30%
Primary Reason				
Cardiovascular	9%	61%	20%	10%
Cancer	13%	46%	21%	19%
Pulmonary	11%	63%	16%	9%
GYN	4%	51%	17%	29%
Internal Medicine	13%	42%	15%	30%
Orthopedic	3%	46%	20%	31%
Non-cardiac surgery	20%	56%	12%	12%

Smith et al., 2002

The following section includes the basic participant data we have collected in our studies.

Tobacco History. The essential tobacco history data include the amount and type of tobacco used prior to hospitalization (e.g., 25 cigarettes/day), and a measure of addiction, either the Fagerstrom Tolerance Questionnaire

(Fagerstrom, 1978) or the modified Fagerstrom Tolerance Questionnaire (Killen & Fortmann, 1994).

Optional information for descriptive and counseling purposes includes a partial or full tobacco use history:

> how old patients were when they started using tobacco

> how many years patients have used tobacco on a regular basis

> reasons patients use tobacco

> how many quit attempts patients have made in the past and whether the quit attempts were voluntary or forced (e.g., hospitalization)

> how long patients' quit attempts lasted

> whether patients have ever quit for at least 7 days

> when was their last quit attempt

> what was their longest quit attempt

> methods patients have used to try to quit

> the most effective methods patients have found for quitting

> reasons for relapsing

> whether patients have used quitting aids, such as nicotine replacement therapy or bupropion, and if they have, how often, what doses, whether they experienced any side-effects, and their perceived efficacy of medication aids

It is important to note that many patients have difficulty remembering specific dates and details about their tobacco history, especially if they have tried multiple times to quit over a number of years, so reliability of recall might be not be high. Patients also have varying interpretations of what they are being asked. For example, what constitutes a quit attempt for one person might not apply to another—some patients consider forced unintended abstinences due to hospitalization as quit attempts whereas others do not, and some patients will report that they have seriously tried to quit hundreds of times but only ever succeed for a few hours before relapsing whereas others will only count attempts longer than one day or one week as an actual quit attempt.

In-Hospital Tobacco Use and Withdrawal. We recommend asking patients if they have used tobacco during their hospitalization, and if so, how much and how often. Although these data might not be very useful in prediction equations because very few patients (about 10%) tend to use tobacco during hospitalization, they can provide insight for counseling purposes—most patients who do use tobacco during hospitalization will continue to use tobacco throughout their stay and post-discharge. Hence, asking the question might allow the patient to be further encouraged to quit during hospitalization, thereby increasing their chances of being tobacco-free post-discharge. We also ask whether patients have experienced withdrawal during hospitalization and how severe it was; it is surprising how few patients do experience withdrawal, and among those who are having difficulty, asking the question can open up a discussion about nicotine replacement therapy. These data have been more useful for counseling than prediction.

Psychosocial. The psychosocial factors most predictive of abstinence that we have found across studies include patients' confidence to remain tobacco-free (self-efficacy), depressed mood in the month prior to hospitalization, and weekly alcohol use (Smith et al., 1999), so we recommend collecting these data at a minimum. For confidence, we use a single-item screen, scored in increments of 10 from 0% to 100%. (We also use a 14-item self-efficacy scale [Baer et al., 1986] for counseling purposes to help patients identify high risk situations for relapse; this scale is best used for counseling purposes only, because high risk situations will differ across patients making it difficult to have much predictive validity for any one situation or item.) For depressed mood, we use a single-item screen, scored from 0 (not at all depressed) to 8 (severely depressed). For alcohol, we measure the frequency of use (six options from never to daily), weekly alcohol intake categorized by beer, wine, highballs, and liqueurs, and the 4-item CAGE alcohol dependence screen (Buchsbaum et al., 1991).

Social-Environmental. Research shows that important factors in remaining tobacco-free are having tobacco-free homes and workplaces (Farkas et al., 2000), so we recommend including a single forced-choice item for smoking bans in the home (completely banned, banned in most rooms, allowed with restrictions, no restrictions) and workplace (not allowed in any areas, allowed in some areas, allowed in all areas, does not apply). Social support for quitting is also an important determinant of abstinence, so we include whether patients have someone they can turn to in times of need, how many others smoke in the house, and whether those closest to them support their quitting (Sherbourne & Stewart, 1991). These latter items are important, but more so for counseling and descriptive purposes rather than for use in prediction equations because the vast majority of patients do have someone they can turn to and others do support their quitting (approximately 90%), so there is little variance within any of the measures. We also ask patients if they live alone.

Medical and Hospitalization-Related Data. The type of hospitalization data collected will vary by the primary aims of the program. For example, if one of the primary aims is to meet the Joint Commission on the Accreditation of Healthcare Organizations standards (JCAHO, 2005), data collected will have to include admission date, birth date, discharge status, and ICD-9-CM principal diagnosis code.

One of the most helpful pieces of information to collect is the primary reason for hospitalization, collected in a forced-choice format as mentioned above. Although the primary reason might include symptoms more so than diagnoses because the data are based on the information provided to the admitting staff, they are easier to collect than discharge diagnoses (as per ICD-9 codes) and we have found that the categories we use (Table 19) tend to correlate highly with discharge diagnoses using the same categories. Discharge diagnoses take more effort to collect because they require retrospective chart reviews (they are not coded until after patients are discharged). So unless discharge diagnoses are required, as they are for JCAHO, we suggest using primary reasons for hospitalization because these data are available on the daily hospital census and are easy to collect.

Optional hospital data include length of stay, use of medication aids such as bupropion and nicotine replacement therapy (NRT) during hospitalization, whether patients received physician advice to quit during hospitalization, and information about previous hospitalizations. These data tend to be informative from a counseling perspective but not very useful for predicting who quits and who does not. This might be due to a variety of reasons. For example, NRT and bupropion data can be cumbersome to collect—patients could potentially begin using these medication aids at any point during hospitalization, which in turn, necessitates repeated review of patients' charts until they are discharged. NRT could be purchased over the counter and therefore not recorded in the chart, or a prescription for bupropion provided during hospitalization might not get filled or used. Physician advice could be missing due to charting inconsistencies. There are multiple determinants of longer hospital stays and previous hospitalizations that could be related to tobacco use in various and inconsistent ways.

Cessation Data

The ideal cessation data include tobacco use data collected at 3, 6, and 12 months post-discharge (longer if possible) using the National Heart, Lung, and Blood Institute's (NHLBI) consensus conference definition of self-reported 7-day point prevalence (not even a puff for a minimum of seven consecutive days prior to the time of assessment) and long-term (continuous) abstinence (self-reported 7-day point-prevalence at all follow-ups, 3, 6, and 12 months) (Ossip-Klein et al., 1986). These definitions of cessation and schedule of data collection allow for comparison across published studies. For patients who are using tobacco at follow-up, it can be informative to ask about the amount and type of tobacco being used (e.g., some patients switch to pipes or cigars believing them to be less harmful than cigarettes). Optional data are corroboration of point-prevalence status at 12-months by saliva cotinine or proxy confirmation, and corroboration of long-term (point-prevalence continuous) abstinence using self-reported continuous abstinence at 3, 6, and 12 months (not even a puff from discharge to the follow-up date).

We also recommend asking patients at all post-discharge scheduled follow-ups whether they used medication to help them quit (e.g., bupropion or NRT) as well as the dose they took and the length of time they used it. Although patient recall is not always good for dose, they can often provide insight that is helpful in determining dose (e.g., purple pill twice a day). We also ask whether patients used other programs or health professionals to help them quit—very few do use other services (less than 4%), so the item is not usually helpful in predicting who quits and who does not. Other helpful information includes recording the number of counseling sessions received to determine fidelity of intervention delivery and to allow cessation data to be analyzed by amount of contact received.

Optional information includes the amount of time patients were tobacco-free before having their first cigarette, number of relapses, the length of each relapse, the average number of cigarettes smoked during each relapse, and the reasons for relapse. Recall may not be reliable unless patients were asked to record this information. Many journal reviewers request information such as how long patients were off tobacco before relapsing or the date of relapse so that survival analyses can be performed, but we have found that patients have difficulty recalling specifics, especially if they have made multiple attempts to quit post-discharge.

15

Program Promotion

One way to enhance the success of an inpatient tobacco cessation program is to increase its visibility through direct marketing and promotion. Ideally, promotion should include a long-range written plan that begins with pre-program announcements and covers at least the first year of the program. Although there are a number of options to choose from for promotion, choices are best made grounded in program goals and keeping to a simple standardized look that becomes a signature of the program. New programs might need more promotion than existing programs, but all programs should be continuously promoted.

In this chapter, we provide an overview of marketing and promoting an inpatient tobacco cessation program. Included are suggestions to cover the basics of promotion, using examples of ways Staying Free has been promoted. We begin with planning promotion, promotion options, and the basics of a standardized look. The chapter ends with suggestions for working with the media. This chapter is not meant to be a definitive source of information on promotion. Rather, the information in this chapter represents our working knowledge of program promotion that has been gleaned from countless experts and experience with promoting Staying Free over the years.

PLANNING PROMOTION

It is helpful to think of the promotion plan in terms of the who, what, where, why, how, when, and the message target, following from the persuasive communication literature. *Who* is the target audience for the message and can include the institution, healthcare providers, patients, patients' families, agencies, and the community in general. *What* is the message content, which will likely differ across different target audiences. *Where* is the placement of the promotion (e.g., patients' rooms, staff lounges). *How* is the delivery medium (e.g., in-service, pamphlets, etc.). *Why* is the reason for the promotion (e.g., to introduce a new program, compliance with asking about tobacco use is low, etc.). *When* is the frequency and/or timing of the promotion. And the *message target* is specifically what the message is designed to accomplish, such as increase awareness, motivation, or behavior. The who, what, where, why, how, when, and message target are most easily identified by using the program goals to plan promotion.

Using Program Goals to Plan Promotion

Achievement of the goals of the inpatient tobacco cessation program should be central to the marketing and promotion of the program. Since program goals will vary across institutions, there is no "one-size fits all" when it comes to marketing and promotion planning. Ideally, messages should be targeted toward benchmark goals, which will, in turn, elucidate the who, what, where, why, how, when, and message target for promotion planning. By their very nature, benchmark goals define the target audience (*who*) and desired outcome (*message target*). The benchmark itself, also helps inform what the promotional message should say (*what*), the media that should be used to promote the message (*how*), the placement of the messages internally and externally to the hospital (*where*), the best time to expose a given target audience to a given message (*when*), and the reason for the promotion (*why*). The key to using benchmark goals to guide promotion is evaluation of all promotion efforts.

An example of a benchmark goal might be to increase to 100% in the first year of the program the percentage of patients who are asked about tobacco use. Assuming that the tobacco use question is added to the admitting records and it is to be asked by admitting staff, achieving this benchmark would require a promotional "campaign" around ensuring all admitting staff are aware of the tobacco use question on the admitting forms and the need to fill it out for every patient. Promotional timing for this benchmark goal should include consideration for front-end loading efforts, beginning prior to the program being officially launched and continuing for at least the first few months of program roll-out. Tracking compliance of completion of the tobacco use item would provide feedback on promotional efforts and indicate whether additional promotion was necessary, and if so, when, how, and for whom.

Other benchmark goals that could be used to guide promotion planning include increasing clinician and/or patient awareness and/or participation. For example, a benchmark goal might be to increase by 10% in the first year of the program the percentage of clinicians who advise their patients to quit using tobacco. Promotional efforts could include developing a series of messages that instruct clinicians to "advise their patients to quit". The messages could all be the same but be disseminated using different media, such as placing posters in staff and physicians' lounges, putting postcard reminders into clinicians' hospital mailboxes, sending out email messages, and/or by providing 5-minute monthly in-services at department meetings. Tracking promotional outcomes is key.

Similarly, a benchmark goal of increasing by 50% in the first year of the program awareness of the program among patients and their families might be chosen. This could involve placing posters and pamphlets in patients' rooms, writing an article for the local newspaper or patient newsletter, giving local radio and cable television interviews about the program, and having staff nurses wear an "Ask me about quitting smoking" badge.

Streamlining Promotion

By using goals as the guide for planning promotion, different messages can be developed for different target audiences and placed in different locations but the same medium and even the same basic background design (for print promotions) can be used, thereby streamlining the promotion efforts and minimizing costs. For example, a series of simple posters could be developed, each using the same basic layout and graphics but tailored to target different program goals by changing only the text lines in the poster and by strategically placing the posters to maximize exposure to the target audiences. Posters could be placed in the admitting department to cue admitting staff to ask the tobacco use question, in patients' rooms to cue those who use tobacco to consider hospitalization as a time to quit, and in staff lounges to remind clinicians to advise patients to quit.

Keeping Messages Fresh

Part of promotion planning should include strategies to keep the promotional messages fresh, so that the target audiences do not habituate to them and no longer notice them. This will be more of an issue for program promotion to staff than it will be to patients, simply because staff have the potential to see the promotional messages every workday of the year whereas patients will usually only be exposed to the messages during their hospital day (an average of 5-6 days at a time). One option for planning might be to simply move the promotional pieces once every one to three months. That is, move them from one wall to another in the staff lounge, from the back of a washroom stall door to beside the mirror, or from the bulletin board to beside the elevator.

Another option for refreshing messages is to provide program updates to map onto existing promotional pieces, much the way some charity campaigns advertise their success by using ladders or thermometers to show benchmark achievements in donations received. For example, posters could be designed with a "tally box" on the right hand side of a poster; this box could be used to provide updates to staff such as the number of patients who have enrolled in the program. A similar design could be used to motivate patients by using the tally box to provide an update of the number of patients who have successfully quit tobacco using the inpatient tobacco cessation program.

Basic Design

Keeping the promotional design and message simple are ultimately important for information processing by all target audiences. If the message is too wordy or complex, or the design is too busy, it will not be able to cut through all the "noise" to reach the target audiences. Within the hospital itself, the program message is not only competing for attention with people's regular daily routines but also with every other program being promoted in the hospital. The program message will also be competing with announcements of new advancements in medicine and patient care, crises such as infection outbreaks, budget announcements and cuts, morale issues, staff shortage issues, charity requests, pro-social causes, social announcements, and continuing education announcements, to name but a few.

Print promotion—pamphlets, posters, articles in newsletters, and memos or postcards, will likely be the mainstay of the promotion plan. For print advertising, it is best to stick to the basics of print advertising[9]. Basics include enhancing readability by keeping the background simple and uncluttered so that the message stands out. Photos of people tend to be more eye-catching than plain text alone. Large font text is easier to read than small font, a mix of upper and lower case text ("Title" or "Sentence case") is easier to read than all capital letters, and dark text on a light background (i.e., black on white) is easier to read than light text on a dark background (i.e., white on black). Simple backgrounds and messages also make easier copy to read when faxed, scanned, published in a newsletter or newspaper, or printed off a website.

Messages focused on a single point and using only a few words are not only visually easier to read, but are also easier to comprehend and remember than messages that include lots of text and lots of information. "Readability" for the general population should be kept at a 6th grade level or lower, and messages should be geared to action by telling people what to do and how to do it. For example, an easy-to-read message for patients, written at the 2nd grade level (according to the Flesch-Kincaid reading level grammar check on a basic word-processing software program), and that tells patients what to do and how to do it, would be: *"Quit smoking. Free. Ask your nurse."* This message could appear on a poster, in a newsletter, on a tent-card in patients' rooms, on a hospital information package, on a lapel button, on a coffee mug, or on a pamphlet, to name a few media amenable to this type of message.

Messages to clinicians do not have to be more complex. Although their reading level might allow them to process material written at higher grade levels, clinicians are usually short on time. Therefore, it might be best to catch their attention with a "sound bite", a condensed but meaningful and catchy message, similar in length to a newspaper or magazine article title (and similar to the

---

[9] Elizabeth Adler wrote a super book on this topic: Everyone's Guide to Successful Publications: How to Produce Powerful Brochures, Newsletters, Flyers, and Business Communications, Start to Finish (Peachprint Press, 1993). Although the book is over 10 years old, the basic principles still apply.

"Quit smoking. Free. Ask your nurse." message above). It might be desirable to complement simple messages by providing an opportunity for target audiences with a high need for cognition to easily access more information. For example, it might be helpful to leave a stack of reprints of a relevant tobacco cessation article published in a medical journal under a poster advertising the inpatient tobacco cessation promotion in the physicians' lounge.

Repetition

Promotion does not need to be elaborate or costly, but it does need to be frequent and repetitive. Promotion plans should include strategies in which the target audience can be exposed to the inpatient tobacco cessation messages at least five times. A rule of thumb in sales is that it takes at least five contacts for people to remember a name, or in this case, a service. It is worth noting that although the tobacco cessation program might have a name (e.g., Staying Free) and there is a push in advertising to "brand" products and services for easy recognition and to enhance customer loyalty and sales, there is some evidence to suggest that in the realm of healthcare, people tend to remember the service they receive (e.g., tobacco cessation counseling) rather than the brand name (Staying Free; Smith & Sieswerda, in progress). As such, repetition might be best served by ensuring that the service being offered (i.e., tobacco cessation) is central to the message rather than spending promotional efforts "branding" the name of the service.

PROMOTION OPTIONS

In-Service Information Sessions

In-services to increase awareness of the program and to provide brief training are a good way to promote the cessation program to clinicians and staff. The key is to keep the in-services brief—5 to 10 minute segments. The reason in-services need to be brief is simply that healthcare workers are busy. They might not be able or willing to process large amounts of information or detail about a tobacco cessation program that they might perceive as peripheral to their daily routine. But keeping the program visible and in front of them is important. We have found with our work that the more visible the cessation counselors are, and the more familiar the cessation counselors become to hospital staff, the more hospital staff work to refer patients to tobacco cessation services. Five minute in-services scheduled as part of regular department meetings is very helpful in keeping the program and the counselors visible.

Staged, regularly-scheduled in-services can be developed that will introduce the program in small increments and keep the staff up to date. For example, the first in-service could announce hospital approval to start an inpatient tobacco cessation program. The first in-service could also introduce who will be delivering the program, the basic components of the program, the projected date of start-up, and how it will affect each department.

Additional in-services could be used to announce the launch of the program, information on how tobacco use status will be added to the admitting records and where to look for it on patients' charts, updates on enrollment (overall and by department), updates on cessation, patient and/or staff testimonials, staff concerns and how they are being dealt with, and even brief content trainings for such things as how to help patients with withdrawal during hospitalization with the use of nicotine replacement. It is important to ensure that the key messages for each audience are stressed. For example, physicians need to be informed about their role in providing a clear message to patients to stop smoking and nurses might need to be reminded to evaluate tobacco use and refer patients to the tobacco cessation counselor.

Prior to beginning the Canadian and Stanford studies, we provided in-service information sessions to physicians, nurses, admitting staff, and other interested hospital staff. Each hospital handled the in-service a little differently. In one hospital, we were invited to the annual general meeting of family physicians and were requested to give a presentation on tobacco dependence and treatment, as well as how the proposed inpatient tobacco cessation program would meet the needs of the patients. In another hospital, we were invited to a family practice monthly meeting and asked to provide only information relevant to what the physicians were being asked to do for the inpatient program. In another hospital, we were asked to provide a symposium for all staff (nurses, physicians, and allied healthcare workers) on inpatient tobacco cessation programs and research, which was held in the hospital auditorium. In a number of hospitals we provided in-service information sessions to admitting staff right in the admitting department because they could not leave their posts. For most initial in-services, we included a standardized presentation that introduced the program and procedures. Each presentation was tailored to the group being addressed, clarifying exactly what they were being asked to do. The in-services were preceded and followed up with letters to the various department heads.

Notices

Brief emails or memos can be sent to hospital staff and physicians following a similar pattern of information dissemination as the brief in-services. Notices can be sent out to announce trainings or even to cue staff to watch for an update of the tobacco cessation program in an upcoming in-service. Brief updates can be included in the hospital newsletter (even one-liners such as how many patients to-date have enrolled). The notices should be brief so that they will be read.

Announcements

Part of program promotion can include various forms of announcements such as memos, letters, and articles in the hospital newsletter. In one of our studies, articles, written by hospital staff, were placed in the hospital newsletters that were sent to all hospital staff and were also available to patients and the community. In that study, the chiefs of staff and directors of nursing at all participating hospitals also sent out a memo to their staff informing them of the inpatient tobacco cessation program and what they were being asked to do. The memos were initially drafted by our research team and provided to the chiefs of staff and directors of nursing to edit as they saw fit and to put on their letterhead for distribution. By having the research team draft the memos, it ensured that all the requisite information was included, avoided putting an extra work burden on the individuals involved, and enhanced the likelihood of timely dissemination.

Postcards

In one of our studies, we followed up an initial program announcement letter and in-service to physicians with small postcards, which were placed in physicians' hospital mailboxes. The cards were intended as the third in a series of announcements of the program launch. On one side of the postcard was an announcement about when the inpatient tobacco cessation study would start, and was meant to remind physicians what they were being asked to do (Figure 13). On the other side was the message physicians were being asked to deliver to their patients (Figure 14). It was a replica of the prompt they would find in the patients' charts when their patients enrolled in the tobacco cessation program.

Figure 13. Announcement Postcard to Physicians Side One

Just a Reminder... 	The tobacco cessation research study begins on Monday, November 9, 1998. When you see the Physician Advice Statement on your patients' charts, please provide them with advice to quit smoking. Thank you,

Figure 14. Announcement Postcard to Physicians Side Two

Hospital Tobacco Cessation Program

Physician Advice Statement

Study after study has shown that physicians play an important role in helping patients to stop smoking. We hope you can take a few minutes to address the following 4 points with your patients. Doing so could have a powerful influence in helping your patients quit.

⊘   Acknowledge that the patient smoked before hospitalization.

⊘   Provide reinforcement for cessation during hospitalization and indicate that the patient will most likely pass through the worst withdrawal during the first 2-3 days of hospitalization.

⊘   Explain why it is important for the patient to quit smoking for good, and personalize this message.

⊘   Ask the patient if there is anything you can do to help him or her to remain a non-smoker.

Letters

One way of bringing providers, especially physicians, into the loop, getting them onboard with the tobacco cessation program, and keeping the program in their awareness is to send them a very brief letter when their patients receive cessation counseling during hospitalization. By creating a template or form letter, this can be an easy method of keeping in touch. It will also enhance continuity of care with cessation support. Hopefully the letters will prompt physicians to follow-up with patients the next time they see them (e.g., *"I see that you enrolled in the tobacco cessation program when you were in the hospital last month and that you were able to quit. How are you doing?"*). Regularly receiving letters about their patients who have received inpatient tobacco cessation services might prompt physicians to advise their other patients who are about to have an upcoming hospitalization that they should consider using the hospitalization as a time to quit.

Pamphlets

It might be desirable to design single page tri-fold pamphlets advertising the inpatient tobacco cessation program to distribute throughout the hospital to staff, to leave in waiting and visitor rooms for patients and their families, to pin to bulletin boards for staff, patients, and visitors, and to hand out to patients or leave in patients' rooms. The pamphlet should include the tobacco cessation counselor contact information, a minimal description of the cessation services offered, the costs involved, how to enroll or access the program, and perhaps some brief advice for quitting (for patients) or strategies for counseling (for staff). Pictures, especially on the front of the pamphlet, can help capture attention, and bullet points rather than paragraphs, can help make it easier to read and comprehend.

It might be helpful to have a simplified black and white electronic version of the pamphlet with minimal graphics and pictures, available for downloading from a website, that can be sent when requested via email, or simply to have as a back-up for easy printing if the stock of pamphlets runs out prior to a scheduled printing run. For an electronic version, it is important to consider that pictures can take a lot of computer memory and take a longer time to download from websites and emails than text alone, that electronic pamphlets might end up being printed on a non-color printer, and that color and pictures are difficult to scan and fax.

Posters

As previously mentioned, posters can be developed to target specific audiences and to promote benchmark goals. In our California dissemination study, we encouraged hospitals to develop posters to be placed in patient rooms, in staff offices, and other places throughout the hospital. The posters included simple messages (e.g. *"Want to Stop Smoking? Ask your nurse about Staying Free."*).

Buttons, Tags, and Other Give Away Items

One hospital in our California dissemination study developed a plastic tag that could be attached to physicians' identification badges. The tag said *"Ask me about staying free"*. Another hospital developed a plastic "job-aid" for physicians that could fit into the package of information many physicians carry. The plastic materials listed the medications available for tobacco cessation use on one side and the interventions physicians were to use on the other.

Newsletters and Websites

In the beginning of the program, it might be difficult to imagine creating a newsletter or website unless they are part of the planned intervention. However, they might both be considerations as the program evolves and expands over time. They could include helpful hints about tobacco cessation, information about tobacco cessation aids, such as nicotine replacement and how to use the various types, success stories and testimonials, and research updates for tobacco issues such as the effects of tobacco on health.

To prepare for creating a newsletter or website, it is helpful to start a file or filing system to systematically collect information that might be of interest to patients, patients' families, and staff. When patients send in letters of appreciation for receiving the program, it is important to acknowledge the letters personally and ask permission to use the letter in a newsletter or article at a later date with full acknowledgement of the sender. Even if a newsletter or website is never created, the file of information can be used in other ways, such as in-services (especially letters of appreciation from patients), articles for the media, and annual reports. In the U.S., however, Health Insurance Portability and Accountability Act (HIPAA) regulations need to be carefully considered in using endorsements from patients (U.S. Department of Health and Human Services. (2005).

STATIONERY AND RELATED ITEMS

It is helpful to have basic stationery that identifies the program—letterhead, envelops, and business cards. Depending on the size of the hospital, a small run of each (about 500), should last at least a year or so. Labels for larger packages and fax sheets are also considerations. If the program is sponsored by the hospital, it would be a good idea to use the hospital's letterhead with a single tag line identifying the tobacco cessation program and if possible, the specific contact information for the program (phone number, email address, and website). This will not only save a lot of time and potentially money (due to volume) during the design phase, but it also clearly identifies the program with the hospital—always a good thing. There might, however, not even be a choice—the hospital might require hospital letterhead to be used.

The key with stationery and related items is to keep them simple. Less is better. Here are some suggestions.

> A simple design should be used that is kept the same across all forms of communication so that it becomes recognizable.

> Since the goal is to keep the design consistent across all forms of communication, including potential future websites, it is important to consider how the stationery will reproduce in various media. For example, many people still use dial-up services for the internet and the more complex the design, the longer it takes to load. If a site takes too long to load, people might lose interest and not wait for it to open.

➤ Stationery and business cards should include only the information necessary to make contact with the program. They should not be used to detail the tobacco cessation services offered, although a tag line of the basic service offered could be included (e.g., "*Free tobacco cessation counseling during hospitalization*").

➤ It is advisable to use white paper with black writing for stationery. Colored paper and light-colored text do not fax or scan well (neither do complex designs, pictures, or too much information).

➤ If it is not clear who will be providing the cessation program or if a number of different clinicians and allied health professionals will be providing the cessation program, it might be more efficient, cost-effective, and logistically simpler to consider using generic business cards that providers can write their names on rather than printing separate cards for everyone.

➤ Standard-sized business cards are a better choice than special oversized business cards because many people have standard-sized business card rolodexes and card files; if a card does not fit into the allotted space, it might get left out.

➤ If possible, business cards should be professionally printed, and the use of inkjet printers for cards should be avoided because the ink can smear or run when it gets wet.

MEDIA

The media can be an important source of free promotion for a cessation program, but dealing with the media can consume a fair amount of time. Sometimes the media hears about the cessation program and approaches the hospital to find out more. Other times, it is in the interests of the program to get free publicity by approaching the media.

The advantage to using the media is that the more the story of the inpatient tobacco cessation program can be kept in the news, the more aware the community will become aware of the program. In turn, the more aware the community is about the program, the more likely it will be that tobacco users will start to think about using hospitalization as an opportunity to quit, the more likely inpatients will be expecting to be offered the program during hospitalization, the more likely patients will enroll, and the more likely community satisfaction with hospital services might increase. The media attention might also serve to positively position the hospital within the community.

In order to effectively use the media as a source of promotion for the cessation program, it is essential to be prepared. It takes more time upfront to prepare for the media, but over time, the initial preparation will save time and help control content and the type and extent of exposure the program gets. There are numerous resources for working with the media (e.g., ASCD, n.d.; Center for the Advancement of Health, 2001; CPA, n.d.).

Newsworthiness

Finding an angle to the tobacco cessation program that makes it newsworthy is what it takes to get media attention. A number of elements make a story newsworthy (Center for the Advancement of Health, 2001):

1. It is a concrete event (e.g., the start of a new cessation program).

2. It has conflict or controversy (e.g., announcement of 100% smoke-free hospital grounds and accompanying cessation program).

3. It is emotional or is sensational (e.g., sensational might be the immediate intra-operative and post-operative complications of continuing to smoke).

4. It provides important new information that can be used (e.g., evidence of an effective new cessation technique, or a new link with tobacco use and illness).

5. It has personal/human interest (e.g., personal success stories of quitting).

6. It is timely (e.g., an inpatient tobacco cessation program is announced just as the hospital grounds goes 100% smoke-free).

The media will spin stories to achieve as many of these key elements as possible. As such, it is important to be prepared for media contact so that the content relative to these areas can be controlled. It is better for the cessation program personnel and patients to define what is newsworthy about the program than it is to leave the definition to reporters who might sensationalize it in ways that have negative repercussions for the program and/or hospital.

For example, information about the cost of smoking to the healthcare system might be spun by the media in a way that angers the public. Whereas a hospital might spin a story about decreased post-surgical complications as a positive (e.g., "Fewer Complications After Surgery for Smokers Who Quit" or "Shorter Healing Time After Surgery for Smokers Who Quit"), the media might spin it to be more controversial (e.g., "Smokers' Increase Their Chance of Surgical Complications" or "Smokers' Heavier Cost the Healthcare System"). If not properly handled, media attention can cause controversies and potential conflict within the hospital that can extend far beyond the cessation program itself.

One of the best ways to control the content of what is presented in the media, is to find as many newsworthy components to the program as possible and prepare a press kit to cover these specific components. It might also be appropriate to prepare a series of articles or potential interview ideas to submit to the media over a given period of time. Being prepared not only helps to control content but also helps ensure that interviews will not require a lot of effort and that the opportunity to publicize a program can be capitalized on at a moment's notice.

The following are some examples of potential newsworthy stories for an inpatient tobacco cessation program:

- the introduction of the program to the hospital, especially if it is offered free of charge to all patients (e.g., concrete event)

- the window of opportunity to quit during hospitalization (e.g., new information that people can use)

- the number of patients who enroll in the program who would not have even tried to quit if they had not been offered the program during hospitalization (e.g., sensational and potentially provides hope to some)

- the number of patients who quit every year (e.g., sensational, new information, potentially provides hope)

- interviews with patients who do quit during hospitalization due to the cessation services provided (e.g., emotional, human interest)

It is also important to ask reporters for the opportunity to review the copy they plan to use for accuracy of facts. Some reporters will allow their work to be previewed, especially in smaller media outlets, others will not and might even get upset, but one never knows unless the question is asked.

Hospital Public Affairs/Relations Department

Before embarking on media preparation, it is important to check with the hospital's public affairs/relations department. They will likely have requirements that must be met when dealing with the media. They might have forms and/or preferred formats for presenting the material. They might have requirements for media releases or limitations about what can be said in the media. They will almost definitely have requirements for how the hospital and funding for the program are acknowledged. And perhaps most importantly, it is likely that promotion of the inpatient tobacco cessation program will fall under their mandate, thereby saving the cessation program substantial time in promoting the program.

It will also be helpful to speak with the hospital's public affairs/relations department to determine who should approach the media (oftentimes only the public affairs/relations department is allowed to), and how and when to approach the media. They can advise on what to include in a press release, who to send a press release to, what type of deadlines the various media have, and how to build the story including the hook or value, angle, key messages, sound bites, facts, and emotional appeal.

The public affairs/relations department can also help with decisions, such as what medium to use, where to place the story within a medium (e.g., front page of the paper versus front page of the lifestyle section), the degree of control over what is said, whether material can be reviewed once reporters have finished the piece, and how to follow-up. They might also be able to help with preparations for live interviews such as briefings on how to avoid "off the cuff" remarks, rehearsing ways to say only what is repeatable, how to anticipate, dodge, bridge, and pull back, and even what to wear for television appearances so as to appear crisp on the screen.

If the public affairs/relations department does not provide any help or forms for the preparation of materials, or if the hospital is sufficiently small enough that media promotion is up to the cessation program personnel, it would be helpful to become acquainted with recommendations for how to work with the media either through a seminar, video, on-line course, or printed material.

Media Kit

Even if the public affairs/relations department will be responsible for dealing with the media, the tobacco cessation program director will nonetheless be responsible for providing the information that will be fed to the media. The best way to prepare the information is to prepare a media kit. The most appropriate format for a media kit will depend upon the hospital and media company requirements. Although it can be time-consuming upfront, it is helpful to create a layered media kit in both electronic and hard copy that can be easily distributed when requested. The public affairs/relations department at the hospital should be able to provide guidance (or see Center for the Advancement of Health, 200, or ASCD, n.d. for ideas).

Setting Boundaries with the Media

When talking to the media, there is always the risk of being misquoted, having information misrepresented, having information not intended for the public leaked, or in some way having the rights and privacy of patients and/or the institution violated. In addition to being proactive with the preparation of a media kit, another way to minimize or manage risk includes setting parameters on what can be discussed. For example, filming patients during interviews performed in the hospital will be off-limits, and for randomized clinical trials there is information that can and cannot be provided to the media prior to and during the study, such as expected findings. Reporters must be told what these parameters are.

If prompted for some insight "off the record", it is important to not be tempted to step past the boundaries of what can be publicly announced. "off the record" is never really off the record. A good rule of thumb is to not say anything that could not be posted on a community or company bulletin board. off the record might also over time become accepted information—reporters can forget where it came from. However, if not doing "hard news", "off the record" will likely not even come up. When it does, it might mean the reporter is looking for something with more of a hook that meets newsworthy criteria (event, conflict, controversy, emotional, or sensational).

Risk management in dealing with the media can also include knowing one's own fatal flaw—some people tend to give *off the cuff* remarks, others provide *off the record* insight, some embellish, and others answer questions they do not have the answers to or that are beyond their expertise. It is, therefore, helpful to identify and practice techniques ahead of time that will compensate for the flaw. For example, if venturing into off-limits material, it is helpful to have a plan to simply stop and start over, or be prepared to give specifics for why the question cannot be answered in a way that does not raise suspicions that something controversial is being withheld. For questions beyond one's expertise, it is helpful to have a stock phrase prepared such as *"It's not really my specialty. I have colleagues who deal with that"*. Another way to manage risk is to set parameters on what can be photographed, and put in controls to ensure that the parameters are adhered to.

It is always important to assess the risks of dealing with the media and the free publicity it can provide compared to the cost of advertising. It might be more in the interests of the hospital to pay for advertising than to *pay* for free publicity.

Part III Ramp Up and Delivery

16

Policies, Procedures, Protocols, and Systems

There are a series of policies, procedures, protocols, and systems that should be clarified, adopted, and/or developed when implementing an inpatient tobacco cessation program. This chapter provides an overview of what to look for and what to consider in terms of policies, procedures, protocols, and systems. Because every hospital will be different, there are no blanket recommendations that will apply across hospitals. The suggestions made here are not exhaustive due to the idiosyncratic nature of hospitals and the programs that will be developed and implemented. Hopefully, however, the suggestions will be directive and help serve to highlight policy and procedure areas that might be relevant to a given program. Some of the information presented here is provided in other chapters but is presented again here to serve as a quick start series of checklists for various aspects of ramping up and preparing for intervention delivery.

HOSPITAL POLICIES AND PROCEDURES

Every hospital will have policies and procedures that must be followed by personnel who provide the tobacco cessation program. These policies and procedures might vary depending on the employment status of the tobacco cessation counselor. Policies and procedures might be different for a full-time employee of the hospital versus volunteers and outside research staff. Policies and procedures might also differ across disciplines and professions. For example, a hospital nurse might have access to patient charts whereas hospital clergy might not. It is important to determine what the specific hospital policies and procedures are for the mix of staff that will be providing the tobacco cessation program.

Orientation and Physical Space Set-Up

Some examples of hospital policies and procedures that might need to be considered include the following.

☐ **New Employees.** Most hospitals have a number of orientation protocols for new personnel, including non-hospital staff who might be involved in the implementation and delivery of the inpatient tobacco cessation program, such as researchers, research nurses, tobacco cessation counselors, and volunteers. New personnel often require orientation on health and safety procedures, disposal of hazardous wastes, emergency procedures, evacuation procedures, infectious disease control protocols, and confidentiality issues.

☐ **Equipment**. In most hospitals, the engineering department and individual hospital units have approval processes for electronic equipment that will be purchased or brought into the hospital including laptop, desktop, and handheld computers, printers, televisions, VCRs/DVDs, and any other type of electronic equipment that might be used for program delivery.

☐ **Sample Collection and Storage**. Most hospitals will have protocols for the collection, use, and storage of human saliva, urine, or blood samples that might be collected in some programs for cotinine verification of tobacco use status. There will also likely be policies and procedures relative to freezer storage for the samples.

☐ **Telecommunications**. There will likely be a series of policies and procedures that need to be followed for telephone and internet hook-up, voice-mail and email set-up, internet and email use (and abuse), and choosing long-distance telephone providers.

Access to Patient Information

All hospitals will have policies regarding access to patients, patients' records, and confidentiality of information. In the United States, healthcare providers need to be aware of confidentiality of information required by the Health Insurance Portability and Accountability Act (HIPAA; U.S. Department of Health and Human Services, 2005b), and are required to demonstrate familiarity with HIPAA rules. It is crucial to determine what the specific hospital policies are for patient access and access to patient information, and to document for tobacco cessation counselors, the protocols for patient access, information access, confidentiality, retrieval, and information storage.

Policies and procedures to check relative to access to patient information:

☐ **Protocols for reviewing patient charts.**
   o   who has access to charts for the tobacco cessation program
   o   how chart access can be obtained for the inpatient tobacco cessation program or research study
   o   access limits on charts for the cessation program
   o   protocols for sharing hard copy charts (for hospitals that are not yet using computerized medical records; protocols might vary by unit)
   o   access codes for electronic charts (including who provides codes)

- o expectations and restrictions for charting tobacco consults including standardization procedures and where tobacco consults should be documented
- o the protocol for notes left in patients' charts to cue physicians to provide cessation advice to patients
- ☐ **Protocols to ensure the privacy and confidentiality of patient information including storage and informed consent.**
  - o determine what documents, if any, are required for informed consent, the information required on the documents, whether standardized forms or formats exist, the review process for the forms, who receives a copy of the consent, and where the documentation must stored and for how long
  - o policies for viewing patient information in charts, and electronic tracking procedures for information viewing
  - o reprimand policies for viewing unauthorized information in patients' charts (e.g., inpatient tobacco cessation program personnel viewing family members' medical information when family members are hospitalized)
  - o determine the training necessary to ensure privacy and confidentiality of patient information
- ☐ **Policies for approaching patients at the bedside.**
  - o determine policies for informed consent and patient information for approaching patients with different aspects of the program (e.g., policies for intervening with and without data collection)
  - o determine definition of medically stable
  - o determine wait periods post-operative

Computer and Printer Access

Access to computers will likely be an important component of the tobacco cessation program. Many programs will have their own computers, but not all will. When computers must be shared with other programs and departments, systems must be developed for computer sharing. For example, in one of our studies, the tobacco cessation program nurses had their own computers for data entry, but the computers were not connected to the hospital's electronic records system so the nurses had to set up a system of sharing computers on each of the units in order to access patient charts. In another hospital, the program nurses had access to electronic medical records through terminals in their office but the terminals could not be connected to their printers so they had to set up an agreement with another department for daily printing of the hospital census.

The following represent some of the policies and procedures that need to be clarified and documented regarding computer and printer access.

☐ If the tobacco cessation program does not have a computer and/or printer, computers and printers within the hospital must be identified for sharing, along with the rules of sharing.

☐ If the tobacco cessation program does have a computer and printer, the level of access to each must be identified. When access is limited (e.g., the daily census cannot be accessed through an individual's desktop computer and can only be printed by certain departments), computers and printers within the hospital for sharing must be identified along with the rules of sharing.

Other policies and procedures to consider relative to computers and access include the following:

☐ How and where to obtain computer access codes when necessary.

☐ Determine the availability of internet connections for the program— who is eligible, how to set up new email and internet accounts within the hospital, determine restrictions on internet providers and software, and determine the availability and rules of wireless connections.

☐ If handheld or laptop computers are used to collect data at the bedside, a protocol for downloading data to a desktop computer for data storage and analysis must be documented.

Bringing Personnel Onboard

All institutions have policies, procedures, and protocols for hiring and terminating employment. It is important to ensure that the hospital's policies are followed. Some of the key issues to consider when bringing personnel onboard include:

☐ Determine the hospital's policies for advertising positions, including job descriptions, policies on internal and external postings, the amount of time advertisements have to be posted, and who is authorized to place advertisements and where.

☐ Determine the institutional policies and requirements regarding hiring from inside and outside the hospital and anti-discrimination hiring policies.

☐ Determine wage and benefit ranges for the positions being considered, as well as policies on wage increases.

☐ Determine what is required for position contracts, including probationary terms and conditions for termination.

☐ Determine policies around interviewing, background checks, making an offer, required documentation (e.g., social security), and hiring.

☐ Determine hospital orientation requirements for new hires.

- ☐ Determine policies for maintaining personnel records required by human resources, such as vacation time, quarterly reviews, etc.
- ☐ Determine policies and required workshops on safe workplaces, sexual harassment in the workplace, emergency evacuation, etc.
- ☐ Determine policies on drug testing.
- ☐ Determine training requirements at the time of hire, availability of hospital funds for ongoing training, professional college requirements for ongoing training (e.g., continuing education credits for nurses), time-off policies for training, etc.
- ☐ Determine dismissal protocols.

In-Service Training

In-service training will be handled differently by each hospital and possibly by each department or unit within a given hospital. Some hospitals might require in-service training to be coordinated by the individual units, which will involve contacting the supervisor of every unit and setting up a series of time slots for training. Some hospitals might be able to coordinate in-service trainings by profession such as including the in-service training as part of an annual general meeting for physicians. A few considerations for in-service training procedures include:

- ☐ Determine the preferences for in-service trainings by contacting the various departments/directors involved.
- ☐ Develop an announcement system such as email, bulletin board, memos, and voice-mail to announce upcoming in-service trainings.
- ☐ Develop a follow-up protocol to solidify in-service trainings.
- ☐ Determine whether all in-service presentations and content must be pre-approved, and if so, by whom.

Ethics and Internal Review Boards

Clarifying the policies and procedure for ethics review is crucial. Ethics committees and internal review boards (IRB) are probably of more relevance to research studies than programs put into standard practice. However, programs in standard practice often involve a research component as part of the program (i.e., data collection that will be reported externally), or statistics that are routinely collected by the hospital as part of the program might be ear-marked for publication, both of which would require IRB clearance.

- ☐ Determine the required documentation and protocol for IRB clearance, including:
  - o the appropriate forms by the necessary dates
  - o the required signatures

- o what formal clearance includes/involves
- o what documentation must be kept on file
- o the protocol and documentation for incident reporting
- o the protocol and documentation for progress reports
- o the notification protocol for completing a study (or data collection).

Purchasing

The purchasing department will likely have requirements, standardized documentation, and approval processes for all types of purchases including furniture, equipment, electronics, and office supplies. Purchasing departments often have exclusive contracts with suppliers that must be honored, certain specifications that must be met for furniture and electronic equipment, and there might be supplier discounts on purchases that can be had only through following the appropriate procedures. It is important to meet with purchasing to find out the details. If the purchasing department uses a variety of forms for different types of purchases, it is helpful to set up a user-friendly binder as a resource for cessation counselors that includes all the forms and when they are to be used. Clarifying the purchasing policies and procedures will include the following steps:

- ☐ Determine purchasing requirements and general protocols for ordering different classes of purchases (equipment, office supplies, furniture, etc.).
- ☐ Determine signing authority protocols for various classes of items.
- ☐ Clarify who the suppliers on contract are for the necessary purchases and what the available discounts are.
- ☐ Clarify the process for ordering, shipping, and receiving patient materials such as books, videos/DVDs, CDs, workbooks, and pamphlets, including those that are donated at no cost to the program and those that have to be purchased.
- ☐ Clarify copyright protocols for material masters that are obtained with permission to print one's own supply.

DOCUMENTATION OF DELIVERY PROTOCOLS

Each aspect of program delivery should have a clearly documented protocol. The protocols will depend on the choices made for patient populations, program components, providers, and reimbursement. Once the protocols are documented, it is helpful to create job aids by creating one-page protocols and laminating them for easy reference.

Overview of Protocols and Systems that Require Documentation

- ☐ Document patient eligibility and exclusion criteria.
- ☐ Document patient screening protocols based on eligibility and exclusion criteria.
- ☐ Document intervention protocols.
- ☐ Document referral systems to the cessation program (e.g., referrals from other departments, referrals from clinicians, etc.).
- ☐ Document procedures for daily recording and monitoring of patient interactions including daily work logs for patient identification, screening, intervention, charting, and insurance reimbursement.
- ☐ Document protocols for clinical consultation assistance for challenging patient cases, including medical queries about patient eligibility.
- ☐ Document procedures for computer and hard copy storage of patient data and records to protect confidentiality of information.
- ☐ Document procedures to be followed when working with steering, advisory, and community committees and upper management such as the requirement for written agendas and minutes, meeting protocols, the types of information appropriate for each type of committee, etc.
- ☐ Document office policies and procedures for personnel such as daily hours, vacation scheduling and coverage, coffee breaks and lunches, overtime, confidentiality of patient information, key control, etc.
- ☐ Develop protocols for keeping patients' physicians apprised of tobacco cessation encounters.
- ☐ Develop protocols for collection and storage of samples for biochemical confirmation, including barriers to infection, awareness/disposal of materials, hand washing, patient comfort, etc.

HOSPITAL INFRASTRUCTURE AND SYSTEMS

There are a number of systems that will need to be developed to ensure program delivery runs smoothly. The basic systems that need to be established include systems for the identification of patients who use tobacco, systems for screening patients, systems to ensure consistent program delivery (including use of electronic equipment), systems to ensure quality assurance, reporting systems, and systems for identifying those most responsible for trouble-shooting various challenges and problems that might arise. These systems will make up the hospital infrastructure required to run the program.

Systems for Identifying Patients Who Use Tobacco

It is essential to establish systems in the hospital to identify patients who use tobacco. The following are three possible systems that can be established—

adding a tobacco use question on the admitting forms, adding it to the vital signs on the history and physical, and doing a bed-to-bed check for tobacco use.

Question on Admitting Forms. As previously mentioned, we believe that the easiest and most effective and efficient way to streamline the identification of patients who use tobacco is to put a single tobacco use item on the admitting forms to be asked by admitting staff. Most hospitals have electronic records for admitting, so adding the tobacco use question and a column on the daily census will usually require the services of the Information Technology (IT) or computer Department. The process of adding the item to the admitting records is relatively simple, but there might be wait times due to project backlogs in the IT department or backlogs due to policy issues involving changing the admitting form. It is important to set up this system as soon as possible because it is central to program delivery. If delays in getting the item on the admitting record are excessive (e.g., more than a few months), it might be helpful to work with the tobacco cessation program champion to see what can be done to speed up the process.

Question on History and Physical. If tobacco use will be recorded in the history and physical, changes to the history and physical form might have to be done, and in-service training will need to be provided to ensure standardized reporting.

Bed-to-Bed Checks for Tobacco Use Status. If tobacco use will be identified using bed-to-bed checks, forms will need to be developed and a system for approaching patients in an orderly and efficient fashion will have to be developed, along with documentation for the need for informed consent (or not).

Systems for Screening Patients Who Use Tobacco

Since some degree of targeting of patients for tobacco cessation intervention might be necessary, a system for screening patients must be devised. In Staying Free, we use a 3-step process that involves reviewing the daily hospital census to identify patients who use tobacco, reviewing medical charts, and approaching patients at the bedside (see Chapter 3). The considerations for creating the screening system used in Staying Free are detailed below. Many of these steps have been noted elsewhere but are included here to provide a coherent flow to the procedures involved. Each step requires a documented data collection procedure, standardized data collection forms, and a data storage system (hard copy files, spreadsheet computer program, or database computer program).

☐ **Step 1 Screening System**. Establishment of this system requires a 3-step process:

1. Establish standardization of the identification of tobacco use on the admitting forms.
2. Expand the daily hospital census to include tobacco use (the IT department might have to reformat the daily census to include the tobacco status).
3. Establish access to a printer for a print-out of the daily census.

☐ **Step 2 Screening System.** Development of this system requires establishing access to patient charts. This system involves obtaining computer access codes for electronic charts and/or protocols for sharing computer access and hard copy files.

☐ **Step 3 Screening System.** Development of this system requires establishing protocols for approaching patients at the bedside and can include consideration of policies and procedures such as obtaining blanket approval from physicians to approach patients, observance of recovery periods post-surgery, and/or informed consent.

Bedside Intervention and Post-Discharge Follow-Up

Depending on the components of the intervention, arrangements might have to be made to set up video or DVD viewing in patients' rooms for tobacco cessation videos. Staying Free, for example, involves in-room viewing of a relapse prevention video. The use of in-room videos or DVDs might involve making arrangements for viewing the film on overhead hospital television monitors. If in-room monitors are not available for use, a television with a VCR/DVD player will have to be wheeled in on an audiovisual (AV) cart.

Moving the AV cart from room to room means obtaining permission for in-room viewing as well as determining how the equipment will fit in each room and where it will be plugged in. Storage for the TV/VCR/DVD when not in use will also have to be arranged. If the hospital is comprised of a number separate buildings that must be accessed by traveling outside, consideration must be given to transporting the electronic equipment between buildings (especially during snow, rain, and other challenging weather systems).

If post-discharge follow-up for counseling or tobacco use status will be performed by telephone, an office that allows privacy must be set-up with the appropriate equipment. Considerations include:

☐ Setting up an office or developing sharing privileges with existing offices.
☐ Arranging telephone service hook-up and payment plans including a long-distance carrier.

- ☐ Optional is the purchase of headsets as an ergonomic aid to prevent neck strain and to assist with simultaneous data entry while speaking with patients on the telephone.
- ☐ Telephone protocol training will be required.

Quality Assurance

A number of quality assurance systems should be put in place to ensure the program is working as intended and to determine where the program might need refinement in order to make it work better. It is helpful to create an annual schedule for fidelity checks (e.g., one, three, six, nine, and twelve months) to ensure procedures and protocols are followed. The following are some areas to consider for quality assurance.

- ☐ Systems to regularly assess whether tobacco use status is being asked and recorded accurately (various checks such as bed-to-bed fidelity checks were mentioned previously in Chapter 10).
- ☐ Systems to regularly assess whether patients in the target audience are receiving the program, and if not, why not. Part of the system should be to determine whether patterns of program acceptance and refusal change over time, and if so, why.
- ☐ Systems to determine whether counselors are following delivery protocols, including telephone follow-up, and whether patients are receiving follow-up as scheduled (and if not, why not).

Reporting Systems

Some hospitals will require quarterly, semi-annual, and annual reports on the progress of the program, others might require weekly reports at department meetings, and still others might only require an annual report. Compliance with reporting schedules requires first, the determination of the reporting schedule(s), the information required at each reporting period, and the reporting format required. Once the details have been identified, a system needs to be developed to ensure adherence to the requirements. This might involve working with the IT department to develop reporting templates that allow quick reports to be made at the push of a button. This is easily done in most database programs. If reports are to be sent to multiple departments or committees, the development of a mailing list database will ease the process.

Who To Go To

As the details of the program are pulled together, it is helpful to provide a complete contact reference list of "who-to-go-to" to trouble shoot problems and challenges. The "who-to-go-to" list will remove the ambiguity of who is the most responsible person to help with each aspect of the program, from computer set-up to ordering patient materials from outside agencies. Each hospital will have its own "who-to-go-to" list. Although hospitals will have a general directory, it is helpful to have the actual name of the person who helped set up the various aspects of the program. A list will hopefully help prevent long delays in trying to track down the appropriate person for the job or to help untangle problems. In most cases, it is helpful to also include the person's supervisor or administrative assistant's name and contact information. This is especially helpful when the designated person is away or terminates employment with the hospital.

The "who-to-go-to" list should probably include the following:

- ☐ Directors and supervisors.
  - o admitting department supervisor or person responsible for ensuring admitting staff ask the tobacco use question
  - o chairperson or representative of the IRB (if reportable data are being collected)
  - o chief of staff
  - o director of nursing
  - o director of research (if involved with the program or if he/she will be helping with data collection, analyses, or evaluation)
  - o director or department head of patient education
  - o pharmacist
  - o public relations for community announcements
- ☐ Information technology representatives.
  - o computer programmer responsible for the tobacco status question on the admitting forms and the daily hospital census
  - o computer technician responsible for internet and email connections
  - o computer technician responsible for setting up, backing up, and trouble-shooting computers and software
- ☐ Telecommunications and hospital infrastructure.
  - o service representatives for all telecommunications (telephone set-up, telephone billing and long-distance, internet, paging, cell phones, etc.)
  - o engineering person responsible for electronic equipment checks
  - o person in charge of the freezer if samples will be collected
  - o key control contact
  - o parking authority if special arrangements are made for patients to return for counseling or to provide samples for cotinine analysis
  - o person in charge of office space

- o purchasing department representative for equipment and supplies
- o shipping and receiving, especially for courier services

It might also be helpful to have a log book to record interactions with the different people and departments for easy reference. The log book should include details of the interaction such as time, person's name, what was discussed, what happened, recommendations, delivery guarantees along with costs, and future actions or options for the area of concern. A log is a good memory container and can prevent a lot of unnecessary "he said/she said" when it comes to problem solving or unraveling difficult situations.

Daily Operations: The First 48 Hours to One Year

This chapter provides an overview of the daily operations of an inpatient tobacco cessation program that uses a centralized counselor approach. It includes examples of tracking logs and organizing tools, and suggests what bigger picture administrative tasks to do throughout the year. This chapter assumes that all the preliminary and developmental work of implementation has been completed—the program has a physical, departmental, and financial home within the hospital, policies and procedures have been checked, protocols and systems have been designed, the hospital infrastructure is set up including the tobacco use question on admitting forms and a column for tobacco status on the daily census, access to patients' charts has been approved, patient charting requirements are documented, funding is in place, counselors have been hired and trained, departments have received in-service training, a database program has been designed, data collection instruments have been incorporated into the database program, all purchases have been made, the intervention has been developed, the program director, champions, and advisory committee are in place, stakeholders and their needs have been identified and incorporated into the implementation and maintenance plan, community resources have been capitalized on, and reporting systems have been set up.

DAILY TASKS, LISTS, LOGS, AND FORMS

Daily To-Do

Like many jobs, one of the most efficient ways to begin the first day of program delivery, and every day after that, is to prepare a daily to-do list. The to-do list is derived from developing a task analysis of the work to be done. The specific work to be done will be determined by the choices made for program delivery and data collection. The easiest way to identify the work to be done is to start at the broadest category of work (see "Duties" in Figure 15) and break the duties up into tasks, tasks into subtasks, and subtasks into steps until the work to be done is clearly identified, narrowly defined, and can be recorded as either completed or not yet completed.

An example of the daily work involved with Staying Free is provided in Figure 15. It includes the four general duties (patient enrollment, intervention delivery, data collection, and administration), broken down into more definable tasks. The task "Complete daily preparation" (see section 1.1 in Figure 15) is broken down further into three subtasks (see section 1.1.1 to 1.1.3). The second subtask "Review previous day's list of patients waiting to be seen" is further broken down into a step (1.1.2.1) that instructs the counselor to review the Daily Screening Log (Figure 17) and the Patient Tracking Form (Figure 18). This example covers only the counseling portion of the job. If the counselors will also assume the role of Program Director, the duties and tasks list would also have to include those administrative responsibilities (see Chapter 4).

Figure 15. Staying Free: Daily To-Do List

Duties	Tasks

1. Patient Enrollment	1.1 Complete daily preparation.
	  1.1.1 Evaluate daily census for tobacco users.
	  1.1.2 Review previous day's list of patients waiting to be seen
	    1.1.2.1 Use the Daily Screening Log and Patient Tracking Form for review
	  1.1.3 Screen patients' medical charts for eligibility
	  1.1.4 Schedule rounds by unit for new and previous day's patients using Patient Tracking Form
	1.2 Visit and enroll patients.
	1.3 Collect baseline data.

2. Intervention Delivery	2.1 Advise all tobacco users to quit. 2.2 Assess willingness to make a quit attempt. 2.3 Assist patients with quitting. 2.4 Arrange & schedule follow-up contact. 2.5 Make follow-up counseling calls.
3. Data Collection	3.1 Record daily patient flow. 3.2 Input baseline data on all tobacco-users. 3.3 Input bedside counseling data. 3.4 Input telephone counseling data.
4. Administration	4.1 Keep daily logs and tracking forms. 4.2 File daily records, forms, and other. 4.3 Make weekly updates to virus protection. 4.4 Make weekly back-ups of data files. 4.5 Answer phone calls, emails, and mail. 4.6 Attend meetings as scheduled 4.7 Provide weekly in-services as per unit schedules 4.8 Prepare weekly, monthly, quarterly, annual reports

The example in Figure 15 is for illustrative purposes only. Ideally, each task would be broken down into subtasks and each subtask would be broken down into steps so that the exact work to be done to complete the job of the tobacco cessation counselor would be so clearly laid out that it could be achieved by a qualified person not yet familiar with the job. This level of detailing is desirable for training purposes, for creating a job aid for those who will cover vacation and sick leave time for the regular cessation counselors, and during the start-up phase of the program to ensure that the program is delivered as intended. This level of detail can also be used as a reference for writing the job description and determining the educational and experiential background needed to do the job. To provide an exceptionally efficient and objective instrument for assessment during training, for assessing job performance, and to use for setting specific performance-related goals, additional columns to record performance could be added to the right of the chart in Figure 15 (e.g., 1st practice, 2nd practice, etc.), and each duty, task, subtask, and step checked off as it is completed.

Assuming a centralized counselor approach is adopted, data collection flows seamlessly from task to task as part of the daily work to be done. For example, once the daily hospital census is printed, it can serve as both an organizing tool for the day's work to identify patients who use tobacco as well as a source of data.

Daily Admissions Data Collection Form

For data collection purposes, it helps to identify the patients who use tobacco with a highlighter pen on the daily census. Data from the daily census can be quickly summarized on the Daily Admissions Data Collection Form (Figure 16).

Figure 16. Daily Admissions Data Collection Form

Week: Jan 9-13, 2006	S	M	T	W	T	F	S	TT
# all new admissions		15						
# patients in units ineligible to screen		6						
OB		1						
Newborns		2						
Pediatrics		1						
Psychiatric		0						
Substance Abuse		2						
# patients in units eligible to screen		9						
# tobacco users in units eligible to screen		2						

The Daily Admissions Data Collection Form (Figure 16) was designed for one of our studies. It provides a quick and easy way to systematically summarize the data provided in the daily hospital census, including the total number of new daily admissions, the number of patients admitted to units considered ineligible to screen, the number of patients admitted to units considered eligible to screen, and the number of patients admitted to units eligible to screen who use tobacco (which in turn, allows easy calculation of tobacco use prevalence as a function of units eligible to screen).

The number of patients in the units eligible to be screened in Figure 16 can be further broken down into age categories. In one of our studies, we separated the data into patients less than 45 years of age and those 45 and older, and recorded the tobacco use prevalence by age (Smith & Corso, submitted). This might be an important consideration as indicated in Chapter 6, because the proportion of older to younger patients will have a direct affect on the overall tobacco use prevalence, which in turn will have implications for program uptake and outcomes.

Daily Screening Log

The nurses in one of our studies designed the Daily Screen Log to systematically organize screening of the patients identified as tobacco users on the daily census (Figure 17).

Figure 17. Daily Screening Log

Date: _____
day/month /year

Purpose:
Data collection tool to track number of patients who are eligible and randomized each day. Can be used to follow patients in hospital and to make weekly reports.

Instructions:
Complete an entry on this screening log for every admitted patient who uses tobacco except those in the ineligible units (e.g., psychiatric, pediatric, etc.).

Medical Record#	Sex	Age (yrs)	Eligible Yes/No	If ineligible, reason	Enrolled Yes/No	If no, why not
458725	F	69	No	palliative	No	Ineligible
556872	M	62	Yes		No	refused
498757	M	63	Yes		Yes	

The nurses found that this log helped them keep track of patients, allowing them to leave the office to see patients and continue to return to the list during day in between their other duties until the list of patients to be seen was completed. Because all the nurses in the study were part-time and job-shared the positions, this daily screening log also allowed all nurses involved with the program to step in and seamlessly carry on with the work to be done at any point during the day. It would be similarly helpful for those covering vacation or sick leave for the tobacco cessation counselor. This screening log also contained all the data needed to complete daily enrollment figures and to determine when and why enrollment into the program was lagging.

Patient Tracking Form

The nurses in one of our studies designed another form, Patient Tracking Form, as a companion piece to the Daily Screening Log. It was designed specifically to organize bedside visits (Figure 18).

Figure 18. Patient Tracking Form

Date: _____
day/month/year

Purpose: Communication tool for cessation providers to keep track of patients who are screened or need to be screened.

Instructions: Use a fresh table each day.

Patient's Name	Age (yrs)	Unit & Room #	Estimated D/C Date	Patient Seen Yes/No	Notes
S. Martin	*45*	*216 W*	*03/21/06*	*Yes*	*enrolled*
J. Smith	*62*	*311 W*	*03/19/06*	*No*	*discharged*
R. Brown	*75*	*421 S*	*03/20/06*		*sedated/revisit*

The nurses found the Patient Tracking Form to be an efficient way to organize daily rounds. This form was used by copying down only the names of patients from the Daily Screening Log who were eligible to be seen at the bedside according to chart reviews (i.e., patients coded as "Yes" eligible to be screened on the Daily Screening Log, Figure 17). The form was also used to schedule bedside visits to patients who did not have tobacco use recorded anywhere in their medical charts. The Patient Tracking Form also helps keep track of patients over time and is especially helpful if more than one provider is seeing patients.

Post-discharge counseling calls and follow-up tobacco use status calls are scheduled according to discharge dates (D/C). Estimated discharge dates are included on the Patient Tracking Form (Figure 18) and can be checked regularly against patient records to verify that enrolled patients are either still in the hospital or if discharged, when they were discharged. If kept up to-date, the Patient Tracking Form can be closely monitored each day to ensure that all hospitalized patients who use tobacco are seen and that their discharge dates are kept under surveillance. This monitoring function should be added to the daily to-do list. Staying Free telephone counseling data collection forms have been previously published (Houston Miller & Taylor, 1995).

When a patient is discharged, all of their future counseling calls and tobacco use status calls should be scheduled according to their discharge date. The calls can be hand-written in a hard copy calendar/day-timer or inputted into a computerized scheduling program. Ideally, the scheduling program should have a prompting feature that lists all calls to be made in a given day and does not remove patients from the list until they are reached or cancelled by the tobacco cessation counselor. We have used both the hand-written and computerized scheduling methods in our work—the computerized version is certainly more efficient and makes it easier for those covering for the tobacco cessation counselor to step in and continue with the work to be done.

DAILY WORKFLOW

Daily Preparation

The work tasks presented in Figure 15 are a good representation of the general daily workflow. The day begins by completing the daily preparation tasks, which involve reviewing the daily hospital census, and filling out the Daily Admissions Data Collection Form (Figure 16), Patient Screening Log (Figure 17), and the Patient Tracking Form (Figure 18). For patients missing the tobacco use status on the daily census, the procedure for determining tobacco use will vary depending on whether the hospital uses electronic or hard copy medical records. If tobacco use status was not asked by the admitting staff (if that is the procedure being used), it might be found elsewhere in the medical records. The most likely places tobacco use would appear is in the interdisciplinary form, nursing notes, history and physical, physician notes, problem list, and/or emergency records. If tobacco use is not listed anywhere in the chart, the unit nurses might be able to provide the information; otherwise, a trip to the bedside to check with the patient will be the only other option, in which case, the patient will be added to the Patient Tracking Form (Figure 18) so that they will be included in the daily rounds and time will not be wasted making a special trip to the bedside in isolation of the other work to be done.

After the new admissions have been evaluated and added to the Daily Screening Log and Patient Tracking Form, patients from previous days who are waiting to be seen need to be determined. For patients on the Patient Tracking Form from previous days, it helps to do a quick check through electronic records to determine whether they are still in the hospital or whether they have been discharged. With this information, the counselor can schedule all new and outstanding patients to be seen, grouping visits according to units/wards when possible. If patients have constraints for visits (e.g., post-operative), they should be flagged on the Patient Tracking Form for a future day. If the hospital uses electronic records and the computers are down for a while, counselors can complete the daily preparation by visiting the various units/wards and talking to the nurses and checking the admission boards, or simply completing work as best as possible on all outstanding patients to be seen.

Unit Rounds

On the unit rounds, the counselors will be engaged in enrolling patients, collecting baseline data, and providing the intervention. Kelly R. Reilly, BScN, MS, the tobacco cessation nurse for the Stanford University Medical Center dissemination project of the inpatient tobacco cessation program (Smith et al., 2002), offered the nurses in the Canadian study of Staying Free, the following suggestions for enrolling patients into an intensive tobacco cessation program.

1. Familiarize yourself with the patients' conditions by reading the H & P, and nursing/physician notes prior to approaching patients at the bedside. This sensitizes you to what patients might have been through, and allows you to provide a more empathic approach. E.g., "Mr. Jones, you were hospitalized two days ago with a heart attack. How are you feeling?"

2. Take time to make a personal connection with the patient.

3. Be calm and slow; approach the patient gently and kindly being sensitive to not offend him or her. If you are too business-like, the patient will not develop rapport with you and might shut you out or get defensive. Use your body language to show the patient that you have all the time in the world for them, even if you don't—most physicians and nurses tend to bustle in and out, often unintentionally giving the message that they are too busy to connect with patients. To make sure, pause outside the patients' door, take a deep breath, let it out slowly, and give your limbs a shake. Sounds odd, but we have found that it works.

4. You will have to adjust your approach to different people; pay attention to visual and auditory cues. This all might seem awkward at first; it becomes more comfortable over time.

5. Remember that you are inviting patients to enroll in a program, you are not telling them to do something you think they should do.

6. Do not judge patients or convey that they are bad people for smoking, silly for not wanting to quit, or that they have done something wrong.

7. When you are first getting started, you can let patients know that you are in the beginning of a new program and are learning the ropes. You might fumble your way through in the beginning, but that is the best way to learn.

Daily Administration

The Daily Screening Log (Figure 17) and the Patient Tracking Form (Figure 18) are completed upon arrival back at the office, and patients' data are entered into the computer (if not done at the bedside with a laptop or handheld computer). If any patients were missed during daily rounds and there is time left in the day, another attempt to see them is often fruitful. Patients not seen one day should be scheduled to be seen the next day. Time to schedule calls and calls themselves should be added to the daily to-do list. Depending on the intervention, post-discharge counseling calls might begin after the first 48 hours of the program being operational.

HOW TO FINISH THE FIRST WEEK

Tracking and Reporting

To finish the first week, it is important to ensure that all patients have been accounted for by checking the Daily Screening Log (Figure 17) and the Patient Tracking Form (Figure 18). The numbers in the Daily Admissions Data Collection Form (Figure 16) should add up, and the daily numbers can be summed to provide a weekly total of the number of new admissions and the tobacco use prevalence. A summary of reasons for ineligibility can be created and a tally of patients who received and refused counseling can be created (data from Figure 17). All of these data should be entered into a computer program, preferably into a database software program. A weekly report can be easily produced after all data are entered and checked for accuracy.

Data Protection

To protect the data, a backup of the database onto a CD or external hard drive should be made every week. Even if the hospital has a backup system, it is a good idea to have an office copy backup (it should only take a few minutes). It is also important to do a live update for virus protection each week (unless this is covered by the hospital IT department), and scan the computer for viruses.

Scheduling

If post-discharge counseling calls will be made, it is important to ensure that the calls for the following week are scheduled, the prompting system is working if using a computerized scheduling program, and that telephone counseling sessions are scheduled in the daily and weekly to-do lists. The end of every day and the end of every week is a good time to check scheduling.

Weekly Review

Finally, a review of the week's activities to determine whether there were any problems or issues that impeded the workflow can be helpful. For example, it is important to determine whether tobacco use is being identified for most, if not all patients. If it is not, it is important to find out why and to problem solve to get the process flowing. It is also helpful to document whether there are any barriers to receiving the daily hospital census in a timely manner. The end of the week is a good time to reflect and analyze what facilitates and inhibits efficient bedside screening and intervention. For example, are bedside rounds scheduled at a good time in terms of connecting with patients or are patients being missed due to meals, procedures, visitors, or because patients are being discharged before the counselor has a chance to see them?

If pharmacy is working with the tobacco cessation program to provide brief counseling for nicotine replacement therapy, ensure that the system is flowing smoothly. It is also helpful to check in with the pharmacy to see if there are any questions or concerns, and to thank the people who work to support the tobacco cessation program and encourage them to continue to help with the program. If insurance plans are being billed for tobacco-cessation services, ensure that all the paperwork is filled out for each patient.

Each week should follow a similar pattern. The keys are to keep good records and keep connected with the people involved with the program—up-to-date logs keep the daily work flowing smoothly so that others can step in to help or cover and good records also keep the lines of communication open among all persons involved with the program. Daily data input into the computer with a weekly check also helps ensure that errors can be caught quickly and reports can be easily generated.

THE FIRST MONTH

Month-End Review

Every month, from the first through to the last in the year, the month-end review should ensure that all daily and weekly logs have been completed, all data have been entered into the computer and cleaned, weekly reports have been generated, the database is backed up, the computer virus protection is updated, the computer is scanned for viruses, billing forms have been completed, and problem areas and solutions have been documented. By the end of the first month, there will be sufficient data to start checking weekly patterns of patient flow and enrollment—it is helpful to graph monthly data to see visual trends.

Monthly Report

In addition to the weekly reports, it is helpful to generate a monthly report for patient flow and enrollment, and distribute it to select stakeholders. The reports should be easy to do if report templates have been designed and the data are stored in a database software program.

Fidelity Check

One month is also a good time to do a bed-to-bed fidelity check on tobacco use status to determine whether all patients are being asked about tobacco use and whether their status is being correctly recorded in their records.

THE FIRST QUARTER

Evaluation

By the end of the first quarter, post-discharge counseling calls will be increasing in number. It might be a good time to do some process and impact evaluation to determine whether there are any areas that could benefit from problem-solving. For example, it would be informative to assess how many patients are receiving their post-discharge calls, the reasons for missed calls, and the number of call attempts to reach patients. Process evaluation could also include brief surveys of patient and staff satisfaction, the number of in-service-trainings that have been completed, changes to the environment, such as a frequency count of nursing units that have tobacco cessation resources available, and the number of nurses who are aware of the available tobacco cessation resources.

Actual Versus Projected Reviews and Fidelity Checks

Three months of data are sufficient to start examining whether patient flow and enrollment are following projections. If numbers are below projected, it is important to determine why. For example, sometimes there are unit closures due to infectious disease outbreaks. Three months is a good time to do another bed-to-bed fidelity check of the accuracy of tobacco-use identification. It is also important to assess to what degree patients are being missed in-hospital by the cessation provider and the reasons why—is it due to short admissions, are patients unavailable at the time the cessation provider is making rounds, or is too much time being spent somewhere else in the workflow process, such as having to share computers and not being able to get access to patients' charts in a timely fashion? It is also a good time to determine the rate of program refusals. If a large percentage of patients are refusing the program, it is important to find out the reasons why. It is also important to ensure that the correct bedside protocol is being followed by counselors and to correct any inconsistencies and breaks from protocol.

Environmental Checks

The end of the first quarter is a good time to check supplies and patient materials to determine if anything needs to be ordered. It might be an optimal time to provide an in-service training update to the various departments, armed with the quarterly report—people like to see what is actually happening in terms of numbers. It is also a good time to refresh the inpatient tobacco cessation program promotional campaigns in the hospital.

Tobacco Use Status Call Scheduling

The end of the first quarter will signal the beginning of 3-month tobacco use status calls if they are being made. It is important to ensure that the system created to track status calls is in place, and that status calls are scheduled into the daily to-list.

TAKING THE PULSE: THE FIRST SIX MONTHS

Fidelity Checks and Evaluation

The work flow by six months should be well-established and monthly fidelity checks should have caught problem areas and barriers to delivery. It might be helpful to continue to continue with process and impact evaluations to ensure that all aspects of the program are flowing smoothly and to provide a progress report to management.

Although most components of the program will be institutionalized by six months, staff attrition within the hospital might have some bearing on the fidelity of the systems in place, such as the assessment of tobacco use by admitting staff. This can be determined by continued evaluation. Evaluation can also include various indicators of program reach such as patient flow and enrollment, the percentage of patients receiving post-discharge counseling, and reasons for refusal of the cessation services. It might also be informative to do another bed-to-bed fidelity check of tobacco use identification. If 3-month post-discharge tobacco use status calls are being made, some cessation data will be available for impact evaluation.

It is also helpful to assess how many patients are receiving their 3-month post-discharge status calls, the reasons for missed calls, and the number of call attempts to reach patients to determine whether there are any areas that could benefit from problem-solving. If 6-month post-discharge calls are being made, it is important to ensure that the scheduling and prompting systems are working. One way to check is to review the 3-month post-discharge calls lists to ensure that the patients appear on the 6-month post-discharge call list—if they do not, it is important to check their records to determine why (e.g., patients might have moved away).

HOW TO FINISH THE FIRST YEAR

One-Year Patient Follow-Up

If 12-month post-discharge status is being collected, it is important to ensure that the calls are scheduled when the patient is discharged from the hospital— otherwise it becomes somewhat of an impossible job to track calls. We prefer using a computerized scheduling software program that prompts all calls to be made on any given day. We also record the date of each call attempt and the reason why the patient was not reached, as well as the date that the patient is reached. These data provide confirmation that patients were called and when or if they were reached. It also allows calculation of the number of calls it takes to reach patients and the window of follow-up in terms of time. Since there will have been six months since the last status call at 6-months post-discharge, it might be slightly more difficult to reach program participants at the 12-month call due to patients moving out of the area or phones being disconnected. It is helpful to realize that some patients might have difficulty recalling participation in the program, especially if they were not reached for the 6-month call. If biochemical confirmation of status is being collected, it might require home visits as it is sometimes difficult to convince participants to return to the hospital or clinic.

Annual Review and Report

The review at one-year can replicate the quarterly and semi-annual reviews. It is important to ensure that all data for the year are in the computer, cleaned, and backed-up on CD or external hard drive. If funding allows, it is important to do an annual process and impact evaluation for the annual report. This should be fairly straight forward and easy to do if the monthly, quarterly, and semi-annual reports have been completed. As part of the review, it is helpful to compare actual outcomes to projected outcomes, and to determine where and why actual numbers do not meet projected. It is also important to determine what areas of the program would benefit from modification, expansion, or general problem-solving. Program goals can be adjusted to reflect these reviews.

Making it through the first year is the culmination of a lot of hard work, dedication, and sufficient funding, but the leverage for success lies in a clear vision, solid planning, a hospital infrastructure and centralized systems to support the program, stakeholder buy-in, a program champion, training and support for the counselors, program promotion, good record keeping, and regular evaluation and reports.

References

Agency for Healthcare Policy and Research (AHQR). (1996). *Smoking cessation clinical practice guideline No. 18.* AHCPR Publication Number 96-0692. Rockville, MD: Agency for Healthcare Policy and Research, U.D. Department of Health and Human Services.

Ahuja, R., Weibel, S. B., & Leone, F. T. (2003). Lung cancer: the oncologist's role in smoking cessation. *Semin Oncol, 30*(1), 94-103.

Aligne, C. A., & Stoddard, J. J. (1997). Tobacco and children. An economic evaluation of the medical effects of parental smoking. *Arch Pediatr Adolesc Med, 151*(7), 648-653.

Altman, D. G., Schulz, K. F., Moher, D., Egger, M., Davidoff, F., Elbourne, D., et al. (2001). The revised CONSORT statement for reporting randomized trials: explanation and elaboration. *Ann Intern Med, 134*(8), 663-694.

American Heart Association. (1990). *An active partnership for the health of your heart.* Dallas: American Heart Association National Center.

American Medical Association. (1994). *American Medical Association guidelines for the diagnosis and treatment of nicotine dependence: how to help patients stop smoking.* Washington DC: American Medical Association.

American Nurses Association. (1995). *Position statement on cessation of tobacco use.* Retrieved May 31, 2005, from http:// www.tobaccofreenurses .org/resources/policy/statements.php#cotu .

American Psychiatric Association. (1996). Practice guideline for the treatment of patients with nicotine dependence. *Am J Psychiatry, 153* (10 (Suppl)), S1-S31.

American Public Health Association. (2003). *Policy Statement: Smoking Cessation within Substance Abuse and/or Mental Health Treatment Settings.* Retrieved May 18, 2005, from http://www.apha.org/legislative/ policy/policysearch/ index.cfm?fuseaction=view&id=1247 .

An, H. S., Simpson, J. M., Glover, J. M., & Stephany, J. (1995). Comparison between allograft plus demineralized bone matrix versus autograft in anterior cervical fusion. A prospective multicenter study. *Spine, 20*(20), 2211-2216.

ANA Nursing World. (2005). *Social Causes and Health Care Position Statements: Tobacco Use Prevention, Cessation, and Exposure to Second-Hand Smoke.* Retrieved December 2005, from http://www.nursingworld.org /readroom/position/social/sctbco.htm .

Annual smoking attributable mortality, years of potential life lost, and economic costs-United States, 1995-1999. (2002). *MMWR Morb Mortal Wkly Rep, 51*(14), 300-303.

Association for Supervision and Curriculum Development (ASCD). (n.d.). *ASCD Advocacy Kit: Working with the Media.* Retrieved January 2006, from: http://www.ascd.org/advocacykit/working_media.html .

Baer, J. S., Holt, C. S., & Lichtenstein, E. (1986). Self-efficacy and smoking reexamined: construct validity and clinical utility. *J Consult Clin Psychol, 54*(6), 846-852.

Bandura, A. (1977). Self-efficacy: toward a unifying theory of behavioral change. *Psych Rev, 84*(2), 191-215.

Bandura, A. (1986). *Social foundations of thought and action: A social cognitive theory.* Englewood Cliffs, NJ: Prentice-Hall.

Barendregt, J. J., Bonneux, L., & van der Maas, P. J. (1997). The health care costs of smoking. *N Engl J Med, 337*(15), 1052-1057.

Berwick, D. M. (2003). Disseminating innovations in health care. *JAMA, 289*(15), 1969-1975.

Bialous, S. A., & Sarna, L. (2004). Sparing a few minutes for tobacco cessation: if only half of all nurses helped one patient per month quit smoking, more than 12 million smokers would overcome their addictions every year. *Am J Nurs, 104*(12), 54-60.

Bock, B. C., Becker, B., Niaura, R., & Partridge, R. (2000). Smoking among emergency chest pain patients: motivation to quit, risk perception and physician intervention. *Nicotine Tob Res, 2*(1), 93-96.

Boudreaux, E. D., Hunter, G. C., Bos, K., Clark, S., & Camargo, C. A. (2004). Multicenter study of smoking, nicotine dependence, and intention to quit among emergency department patients and visitors. *Acad Emerg Med, 11*(5), 548-549.

British Thoracic Society. (1998). Smoking cessation guidelines and their cost-effectiveness. *Thorax, 53*(Suppl 5, part1), S1-S38.

Browman, G. P., Wong, G., Hodson, I., Sathya, J., Russell, R., McAlpine, L., et al. (1993). Influence of cigarette smoking on the efficacy of radiation therapy in head and neck cancer. *N Engl J Med, 328*(3), 159-163.

Brown, C. W., Orme, T. J., & Richardson, H. D. (1986). The rate of pseudarthrosis (surgical nonunion) in patients who are smokers and patients who are nonsmokers: a comparison study. *Spine, 11*(9), 942-943.

Buchsbaum, D. G., Buchanan, R. G., Centor, R. M., Schnoll, S. H., & Lawton, M. J. (1991). Screening for alcohol abuse using CAGE scores and likelihood ratios. *Ann Intern Med, 115*(10), 774-777.

Burgess, E., Taenzer, P., & Smith, P. M. (in progress). *A Hospital-Based Smoking Cessation Program: Helping Cardiac Patients Make a Fresh Start.* Foothills Hospital Health Promotion Program: Calgary, Alberta. Unpublished manuscript.

Cabana, M. D., Rand, C. S., Powe, N. R., Wu, A. W., Wilson, M. H., Abboud, P. A., et al. (1999). Why don't physicians follow clinical practice guidelines? A framework for improvement. *JAMA, 282*(15), 1458-1465.

Calgary Health Region (CHR). (2000). *Regional policy. Tobacco reduction.* Retrieved January 3, 2006, from http://www.calgaryhealthregion.ca/ policydb/ShowPolicy?policy_id=1325 .

Calgary Health Region (CHR). (2003). *Tobacco reduction policy evaluation: Creating smoke free property.* Retrieved January 3, 2006, from http:// www.calgaryhealthregion.ca/hecomm/tobacco/pdf/Policy%20Evaluation%2 0Booklet.pdf .

Calgary Health Region (CHR). (2004). *Tobacco reduction policy information.* Retrieved January 3, 2006, from http://www.calgaryhealthregion.ca/ hecomm/tobacco/policies.htm .

Cameron, R. P., Taylor, C. B., Miller, N. H., & Fagans, E. F. (submitted). *Dissemination and implementation of inpatient tobacco cessation interventions.* Unpublished manuscript.

Canadian Institutes for Health Information. (n.d.). *Hospital Morbidity Database.* Retrieved January 3, 2006, from http://secure.cihi.ca/ cihiweb/dispPage.jsp?cw_page=statistics_results_source_hmdb_e .

Canadian Psychological Association (CPA). (n.d.). *Working with the Media: A Guide for Psychologists.* Retrieved January 2006, from: http://www.cpa .ca/media.html .

Canadian Thoracic Society Workshop Group. (1992). Guidelines for the assessment and management of chronic obstructive pulmonary disease. *CMAJ, 147*(4), 420-428.

Cataldo, J. K. (2001). The role of advanced practice psychiatric nurses in treating tobacco use and dependence. *Arch Psychiatr Nurs, 15*(3), 107-119.

Cavender, J. B., Rogers, W. J., Fisher, L. D., Gersh, B. J., Coggin, C. J., & Myers, W. O. (1992). Effects of smoking on survival and morbidity in patients randomized to medical or surgical therapy in the Coronary Artery Surgery Study (CASS): 10-year follow-up. CASS Investigators. *J Am Coll Cardiol, 20*(2), 287-294.

Celli, B. R., Snider, G.L., Heffner, J., Tiep, B., Ziment, I., Make, B., et al. (1995). Standards for the diagnosis and care of patients with chronic obstructive pulmonary disease. *Am J Respir Crit Care Med, 152*, S77-S120. Retrieved May 5, 2005, from http://www.thoracic.org/adobe/statements/ copd1-45.pdf .

Center for Tobacco Cessation. (2005a). Resources: Toolkits. Retrieved January 3, 2006, from http://ctcinfo.org/resources/toolkits.asp .

Center for Tobacco Cessation. (2005b). E-newsletter. Retrieved January 3, 2006, from http://ctcinfo.org/enewsletter/default.asp .

Centers for Disease Control and Prevention (CDC). (2002). Cigarette smoking among adults—United States, 2002. *MMWR, 53(20)*, 427-430.

Centers for Disease Control and Prevention (CDC). (2004). *The Health Consequences of Smoking Database.* Retrieved January 3, 2006, from http://apps.nccd.cdc.gov/sgr/ .

Centers for Medicare and Medicaid Services. (2003). *Medicare gets first database measuring quality of medical care delivered to beneficiaries.* Retrieved February 25, 2005, from http://www.cms.hhs.gov/media/press/release.asp?Counter=385 .

Center for the Advancement of Health. (2001). *Communicating health behavior science in the media: tips for researchers.* Retrieved January 2006, from http://www.cfah.org/pdfs/ResearchTipsBooklet.pdf .

Cohen, S., Lichtenstein, E., Prochaska, J. O., Rossi, J. S., Gritz, E. R., Carr, C. R., et al. (1989). Debunking myths about self-quitting. Evidence from 10 prospective studies of persons who attempt to quit smoking by themselves. *Am Psychol, 44*(11), 1355-1365.

COMMIT Research Group. (1995). Community intervention trial for smoking cessation (COMMIT): II. Changes in adult cigarette smoking prevalence. *Am J Public Health, 85*(2), 193-201.

Critchley, J. A., & Capewell, S. (2003). Mortality risk reduction associated with smoking cessation in patients with coronary heart disease: a systematic review. *JAMA, 290*(1), 86-97.

Cromwell, J., Bartosch, W. J., Fiore, M. C., Hasselblad, V., & Baker, T. (1997). Cost-effectiveness of the clinical practice recommendations in the AHCPR guideline for smoking cessation. Agency for Health Care Policy and Research. *JAMA, 278*(21), 1759-1766.

Cummings, S. R., Rubin, S. M., & Oster, G. (1989). The cost-effectiveness of counseling smokers to quit. *JAMA, 261*(1), 75-79.

Curran, V. R., Hoekman, T., Gulliver, W., Landells, I., & Hatcher, L. (2000). Web-based continuing medical education. (II): Evaluation study of computer-mediated continuing medical education. *J Contin Educ Health Prof, 20*(2), 106-119.

Curry, S. J., Grothaus, L. C., McAfee, T., & Pabiniak, C. (1998). Use and cost effectiveness of smoking-cessation services under four insurance plans in a health maintenance organization. *N Engl J Med, 339*(10), 673-679.

Dalack, G. W., & Meador-Woodruff, J. H. (1996). Smoking, smoking withdrawal and schizophrenia: case reports and a review of the literature. *Schizophr Res, 22*(2), 133-141.

DeBusk, R. F., Miller, N. H., Superko, H. R., Dennis, C. A., Thomas, R. J., Lew, H. T., et al. (1994). A case-management system for coronary risk factor modification after acute myocardial infarction. *Ann Intern Med, 120*(9), 721-729.

Delgado-Rodriguez, M., Medina-Cuadros, M., Martinez-Gallego, G., Gomez-Ortega, A., Mariscal-Ortiz, M., Palma-Perez, S., et al. (2003). A prospective study of tobacco smoking as a predictor of complications in general surgery. *Infect Control Hosp Epidemiol, 24*(1), 37-43.

Dennis, K. E., & Prescott, P. A. (1985). Florence Nightingale: yesterday, today, and tomorrow. *ANS Adv Nurs Sci, 7*(2), 66-81.

DiFranza, J. R., & Lew, R. A. (1996). Morbidity and mortality in children associated with the use of tobacco products by other people. *Pediatrics, 97*(4), 560-568.

Egan, T. D., & Wong, K. C. (1992). Perioperative smoking cessation and anesthesia: a review. *J Clin Anesth, 4*(1), 63-72.

Eisenberg, J. M. (2002). Physician utilization: the state of research about physicians' practice patterns. *Med Care, 40*(11), 1016-1035.

Enstrom, J. E. (1999). Smoking cessation and mortality trends among two United States populations. *J Clin Epidemiol, 52*(9), 813-825.

Esterberg, M. L., & Compton, M. T. (2005). Smoking behavior in persons with a schizophrenia-spectrum disorder: a qualitative investigation of the transtheoretical model. *Soc Sci Med, 61*(2), 293-303.

Etter, J. F., Bergman, M. M., Humair, J. P., & Perneger, T. V. (2000). Development and validation of a scale measuring self-efficacy of current and former smokers. *Addiction, 95*(6), 901-913.

Fagerstrom, K. O. (1978). Measuring degree of physical dependence to tobacco smoking with reference to individualization of treatment. *Addict Behav, 3*(3-4), 235-241.

Farkas, A. J., Gilpin, E. A., White, M. M., & Pierce, J. P. (2000). Association between household and workplace smoking restrictions and adolescent smoking. *JAMA, 284*(6), 717-722.

Faulkner, A., & Ward, L. (1983). Nurses as health educators in relation to smoking. *Nurs Times, 79*(15), 47-48.

Fellows, J. F., Rehm, R., Hornbrook, M., Hollis, J., Haswell, T. C., Dickerson, J., & Volk, C. (2004). *Making the business case for smoking cessation and ROI calculator*: Center for Health Research. Retrieved January 3, 2006, from http://www.businesscaseroi.org/roi/apps/execsum.aspx .

Fiore, M. C., Bailey, W. C., Cohen, S. J., Dorfman, S. F., Gritz, E. R., Heyman, R. B., et al. (2000). *Treating Tobacco Use and Dependence, Clinical Practice Guideline*. Rockville, MD: U.S. Department of Health and Human Services. Public Health Service.

Fishbein, M., & Ajzen, I. (1975). *Belief, Attitude, Intention and Behavior: An Introduction to Theory and Research*. Reading, Mass: Addison-Wesley.

France, E. K., Glasgow, R. E., & Marcus, A. C. (2001). Smoking cessation interventions among hospitalized patients: what have we learned? *Prev Med, 32*(4), 376-388.

Francis, B., Mauriello, S. M., Phillips, C., Englebardt, S., & Grayden, S. K. (2000). Assessment of online continuing dental education in North Carolina. *J Contin Educ Health Prof, 20*(2), 76-84.

Galen, K. M., Deligonul, U., Kern, M. J., Chaitman, B. R., & Vandormael, M. G. (1988). Increased frequency of restenosis in patients continuing to smoke cigarettes after percutaneous transluminal coronary angioplasty. *Am J Cardiol, 61*(4), 260-263.

Gielen, A. C., & McDonald, E. M. (1997). The Precede-Proceed Planning Model. In K. Glanz, F. M. Lewis & B. K. Rimer (Eds.), *Health behavior and health education: Theory, research, and practice* (2 ed.). San Francisco, CA: Jossey-Bass Publishers.

Glasgow, R. E., Klesges, L. M., Dzewaltowski, D. A., Bull, S. S., & Estabrooks, P. (2004). The future of health behavior change research: what is needed to improve translation of research into health promotion practice? *Ann Behav Med, 27*(1), 3-12.

Glasgow, R. E., Stevens, V. J., Vogt, T. M., Mullooly, J. P., & Lichtenstein, E. (1991). Changes in smoking associated with hospitalization: quit rates, predictive variables, and intervention implications. *Am J Health Promot, 6*(1), 24-29.

Goldman, L., Garber, A. M., Grover, S. A., & Hlatky, M. A. (1996). 27th Bethesda Conference: matching the intensity of risk factor management with the hazard for coronary disease events. Task Force 6. Cost effectiveness of assessment and management of risk factors. *J Am Coll Cardiol, 27*(5), 1020-1030.

Goldstein, A. O., Hellier, A., Fitzgerald, S., Stegall, T. S., & Fischer, P. M. (1987). Hospital nurse counseling of patients who smoke. *Am J Public Health, 77*(10), 1333-1334.

Green, L. W., & Kreuter, M. W. (1991). *Health Promotion Planning: An Educational And Environmental Approach* (2 ed.). Mountain View, CA: Mayfield.

Green, L. W., Richard, L., & Potvin, L. (1996). Ecological foundations of health promotion. *Am J Health Promot, 10*(4), 270-281.

Groupe d'analyse Economique. (2002). *Impact of an anti-smoking campaign on direct healthcare costs in Canada. Report to the Canadian Council for Tobacco Control, April 2002.* Retrieved January 3, 2006, from: http://www.cqct.qc.ca/Documents_docs/DOCU_2002/BRIE_02_04_09_Etu deEconomiqueCanadaENG.PDF .

Grumbach, K., & Bodenheimer, T. (2002). A primary care home for Americans: putting the house in order. *JAMA, 288*(7), 889-893.

Haapanen-Niemi, N., Miilunpalo, S., Vuori, I., Pasanen, M., & Oja, P. (1999). The impact of smoking, alcohol consumption, and physical activity on use of hospital services. *Am J Public Health, 89*(5), 691-698.

Harden, R. M., & Hart, I. R. (2002). An international virtual medical school (IVIMEDS): the future for medical education? *Med Teach, 24*(3), 261-267.

Hartmann, K. E., Espy, A., McPheeters, M., & Kinsinger, L. S. (2004). Physicians taught as residents to conduct smoking cessation intervention: a follow-up study. *Prev Med, 39*(2), 344-350.

Health Canada. (1993). *Laboratory Centre for Disease Control.* Ottawa: Health Canada.

Heath, J., Andrews, J., Kelley, F. J., & Sorrell, J. (2004). Caught in the middle: experiences of tobacco-dependent nurse practitioners. *J Am Acad Nurse Pract, 16*(9), 396-401.

Hermanson, B., Omenn, G. S., Kronmal, R. A., & Gersh, B. J. (1988). Beneficial six-year outcome of smoking cessation in older men and women with coronary artery disease. Results from the CASS registry. *N Engl J Med, 319*(21), 1365-1369.

Hodgson, T. A. (1992). Cigarette smoking and lifetime medical expenditures. *Milbank Q, 70*(1), 81-125.

Hoffman, A. L., & Slade, J. (1993). Following the pioneers. Addressing tobacco in chemical dependency treatment. *J Subst Abuse Treat, 10*(2), 153-160.

Hollis, J. F., Lichtenstein, E., Vogt, T. M., Stevens, V. J., & Biglan, A. (1993). Nurse-assisted counseling for smokers in primary care. *Ann Intern Med, 118*(7), 521-525.

Houston Miller, N., Smith, P. M., DeBusk, R. F., Sobel, D. S., & Taylor, C. B. (1997). Smoking cessation in hospitalized patients. Results of a randomized trial. *Arch Intern Med, 157*(4), 409-415.

Houston Miller N., & Taylor, C. B. (1995). Lifestyle management for patients with coronary heart disease. *Current Issues in Cardiac Rehabilitation, Monograph Number 2*. Champaign, IL: Human Kinetics.

Hughes, J. R. (1993). Possible effects of smoke-free inpatient units on psychiatric diagnosis and treatment. *J Clin Psychiatry, 54*(3), 109-114.

Hughes, J. R., Hatsukami, D. K., Mitchell, J. E., & Dahlgren, L. A. (1986). Prevalence of smoking among psychiatric outpatients. *Am J Psychiatry, 143*(8), 993-997.

Humair, J. P., & Ward, J. (1998). Smoking-cessation strategies observed in videotaped general practice consultations. *Am J Prev Med, 14*(1), 1-8.

Hurt, R. D., Eberman, K. M., Croghan, I. T., offord, K. P., Davis, L. J., Jr., Morse, R. M., et al. (1994). Nicotine dependence treatment during inpatient treatment for other addictions: a prospective intervention trial. *Alcohol Clin Exp Res, 18*(4), 867-872.

Joint Commission on Accreditation of Healthcare Organizations (JCAHO). (n.d.[a]) *Quality Check.* Retrieved May 16, 2005, from http://www.jcaho.org/quality+check/index.htm .

Joint Commission on Accreditation of Healthcare Organizations (JCAHO). (2005). *Specifications Manual for National Hospital Quality Measures.* Retrieved November 27, 2005, from http://www.jcaho.org/pms/ core+measures/aligned_manual.htm .

Joint Commission on Accreditation of Healthcare Organizations (JCAHO). (n.d.[b]). *A comprehensive review of development and testing for national implementation of hospital core measures.* Retrieved February 25, 2005, from http://www.jcaho.org/pms/core+measures/cr_hos_cm.htm .

Joint Commission on Accreditation of Healthcare Organizations (JCAHO). (n.d.[c]). *NQF-endorsed voluntary consensus standards for hospital care*

(Measure set: Acute Myocardial Infarction, AMI-4, Adult Smoking Cessation Advice/Counseling). Specifications Manual for National Hospital Quality Measures. Retrieved May 16, 2005, from http://www.jcaho.org/pms/core+measures/2eami4.pdf .

Joint Commission on Accreditation of Healthcare Organizations (JCAHO). (n.d.[d]). *NQF-endorsed voluntary consensus standards for hospital care (Measure set: Heart Failure, HF-4, Adult Smoking Cessation Advice/Counseling). Specifications Manual for National Hospital Quality Measures.* Retrieved May 16, 2005, from http://www.jcaho.org/pms/core+measures/2thf4.pdf .

Joint Commission on Accreditation of Healthcare Organizations (JCAHO). (n.d.[e]). *NQF-endorsed voluntary consensus standards for hospital care (Measure set: Pneumonia, PN-4, Adult Smoking Cessation Advice/Counseling). Specifications Manual for National Hospital Quality Measures.* Retrieved May 16, 2005, from http://www.jcaho.org/pms/core+measures/2zpn4.pdf .

Katz, D. A., Brown, R. B., Muehlenbruch, D. R., Fiore, M. C., & Baker, T. B. (2004). Implementing guidelines for smoking cessation: comparing the efforts of nurses and medical assistants. *Am J Prev Med, 27*(5), 411-416.

Killen, J. D., & Fortmann, S. P. (1994). Role of nicotine dependence in smoking relapse: results from a prospective study using population-based recruitment methodology. *Int J Behav Med, 1*(4), 320-334.

King, A. C., Taylor, C. B., Haskell, W. L., & DeBusk, R. F. (1989). Influence of regular aerobic exercise on psychological health: a randomized, controlled trial of healthy middle-aged adults. *Health Psychol, 8*(3), 305-324.

Kottke, T. E., Battista, R. N., DeFriese, G. H., & Brekke, M. L. (1988). Attributes of successful smoking cessation interventions in medical practice. A meta-analysis of 39 controlled trials. *JAMA, 259*(19), 2883-2889.

Kottke, T. E., Solberg, L. I., Brekke, M. L., Conn, S. A., Maxwell, P., & Brekke, M. J. (1992). A controlled trial to integrate smoking cessation advice into primary care practice: Doctors Helping Smokers, Round III. *J Fam Pract, 34*(6), 701-708.

Kottke, T. E., Willms, D. G., Solberg, L. I., & Brekke, M. L. (1994). Physician-delivered smoking cessation advice: issues identified during ethnographic interviews. *Tob Control, 3*, 46-49.

Krejci, R. (2000). Tobacco cessation program implementation-from plans to reality: skill building workshop-network model. *Tob Control, 9 Suppl 1*, I33-36.

Kroenke, K., Spitzer, R. L., & Williams, J. B. (2003). The Patient Health Questionnaire-2: validity of a two-item depression screener. *Med Care, 41*(11), 1284-1292.

Krumholz, H. M., Cohen, B. J., Tsevat, J., Pasternak, R. C., & Weinstein, M. C. (1993). Cost-effectiveness of a smoking cessation program after myocardial infarction. *J Am Coll Cardiol, 22*(6), 1697-1702.

Lancaster, T., Silagy, C., & Fowler, G. (2000). Training health professionals in smoking cessation. *Cochrane Database Syst Rev*(3), CD000214.

Leong, S. L., Baldwin, C. D., & Adelman, A. M. (2003). Integrating web-based computer cases into a required clerkship: development and evaluation. *Acad Med, 78*(3), 295-301.

Leung, G. M., Ho, L. M., & Lam, T. H. (2003). The economic burden of environmental tobacco smoke in the first year of life. *Arch Dis Child, 88*(9), 767-771.

Lightwood, J. M., & Glantz, S. A. (1997). Short-term economic and health benefits of smoking cessation: myocardial infarction and stroke. *Circulation, 96*(4), 1089-1096.

Lightwood, J. M., Phibbs, C. S., & Glantz, S. A. (1999). Short-term health and economic benefits of smoking cessation: low birth weight. *Pediatrics, 104*(6), 1312-1320.

Lyon, E. R. (1999). A review of the effects of nicotine on schizophrenia and antipsychotic medications. *Psychiatr Serv, 50*(10), 1346-1350.

Makomaski Illing, E. M., & Kaiserman, M. J. (1999). Mortality attributable to tobacco use in Canada and its regions, 1994 and 1996. *Chronic Dis Can, 20*(3), 111-117.

Manley, M. W., Griffin, T., Foldes, S. S., Link, C. C., & Sechrist, R. A. (2003). The role of health plans in tobacco control. *Annu Rev Public Health, 24*, 247-266.

Marbella, A. M., Riemer, A., Remington, P., Guse, C. E., & Layde, P. M. (2003). Wisconsin physicians advising smokers to quit: results from the Current Population Survey, 1998-1999 and Behavioral Risk Factor Surveillance System, 2000. *WMJ, 102*(5), 41-45.

Marlatt, G. A., & Gordon, J. R. (1985). *Relapse prevention: Maintenance strategies in the treatment of addiction.* New York: Guilford Press.

McBride, C. M., & Pirie, P. L. (1990). Postpartum smoking relapse. *Addict Behav, 15*(2), 165-168.

McBride, P. E., Plane, M. B., Underbakke, G., Brown, R. L., & Solberg, L. I. (1997). Smoking screening and management in primary care practices. *Arch Fam Med, 6*(2), 165-172.

McPhillips-Tangum, C., Bocchino, C., Carreon, R., Erceg, C., & Rehm, B. (2004). Addressing tobacco in managed care: results of the 2002 survey. *Prev Chronic Dis, Oct.* Retrieved May 6, 2005, from http://www.cdc.gov/pcd/issues/2004/oct/04_0021.htm .

Miller, J. E., Russell, L. B., Davis, D. M., Milan, E., Carson, J. L., & Taylor, W. C. (1998). Biomedical risk factors for hospital admission in older adults. *Med Care, 36*(3), 411-421.

Moller, A. M., Villebro, N., Pedersen, T., & Tonnesen, H. (2002). Effect of preoperative smoking intervention on postoperative complications: a randomized clinical trial. *Lancet, 359*(9301), 114-117.

Murray, C. J., Kreuser, J., & Whang, W. (1994). Cost-effectiveness analysis and policy choices: investing in health systems. *Bull World Health Organ, 72*(4), 663-674.

Naidoo, B., Stevens, W., & McPherson, K. (2000). Modelling the short term consequences of smoking cessation in England on the hospitalisation rates for acute myocardial infarction and stroke. *Tob Control, 9*(4), 397-400.

National Center for Chronic Disease Prevention and Health Promotion (CDC). (2005). *Tobacco Information and Prevention Source (TIPS). Introduction to Program Evaluation for Comprehensive Tobacco Control Programs.* Retrieved January 2006, from, http://www.cdc.gov/tobacco/evaluation_ manual/contents.htm .

National Committee for Quality Assurance (NCQA). (2004). *The State of Healthcare Quality 2004: Medical Assistance with Smoking Cessation.* Retrieved May 16, 2005, from http://www.ncqa.org/Communications /SOHC2004/ma_smoking.htm .

Ockene, J. K., Kristeller, J., Pbert, L., Hebert, J. R., Luippold, R., Goldberg, R. J., et al. (1994). The physician-delivered smoking intervention project: can short-term interventions produce long-term effects for a general outpatient population? *Health Psychol, 13*(3), 278-281.

Ockene, J. K., Quirk, M. E., Goldberg, R. J., Kristeller, J. L., Donnelly, G., Kalan, K. L., et al. (1988). A residents' training program for the development of smoking intervention skills. *Arch Intern Med, 148*(5), 1039-1045.

O'Donnell, D. E., Hernandez, P., Aaron, S., Bourbeau, J., Marciniuk, D., Hodder, R., et al. (2003). Canadian Thoracic Society COPD Guidelines: summary of highlights for family doctors. *Can Respir J, 10*(4), 183-185.

Orleans, C. T., & Hutchinson, D. (1993). Tailoring nicotine addiction treatments for chemical dependency patients. *J Subst Abuse Treat, 10*(2), 197-208.

Ossip-Klein, D. J., Bigelow, G., Parker, S. R., Curry, S., Hall, S., & Kirkland, S. (1986). Classification and assessment of smoking behavior. *Health Psychol, 5 Suppl*, 3-11.

Oster, G., Huse, D. M., Delea, T. E., & Colditz, G. A. (1986). Cost-effectiveness of nicotine gum as an adjunct to physician's advice against cigarette smoking. *JAMA, 256*(10), 1315-1318.

Pacific Center On Health and Tobacco. (2003). *Linking a Network: Integrate Quitlines with Health Care Systems.* Retrieved January 2006, from: http:// www.paccenter.org/public/reports_folder/linking_broch_web.pdf .

Pbert, L., Ockene, J. K., Ewy, B. M., Leicher, E. S., & Warner, D. (2000). Development of a state wide tobacco treatment specialist training and certification programme for Massachusetts. *Tob Control, 9*(4), 372-381.

Pederson, L. L., Baskerville, J. C., & Wanklin, J. M. (1982). Multivariate statistical models for predicting change in smoking behavior following physician advice to quit smoking. *Prev Med, 11*(5), 536-549.

Peters, T. (1994). *The pursuit of WOW!* New York: Vintage Books.

Prochaska, J. O., & DiClemente, C. C. (1983). Stages and processes of self-change of smoking: toward an integrative model of change. *J Consult Clin Psychol, 51*(3), 390-395.

Ratner, P. A., Johnson, J. L., Richardson, C. G., Bottorff, J. L., Moffat, B., Mackay, M., et al. (2004). The efficacy of a smoking-cessation intervention for elective-surgical patients. *Res Nurs Health; 27(3)*, 148-161.

Revell, C. C., & Schroeder, S. A. (2005). Simplicity matters: using system-level changes to encourage clinician intervention in helping tobacco users quit. *Nicotine Tob Res, 7 Suppl 1*, S67-69.

Rice, V. H. (1999). Nursing intervention and smoking cessation: A meta-analysis. *Heart Lung, 28*(6), 438-454.

Rice, V. H., & Stead, L. F. (2000). Nursing interventions for smoking cessation. *Cochrane Database Syst Rev*(2), CD001188.

Rigotti, N. (2005). *View public comment for smoking & tobacco use cessation counseling* (No. CAG-00241N). Retrieved February 25, 2005, from http://www.cms.hhs.gov/mcd/publiccomment_popup.asp?comment_id=865 .

Rigotti, N. A., Munafo, M. R., Murphy, M. F., & Stead, L. F. (2003). Interventions for smoking cessation in hospitalised patients. *Cochrane Database Syst Rev(1):*CD001837. Review.

Rigotti, N. A., Quinn, V. P., Stevens, V. J., Solberg, L. I., Hollis, J. F., Rosenthal, A. C., et al. (2002). Tobacco-control policies in 11 leading managed care organizations: progress and challenges. *Eff Clin Pract, 5*(3), 130-136.

Rosenthal, A. C. (2000). Addressing Tobacco in Managed Care program. *Tob Control, 9 Suppl 1*, I71.

Samet, J. M. (1992). The health benefits of smoking cessation. *Med Clin North Am, 76*(2), 399-414.

Sarna, L., Wewers, M. E., Brown, J. K., Lillington, L., & Brecht, M. L. (2001). Barriers to tobacco cessation in clinical practice: report from a National Survey of Oncology Nurses. *Nurs Outlook, 49*(4), 166-172.

Sherbourne, C. D., & Stewart, A. L. (1991). The MOS social support survey. *Soc Sci Med, 32*(6), 705-714.

Siahpush, M., Heller, G., & Singh, G. (2005). Lower levels of occupation, income and education are strongly associated with a longer smoking duration: multivariate results from the 2001 Australian National Drug Strategy Survey. *Public Health, 119*, 1105-1110.

Simon, J. A., Solkowitz, S. N., Carmody, T. P., & Browner, W. S. (1997). Smoking cessation after surgery. A randomized trial. *Arch Intern Med, 157*(12), 1371-1376.

Single, E., Robson, L., Xie, X., & Rehm, J. (1998). The economic costs of alcohol, tobacco and illicit drugs in Canada, 1992. *Addiction, 93*(7), 991-1006.

Sivarajan Froelicher, E. S., Miller, N. H., Christopherson, D. J., Martin, K., Parker, K. M., Amonetti, M., et al. (2004). High rates of sustained smoking cessation in women hospitalized with cardiovascular disease: the Women's Initiative for Nonsmoking (WINS). *Circulation, 109*(5), 587-593.

Smith, P.M. (2001, March 21-24). *Effectiveness of A Nurse Case-Managed Inpatient Smoking Cessation Program for Hospitalized Smokers.* Paper presented at the Society of Behavioral Medicine Annual Conference, Seattle, Washington.

Smith, P. M., Cameron, R., McDonald, P. W., Kawash, B., Madill, C., & Brown, K. S. (2004). Telephone counseling for population-based smoking cessation. *Am J Health Behav, 28*(3), 231-241.

Smith, P. M., & Corso, L. (submitted). *Estimating Enrollment in an Inpatient Tobacco Cessation Program.* Unpublished manuscript.

Smith, P. M., Corso, L., Brown, K. S., Cameron, R., & Winfield, K. D. (submitted). *Nurse Case-Managed Tobacco Cessation Interventions for General Hospital Patients: Results of a Randomized Clinical Trial.* Unpublished manuscript.

Smith, P. M., Kraemer, H. C., Miller, N. H., DeBusk, R. F., & Taylor, C. B. (1999). In-hospital smoking cessation programs: who responds, who doesn't? *J Consult Clin Psychol, 67*(1), 19-27.

Smith, P. M., Miller, N. H., DeBusk, R. F., & Taylor, C. B. (1997, June 29 - July 3). *Dissemination of an Inpatient Smoking Cessation Programme.* Paper presented at The 4th International Conference on Preventive Cardiology, Montreal, PQ.

Smith, P. M., Reilly, K. R., Houston Miller, N., DeBusk, R. F., & Taylor, C. B. (2002). Application of a nurse-managed inpatient smoking cessation program. *Nicotine Tob Res, 4*(2), 211-222.

Smith, P. M., & Sieswerda, L. (in progress). *District Health Unit Program Awareness and Utilization: A Community Survey.* Unpublished manuscript.

Solberg, L. I., Boyle, R. G., Davidson, G., Magnan, S. J., & Carlson, C. L. (2001). Patient satisfaction and discussion of smoking cessation during clinical visits. *Mayo Clin Proc, 76*(2), 138-143.

Sorensen, L. T., Horby, J., Friis, E., Pilsgaard, B., & Jorgensen, T. (2002). Smoking as a risk factor for wound healing and infection in breast cancer surgery. *Eur J Surg Oncol, 28*(8), 815-820.

Spangler, J. G., George, G., Foley, K. L., & Crandall, S. J. (2002). Tobacco intervention training: current efforts and gaps in US medical schools. *JAMA, 288*(9), 1102-1109.

Sparrow, D., & Dawber, T. R. (1978). The influence of cigarette smoking on prognosis after a first myocardial infarction. A report from the Framingham study. *J Chronic Dis, 31*(6-7), 425-432.

Stephens, T., Kaiserman, M. J., McCall, D. J., & Sutherland-Brown, C. (2000). School-based smoking prevention: economic costs versus benefits. *Chronic Dis Can, 21*(2), 62-67.

Stokols, D. (1996). Translating social ecological theory into guidelines for community health promotion. *Am J Health Promot, 10*(4), 282-298.

Sullivan, P., & Kothari, A. (1997). Right to bill may affect amount of tobacco counselling by MDs. *CMAJ, 156*(2), 241-243.

Taylor, C. B., Y Curry, S. J. (2004). Implementation of evidence-based tobacco use cessation guidelines in managed care organizations. *Ann Beh Med, 27*, 13-21.

Taylor, C. B., Houston-Miller, N., Killen, J. D., & DeBusk, R. F. (1990). Smoking cessation after acute myocardial infarction: effects of a nurse-managed intervention. *Ann Intern Med, 113*(2), 118-123.

Taylor, C. B., Miller, N. H., Cameron, R. P., Fagans, E. W., & Das, S. (2005). Dissemination of an effective inpatient tobacco use cessation program. *Nicotine Tob Res, 7*(1), 129-137.

Taylor, C. B., Miller, N. H., Herman, S., Smith, P. M., Sobel, D., Fisher, L., et al. (1996). A nurse-managed smoking cessation program for hospitalized smokers. *Am J Public Health, 86*(11), 1557-1560.

Taylor, D. H., Hasselblad, V., Henley, S. J. Thun, M. J., & Sloan, F. A. (2002). Benefits of smoking cessation for longevity. *Am J Public Health, 92*(6), 990-996.

Thalgott, J. S., Cotler, H. B., Sasso, R. C., LaRocca, H., & Gardner, V. (1991). Postoperative infections in spinal implants. Classification and analysis--a multicenter study. *Spine, 16*(8), 981-984.

Thorndike, A. N., Ferris, T. G., Stafford, R. S., & Rigotti, N. A. (1999). Rates of U.S. physicians counseling adolescents about smoking. *J Natl Cancer Inst, 91*(21), 1857-1862.

Thorndike, A. N., Rigotti, N. A., Stafford, R. S., & Singer, D. E. (1998). National patterns in the treatment of smokers by physicians. *JAMA, 279*(8), 604-608.

Tobacco Free Nurses. (2004a). *Policy. Policy Statements.* Retrieved December 2005, from http://www.tobaccofreenurses.org/resources/policy/statements.php#cotu .

Tobacco Free Nurses. (2004b). *Leadership.* Retrieved December 2005, from http://www.tobaccofreenurses.org/summit.php .

Tobacco Free Nurses. (2004c). Retrieved December 2005, from http://www.tobaccofreenurses.org/ .

Treating Tobacco Use and Dependence: Online Continuing Medical Education Course. (2003). University of Wisconsin Medical School. Agency for Healthcare Research and Quality. Rockville, MD. Retrieved May 2005, from http://www.ahrq.gov/clinic/ttudcme.htm .

Tsevat, J. (1992). Impact and cost-effectiveness of smoking interventions. *Am J Med, 93*(1A), 43S-47S.

U.S. Department of Health and Human Services. (1991). *Strategies to control tobacco use in the United States: A blueprint for public health action in the 1990's. Smoking and Tobacco Control Monographs 1* (NIH Publication No. 92-3316): Public Health Service, National Institutes of Health, National Cancer Institute.

U.S. Department of Health and Human Services. (2004). *The health consequences of smoking: a report of the Surgeon General.* Atlanta, GA: Centers for Disease Control and Prevention, National Center for Chronic Disease Prevention and Health Promotion. office on Smoking and Health. Retrieved May 5, 2005, from http://www.cdc.gov/tobacco/sgr/sgr_2004/index.htm .

U.S. Department of Health & Human Services (USDHHS) Centers for Medicare & Medicaid Services (CMS). (2005a). *CMS Manual System. Publ.100-04 Medicare Claims Processing.* May 20, 2005. Retrieved June 22, 2005, from http://www.cms.hhs.gov/manuals/pm_trans/R562CP.pdf .

U.S. Department of Health and Human Services. (2005b). *office for Civil Rights – HIPAA. Medical Privacy - National Standards to Protect the Privacy of Personal Health Information.* Retrieved November 2005, from http://www.hhs.gov/ocr/hipaa/ .

U.S. Department of Health, Education, and Welfare. (1964). *Smoking and Health: Report of the Advisory Committee to the Surgeon General of the Public Health Service.* Washington: U.S. Department of Health, Education, and Welfare, Public Health Service, Center for Disease Control. PHS Publication No. 1103.

U.S. Department of Health and Human Services. (n.d.). *Reports of the Surgeon General, U.S. Public Health Service.* Retrieved January 3, 2006, from, http://www.surgeongeneral.gov/library/reports.htm .

van Domburg, R. T., Meeter, K., van Berkel, D. F., Veldkamp, R. F., van Herwerden, L. A., & Bogers, A. J. (2000). Smoking cessation reduces mortality after coronary artery bypass surgery: a 20-year follow-up study. *J Am Coll Cardiol, 36*(3), 878-883.

Vitale, F. (2000). Professional Intervention for smoking cessation: The contribution of the pharmacist. *Eur J Public Health, 10,* 21-24.

Voors, A. A., van Brussel, B. L., Plokker, H. W., Ernst, S. M., Ernst, N. M., Koomen, E. M., et al. (1996). Smoking and cardiac events after venous coronary bypass surgery. A 15-year follow-up study. *Circulation, 93*(1), 42-47.

Wagner, E. H., Curry, S. J., Grothaus, L., Saunders, K. W., & McBride, C. M. (1995). The impact of smoking and quitting on health care use. *Arch Intern Med, 155*(16), 1789-1795.

Warner, K. E., Mendez, D., & Smith, D. G. (2004). The financial implications of coverage of smoking cessation treatment by managed care organizations. *Inquiry, 41*(1), 57-69.

West, R., McNeill, A., & Raw, M. (2000). Smoking cessation guidelines for health professionals: an update. Health Education Authority. *Thorax, 55*(12), 987-999.

Zeldman, M. (1999). *Keeping technical projects on target.* Pittsburgh, Pennsylvania: EMZEE Associates Inc.

Zhu, S. H., Stretch, V., Balabanis, M., Rosbrook, B., Sadler, G., & Pierce, J. P. (1996). Telephone counseling for smoking cessation: effects of single-session and multiple-session interventions. *J Consult Clin Psychol, 64*(1), 202-211.

Author Index

Subject Index